WAR SHOTS

WAR SHOTS

Norm Hatch and the U.S. Marine Corps
Combat Cameramen of World War II

Charles Jones

STACKPOLE
BOOKS

Published by
STACKPOLE BOOKS
5067 Ritter Road
Mechanicsburg, PA 17055

Printed in the United States of America

ISBN 978-0-8117-0631-5

To my wife, Deborah White Jones

CONTENTS

FOREWORD

War Shots offers the reader a fascinating account of the life of one of the Marine Corps' most quietly distinguished twentieth-century leaders. Joining the Marines as an enlisted Marine in 1939 and rising rapidly to the rank of staff sergeant, Norm Hatch's World War II experiences not only give us a new insight into his very personal experiences—from the Tarawa Atoll to the second atomic bomb on Nagasaki—but also into the development of the Marine Corps' combat photographer/reporter occupational field.

Along the way, the reader is treated to fresh details of the raising of the flag on Iwo Jima, as well as to issues concerning the very survival of the Marine Corps as one of our nation's services in the aftermath of the war.

Norm Hatch was most well-positioned when and where the Marines needed him most. In fact, he seemed to have a knack for being in the right place at the right time; some might even say the wrong place at the wrong time!

Admirably well researched by the author, *War Shots* will fascinate those who crave a deeper understanding of the pivotal amphibious assaults in the Pacific theater. Norm Hatch, an eyewitness to the turning point of the war on the ground in the island campaigns and immediately after the nuclear attack on Japan, tells the story as only an enlisted Marine can.

Charles Jones's superb recounting of Major Hatch's career, adds significantly to the lore of the most important moments in our nation's history. *War Shots* ranks as one of the most riveting personal accounts of the horrific and heroic times of this epic war which propelled the United States into a position of international leadership responsibility that endures today.

Like so many Marines past and present, he joined the Marine Corps because he wanted a better life for himself. Readers will discover that the Navy was his first choice, but administrative delays in processing his enlistment caused the impatient young man to turn to the Marines, who, much like during today's competitive recruiters, welcomed him immediately.

His is a story of patriotism, courage, loyalty, and a refreshing sense of honor. Our young people who are considering joining one of the Armed Services today would do well to read *War Shots*; our veterans will appreciate Charles Jones's accurate treatment of the war that gave rise to "the greatest generation."

Gen. James L. Jones, Jr.
32nd Commandant of the U.S. Marine Corps
and Former National Security Advisor
to President Barack Obama

CHAPTER ONE

"Stay the Hell Out of My Way"

Whenever he was on a ship at sea, Norm Hatch always searched for the best possible vantage point. Usually he found it on the flying bridge—the open space by the pilothouse—where he could escape the noise and crowding below deck among his fellow Marines. Growing up in Gloucester, Massachusetts, a fishing village thirty miles northeast of Boston, Hatch was a gangly and gregarious youth who spent his summers playing and working in and around the ocean. Sometimes he crewed for the well-heeled owners of sailboats and schooners docked in Gloucester and watched rum-runners skirting federal agents intent on intercepting illicit booze during Prohibition.

Much of the work wasn't that glamorous, such as scraping the interiors of fishing boats and painting their hulls. It was while doing the grunt work of the seafaring life that he learned from old sea dogs that it's always better to ride out a storm in the open rather than down in the hatches below.

But in late November 1943, leaning against the flying bridge rail of a U.S. Navy transport ship, the *Heywood*, S/Sgt. Norman T. Hatch sensed there would be no way to find shelter from the man-made storm about to break across the calm expanse of the mid-Pacific.

Awestruck by the size of the armada of ships slicing through the dark blue waves shortly before dawn, he pondered the importance of gaining the best perspective to succeed in a unique and dangerous mission: to film the United States Marine Corps' first large-scale assault from the sea against the heavily fortified beachhead of Betio in the Tarawa Atoll. The tiny island (pronounced *bay-SHEE-O*) was defended by a garrison of 4,800 Japanese troops, including some 2,600 men from Emperor Hirohito's most elite naval defense forces.

These Japanese defenders should not be taken lightly, warned Col. Merritt A. "Red Mike" Edson, chief of staff of the 2nd Marine Division. Edson, known for his fiery temper and tactical brilliance, had been assigned by his more cerebral boss, Maj. Gen. Julian C. Smith, to train thousands of veteran leathernecks and more recent recruits into a lethal amphibious force. A hero of the recent battle of Guadalcanal, the largest clash with Japanese ground forces thus far in the war, Edson cautioned that the Imperial Japanese Marines were "the best Tojo's got."[1] Only a few months before, Edson's 1st Raider Battalion had suffered eighty-eight casualties in taking the island of Tulagi from the 3rd Kure Special Naval Landing Force.

Now, according to American intelligence, the Japanese were dug into heavily fortified positions buttressed by sand, coconut logs, and concrete on this former British trading post. Less than three miles long and no wider than 800 yards, Betio Island was nearly as flat as a parking lot; its 300 acres were equal in size to the Pentagon and its surrounding space. The flat terrain made Betio relatively easy to defend—and most treacherous to attack. Though they were duly warned, many of the Marines aboard the ship with Hatch simply dismissed the fighting spirit of the Japanese and ignored the perils lurking over the horizon.

They should have known better. Emperor Hirohito's forces had already fought bravely against Gen. Douglas MacArthur's forces in the jungles of New Guinea, stalling the American army commander's plan to launch an island-hopping campaign in the Southwest Pacific. In

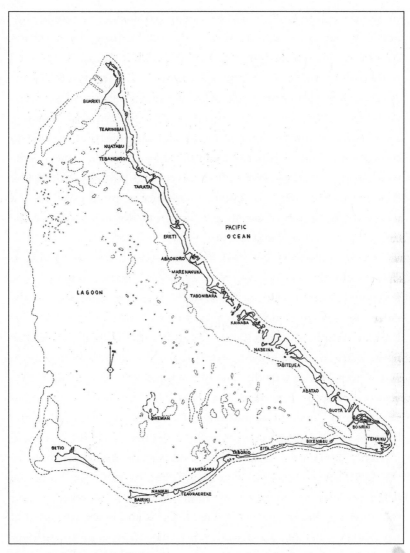

Tarawa Atoll, invaded by the Marines in November 1943. Betio, the battle's focal point, is at lower left. U.S. MARINE CORPS

those days before satellite photos and global media and intelligence networks, Japanese military strategists could only guess about the Americans' intentions. But they weren't taking anything for granted in the Gilbert Islands along the equator in the Central Pacific. Japanese Rear Adm. Tomanari Saichiro had personally supervised an elaborate construction plan on Betio's spit of palm-covered earth, building a sophisticated line of defense to protect his prime asset, an airfield that gave the empire superiority in the skies above the sixteen scattered atolls of Tarawa. Normally peaceful and lightly populated by fishermen and traders, the Gilberts had once inspired novelists and painters with visions of earthly paradise, from *Robinson Crusoe* to the tropical paintings of Paul Gauguin.

But by mid-December 1941, any dreams of earthly Eden had been shattered by the brutal Japanese invasion force that scattered the few remaining British traders on Betio. Japan claimed sovereignty over the entire equatorial island chain as part of its "Greater East Asia Co-Prosperity Sphere." Thus Tarawa Atoll became part of the defense perimeter against the growing American naval, air, and ground forces that were poised to start the long slog across the Pacific toward Tokyo. Betio's defenses were more than a year in the making after a report to the Imperial General Headquarters exposed the weaknesses of Japan's defenses in the Gilberts and pointed out the need to build an airbase.

The 1,600 men of Japan's 111th Construction Battalion (similar to the U.S. Navy's Seabees) were dispatched to begin building the defenses, along with nearly 1,000 unskilled civilian laborers. On their way to Betio, this engineering group acquired an impressive arsenal of naval and air defense guns. But even as the Japanese unloaded their armaments, American bombers started pestering them with random air raids in late 1942.

Nonetheless, the Japanese spent the better part of 1943 erecting the Betio fortifications. They built reinforced-concrete command posts and set up 8-inch naval cannons and turrets, along with 127-millimeter and 140-millimeter antiaircraft guns. The gun positions were protected by revetments using the plentiful material at hand, coconut logs and coral rock. The 111th Pioneers, as they were known, bolstered the gun positions with other features, from range finders to signal stations to barracks.[2]

In addition, Saichiro ordered the construction of concrete and steel tetrahedrons, minefields, and long strings of double-apron barbed wire on the beach and out into the coral reef beyond. This was buttressed by a barrier wall of logs and coral around much of the island. The Japanese planned to defend the island on its perimeter, as stated in a directive to the newly arrived Yokosuka 6th Special Landing Force, which had been designated as the *tokususetsu konkyochitai,* or special base defense forces, according to Marine historian Col. Joseph H. Alexander. "Knock out the landing boats with mountain gun fire, tank guns and infantry guns," the directive ordered, "then concentrate all fires on the enemy's landing point and destroy him at the water's edge."[3]

To execute this shore defense plan, the Japanese built 500 pillboxes protected by coconut logs, steel plates, and sand. Betio was also armed with turret-mounted 8-inch naval rifles known as "Singapore guns," which, according to legend, were taken from the British colony of Singapore after it fell to the Japanese. In fact, the Japanese had purchased the guns from their British manufacturer, Vickers, in 1905 during Japan's earlier war with Russia, according to Alexander.[4] Thus, by late 1943, Betio bristled with a mix of old and new, light and heavy, weaponry: machine guns, cannons, mortars, light tanks, and antiaircraft guns.

Yet even this steel ring wasn't enough protection against the Americans to satisfy Prime Minister Hideki Tojo, the former general known as "the Razor." In August 1943, Tojo replaced the defensive-minded Saichiro with Rear Adm. Keiji Shibisaki, a forty-nine-year-old veteran known for his work as a naval officer and spirited leadership of the Japanese Navy's special landing forces. "Saichiro had been more engineer than combat leader," wrote Martin Russ, while

Shibasaki "was strictly tactical—and quite ready to defend Betio to the last man."[5]

True to the *samurai* warrior code of *bushido*, the boyish-looking Shibisaki strode onto the coral atoll with a chest full of medals and a bravado that lifted his fighters' morale. He reportedly boasted to cheering troops that "a million Americans couldn't take Tarawa in 100 years." The claim would soon be put to the test.

Hatch and his fellow Marines had been training for nearly a year for this clash, and they were equally determined to be true to their own warrior code—*Semper Fidelis*, "always faithful." Shibisaki's hyperbole notwithstanding, the American invaders were nowhere near one million strong. Overcoming logistical problems that stretched thousands of miles from southern California to New Zealand, they had cobbled together a force of 18,088 men of the 2nd Marine Division who were joined by hundreds more sailors and engineers in the escort and troop ships bearing down on the Tarawa Atoll on D-Day, November 20, 1943.

Hatch, a natural-born reporter with a penchant for picking up the latest scuttlebutt, learned all he could from officers and noncommissioned officers about the furious planning for the invasion. Based on his extensive training in film and Corps maneuvers, he instinctively knew that knowledge was power when it came to photojournalism. Knowing the basic invasion plan would help him get in the best position to chronicle the story.

The Marine Corps' planning team was headed by David M. Shoup, a thirty-eight-year-old Indiana native only recently promoted to colonel when his predecessor became ill. Hatch became aware of the sand tables Shoup used to simulate positions of enemy and friendly troops on the island. Betio was shaped like a bird lying on its back, with its breast facing north into a lagoon. The Japanese concentrated their defenses on the southern and western coasts—the bird's head and back—because this was where they had landed months before. Shoup recognized that the lagoon and beaches on Betio's northern shore presented the best, if imperfect, site for an amphibious assault.

As the Marines prepared to test Admiral Shibisaki's orders "to defend to the last man all vital areas and destroy the enemy at the water's edge," Hatch worried about the inherent cockiness of his fellow leathernecks. "The only reason we're carrying entrenching tools," the Marines were saying, "is to bury the Japanese."

The 2nd Marine Division had been training for more than a year, first in southern California and finally in New Zealand, practicing and refining the latest techniques of amphibious warfare. (With many of its young men gone to fight the Germans, New Zealand's attractive young ladies had provided a welcome distraction for the Marines.)

The Americans hoped to continue the momentum achieved at Guadalcanal, where the 1st Marine Division, aided by elements of the 2nd Marine Division, initially sent the Japanese scurrying inland for cover. But Guadalcanal was no cake walk, and after the Japanese brought in 50,000 troops as reinforcements, it took nearly six months for the Marines to finally prevail by killing more than 25,000 of the enemy. On the American side, the toll was not as bad, but still steep: 1,044 Marines killed in action, with 2,894 wounded, 55 missing, and 8,580 recorded cases of malaria. The U.S. Army lost 446 soldiers, with 1,910 wounded. And the Marine air wing lost 55 men, with 127 wounded and 85 missing. Both nations' navies sustained heavy losses of tonnage in the prolonged fighting.

Tarawa, by contrast, seemed to be a smaller, simpler target, which explained the early optimism among the troops that this would be a quick and almost surgical assault starting with the large scalpel of naval gunfire. Though Hatch doubted it would be as easy a fight as some were saying, he was quite sure that this massive amphibious operation would give all of the combat cameramen a rare and even historic opportunity to chronicle a pivotal moment for the Marine Corps: a major amphibious attack on a fortified beachhead.

Hatch had joined the Marines four years earlier at the tender age of eighteen after the U.S. Navy kept sinking his hopes of ever becoming a sailor. This child of the Depression had grown weary of working odd jobs around Boston, and his parents couldn't afford to send him to college. Enlisting in the military was a natural option.

After boot camp at Parris Island, the Marine Corps provided a unique brand of postgraduate education for Hatch. He began as an English instructor and then became a magazine editor. His creative career path would take him to New York City, where he worked for the newsreel series produced by Henry Luce's *Time* magazine—*The March of Time*—studying the new art of documentary filmmaking. Now he was poised to test his professional training under fire. Along with his assistant, Bill Kelliher, Hatch surveyed their supplies:

Handheld 35-millimeter Bell & Howell Eyemo camera. Check.

Forty-five rolls of black-and-white film, each 100 feet long, totaling 4,500 feet of film. Check.

Field pack. Check.

.45-caliber pistol. Check.

Hatch pulled out the Eyemo and began shooting through its three lenses that protruded like a triple-barreled, sawed-off shotgun. He wanted to capture for posterity the memorable sight of thousands of Marines clambering onto the Higgins boats several miles out at sea.

The plan was to transfer troops from the wooden boats, which lacked armor, onto bulky amphibious tractors designed to roll like tanks over the reef and onto shore. The time-consuming troop transfers were necessary because the LVTs (landing vehicles, tracked) lacked the handling capability to draw beside the transport ships to collect the Marines. There were actually two kinds of these lightly armored vehicles that were originally meant to serve as supply vehicles to ferry goods from ships at sea to Marines on land. The first version of the "Swamp Gator," the LVT-1 Alligator, gave the Corps an amphibious vehicle capable of churning through sea and surf and onto land. But these early models were prone to breaking down in the mud or saltwater; at times, as Hatch witnessed firsthand, they took a toll in lives.

A more advanced LVT-2 Water Buffalo had been developed, but as D-Day at Tarawa neared, the Marines were nervously awaiting their delivery from San Diego. Even if the vehicles did make it, there would be no time for training or shaking out any of the bugs in the new equipment.

Now, early on D-Day, Hatch was getting an eyeful in his Eyemo. Before the Marines scurried down the cargo nets, the Navy battlewagons opened up 8-inch and 16-inch guns whose barrels erupted with flames in the predawn darkness. Surely, Hatch thought, their destructive power would wipe Betio off the map. The gunfire was deafening and drowned out the sound of men hollering and cursing and joking as they climbed down the wide cargo nets to the Higgins boats bobbing alongside. The time had come for Hatch to stow his camera and get in position. True to his surname, he had hatched this part of his plan several weeks earlier, before they left their training ground in a country he had grown to love, New Zealand.

As the senior NCO of the photography section, Hatch was responsible for positioning the men for their combat assignments. He also had to figure out how he would cover the operation. He finally turned his attention to one of the heroes of Guadalcanal, Maj. Henry P. "Jim" Crowe, a Kentucky native who, like Hatch, became a Marine at least in part to escape economic hardship. Crowe had enlisted in the Marines a quarter of a century earlier during World War I and stood guard in France while President Woodrow Wilson visited victorious American troops.

Crowe later served as an ordnance officer in China in the 1920s, where he drank *sake* with some Japanese embassy colleagues to celebrate the emperor's birthday. The military attaches had tried—and failed—to drink Crowe under the table. This Old Corps Marine loved to regale young officers and more seasoned NCOs with colorful tales of his hell-raising with those sons of the Rising Sun. As he approached Tarawa, Crowe must have known that his old drinking buddies could be leading some of the enemy forces at Betio.

As a "mustang"—an enlisted man who worked his way up to become an officer—Jim Crowe was the kind of battalion commander who inspired equal parts admiration and fear from his men. This was especially true of anyone who witnessed the performance of the big, burly, red-bearded Marine captain on Guadalcanal. After leading his weapons company in half-tracks through a fusillade of machine-gun fire, Crowe abandoned his vehicle and hoisted a shotgun as though he was going on a hunting trip. Indeed, he packed impressive credentials as an award-winning marksman, holding the national record for the Browning automatic rifle (BAR), and had been coach of the Marine Corps Rifle Team.

When he found a group of dazed Marines cowering in a shell hole at Guadalcanal, Crowe bellowed, "Goddamn it, you'll never get the Purple Heart hiding in a foxhole! Follow me!" Galvanized by this fierce, cigar-chomping figure, the reluctant combatants scrambled out of the hole and followed Crowe's rifle-and-grenade charge that wiped out the machine-gun emplacement.[6]

After learning of Crowe's legendary exploits—and how he miraculously avoided getting so much as a scratch in the battle—Hatch knew this was exactly the kind of gung-ho leader he wanted to trail. However, his introduction to Crowe in his office in New Zealand had not gone well. Crowe commanded the more than 900 men of 2nd Battalion, 8th Marines, one of the four battalion landing teams that would spearhead the attack at Betio.

"Good morning, sir. I'm Staff Sergeant Hatch with division photo."

Shuffling papers on his desk, Crowe seemed distracted and barely looked up. "Why are you here?"

"Well, sir," Hatch replied carefully, "I have been assigned to 2/8 for the upcoming island invasion."

The stern CO, who now sported a red mustache, looked him squarely in the eye, staring him down. Sensing he was being tested, Hatch didn't flinch. "What exactly do you do?" Crowe finally asked with a touch of annoyance.

"I work at headquarters, and I'm a combat cinematographer," Hatch replied evenly.

Crowe lit a cigar. Leaning back, he exhaled a plume of smoke. "Sergeant, I really don't want any goddamn Hollywood Marines with me."

This cool reception was to be expected, though, especially in the early days of the war. The Marines had only recently formed a Division of Public Relations and, concurrently, started their first-ever photographic services, to which Hatch was assigned. The innovations in both public relations and photojournalism either confused or rankled some in the officer corps. When the Commandant, Maj. Gen. Thomas Holcomb, hand-picked Col. Robert L. Denig to head the new public-relations unit and promoted him to brigadier general, he asked, "Well, Denig, what do you know about public relations?"

"I don't know anything about it, never heard of it," Denig replied with characteristic frankness.

Holcomb duly informed him, "You better learn about it, because that's what you're going to be!"

It was an inauspicious beginning, but the public-relations branch of the Marine Corps soon became known as "Denig's Demons" for its effective recruitment of newspaper professionals—basically the decimation of wide swaths of the city rooms of the *Washington Post*, *Times-Herald*, and other publications. Eventually, the *Times-Herald*'s publisher-owner, Cissie Patterson, protested to President Roosevelt about the raid on her veteran staff. This complaint led Holcomb to order Denig to look elsewhere for reporters and photographers.[7]

Despite the Marines' rapid-fire recruitment of a new group of professionals who were anointed as "combat correspondents," the attitude in the field typically mirrored Crowe's resistance to working with

Hatch. The frequent response to a newly arrived correspondent, according to historian Benis Frank, was "Where the hell are we going to put them? What can they do for us? They'll only be in the way."[8]

Nonetheless, Hatch, who joined the Corps well before the public-relations branch opened for business, simply refused to melt under Crowe's reproving glare.

"Sir," Hatch asserted, "I'm a regular Marine with five years' service. If I need a rifle, all I have to do is bend down and pick one up."

Crowe puffed his cigar and thought it over. Finally, he growled, "All right, but stay the hell out of my way!"

Two weeks later, on November 20, 1943, Hatch was waiting for the no-nonsense major to step over the *Heywood*'s rail to climb down the cargo net into one of the Higgins boats bobbing on the rough water below. Shells from the Navy's big guns were exploding along the Betio shoreline. The battle for Tarawa Atoll had begun. Surely the Japanese couldn't survive such a show of force, Hatch thought. And even if they do, they would be stunned silly by the salvos that seemed to confirm all the boasting from the troops and their leaders. One naval commander guaranteed that his fire-support group would "obliterate" Betio. After taking the haymaker punches of the Seventh Fleet, the Japanese certainly couldn't find the fortitude to repulse these highly trained troops waiting to storm the beach and quickly complete their mission. The Marines were well armed with fairly new Garand M-1 semiautomatic rifles, Browning automatic rifles and machine guns, flame throwers, dynamite, and other high explosives.

Hatch, for his part, carried only a .45-caliber pistol. Otherwise, except for his bulky Eyemo and canisters of film, his gear was the same as his fellow infantrymen: knapsack, poncho, entrenching tool, bayonet, field rations, and a gas mask, which was swiftly discarded.

The 2nd Battalion, 8th Marines, under Major Crowe's command was slated to land at one of the three beach areas, each about 600 yards long, beyond Betio's blue lagoon.

It was part of a hastily crafted assault plan, developed throughout that autumn by order of the Joint Chiefs of Staff, to launch three amphibious assaults—dubbed Operation Galvanic—in the mid-Pacific. (Besides Tarawa, the Chiefs ordered attacks on two other islands in the Gilbert chain, Makin and Apamama.) The 2nd Marine Division was given the biggest challenge, Tarawa's heavily fortified island of Betio. The division was commanded by Maj. Gen. Julian C. Smith, a bespectacled, soft-spoken gentleman who—like Jim Crowe—was a top-notch marksman and former rifle team coach. Though his combat command experience was limited, Smith was known as a hands-on leader, one Hatch had seen out in the field getting his hands—and boots—dirty.

Major Crowe no doubt understood that despite his superiors' best attempts at surprising the Japanese, there was zero chance they would reach the beach undetected. Indeed, this exposure had led Smith to raise holy hell at an earlier planning conference in Honolulu with Adm. Chester Nimitz, commander of the Pacific Fleet, and the rest of the Navy and Marine brain trust for Operation Galvanic.

The June 1943 meeting took place as American forces began to retake the central Solomon Islands and the Aleutians; offensive campaigns also were being hatched against the northern Solomons, New Britain, and Bougainville. The framework for America's Pacific strategy had been set that spring as Roosevelt, Churchill, and their military staffs met in Casablanca, Washington, and Quebec. Once the cross-channel invasion of France was delayed until 1944, the U.S. Navy's amphibious ships and landing craft were freed up for the Pacific theater. But the clock was ticking on having access to all of that equipment to attack Japan.

So the Joint Chiefs gave the 2nd Marine Division about five months to prepare to launch the island-hopping campaign that would start in the Gilberts and drive north to the Marshall Islands, putting U.S. air assets within striking distance of Japan as well as establishing safe harbors for the Navy to fight farther west.

Fearful of getting his fleet tied up off the coast of Tarawa—or sunk by enemy submarines—Nimitz declared that gaining the element of strategic surprise meant limiting the pre-assault naval bombardment of Betio to about three hours on the morning of D-Day. He also ruled out any decoy landings or grabbing any of the islands surrounding Betio.

Adding to these weighty restrictions, V Amphibious Corps' commander, Maj. Gen. Holland Smith, the hot-headed Alabaman known as "Howlin' Mad," dropped his own bombshell on Smith: the 6th Marines, which represented a full third of the division's combat power, would be kept from the initial invasion as a reserve force, thus further diluting Julian Smith's troop assets.

"All of Julian Smith's tactical options had been stripped away," Alexander wrote in the Marine Corps' history of the battle. "The 2d Marine Division was compelled to make a frontal assault into the teeth of Betio's defenses with an abbreviated preparatory bombardment. Worse, the loss of the 6th Marines meant he would be attacking the island fortress with only a 2-to-1 superiority in troops, well below the doctrinal minimum. Shaken, he insisted that Holland Smith absolve him of any responsibility for the consequences. This was done."[9]

When Japanese coast watchers spotted the approaching armada at 5:07 A.M. on D-Day, November 20, 1943, Rear Admiral Shibisaki's 8-inch shore battery responded with a full-throated dragon's roar. The battleships *Colorado* and *Maryland* delivered counterbattery fire. One 14-inch shell found its mark early on, hitting the magazine of one of the Japanese guns. A fireball lit the pale sky, followed by a series of explosions.

Despite this early marksmanship, the incessant shelling by Shibisaki's shore guns prompted Adm. Harry Hill, the amphibious task force's commander, to order his troop transports to shift their anchorages to get out of the way of his gun support ships. This did not sit well with the Marines who were halfway down the cargo nets to the Higgins boats when the mother ships weighed anchor. Some Marines worried about getting run over by their own ships even as waterspouts shot up around them from the guns on the distant shore. The amphibious operation—which had gone so well during months of training—quickly became chaotic.

The chaos continued into mid-morning, when Hatch was perched on the engine hatch of a Higgins boat next to Major Crowe, watching the drama unfold in the surf and on the shore. The first wave of the 2nd Battalion's LVTs struggled to make it across the reef and over the seawall onto shore as the Japanese raked them with machine-gun, small-arms, and mortar fire.

Another decision made earlier by the U.S. Navy's leadership—limiting the number of better-armored LVT-2s for the Marines—was also costing the Marines dearly. Casualties mounted.

Instinctively, the drivers of the thinly armed LVT-1s took cover next to a 1,000-yard-long pier jutting like a compass dial due north into the lagoon.

"Jesus!" exclaimed Crowe, the battalion commander. "I'm losing my goddamn front. Coxswain, put this damned boat in."

Crowe's boat was not due to land until after the first three waves of LVTs made it ashore. By then, the other mode of transport—the wooden Higgins boats—were getting hung up on the shallow water of the lagoon's reef. They needed at least four feet of water to maneuver, but the water depth on the lagoon's reef had fallen to about three feet. The one-foot difference proved deadly for hundreds of Marines who were forced to bail out of their boats and wade ashore for up to half a mile. Traversing the length of eight football fields made the Marines easy pickings for the dug-in defenders. The *samurai* fighters would make the Americans pay dearly for their audacious assault. The water in Betio's lagoon began to turn red from the blood of the Marines.

Norm Hatch stood by Major Crowe as the coxswain gunned the boat's engine toward Red Beach Three. It hit the reef hard, throwing everyone into a heap on the boat's deck. But they got up. It was time to start shooting.

CHAPTER TWO

From Capone to the Corps

If Shakespeare is right and "what's past is prologue," then the tempestuous Roaring Twenties and the subsequent hardships of the 1930s and the Great Depression forever marked the minds and hearts of the young men who would one day storm the beaches at Betio.

In late summer of 1929—when Norm Hatch was an eight-year-old boy settling into his new home in Chicago—a heat wave scorched the streets from New York to Kansas City. In this big city where his father had found work as a car salesman, Hatch watched the businessmen crossing Michigan Avenue wearing starched collars, waistcoats, and hats. The ladies dressed more daringly, wearing short skirts that would have scandalized his grandmother back in Boston, even those that fell a mere two inches below the knee. And the V-necked blouses offered further evidence to the prim and proper ladies of the Temperance Movement that the country was going to hell in a whiskey bucket. With Prohibition the law of the land, drinking created a cultural division (much as marijuana would in the 1960s and 1970s), not to mention a black market for liquor sales and distribution that corrupted politicians and police across the United States.

Nowhere was this truer than Chicago, where a bootlegger named Al Capone lorded over an illicit liquor syndicate. To young Hatch, though, he was just a friendly man in his apartment building, one of the first men he would ever meet who made a living by violent means.

Steam shovels were tearing up downtown lots as America was on a vertical growth spurt. New office towers seemed to rise as randomly as all the new musical and drama fads driven by recent advances in radio and movies. Hatch heard people whistling "Singin' in the Rain" and the latest hits by Al Jolson.

His local paper, the *Chicago Tribune*, carried international news of an address to the League of Nations by British Prime Minister Ramsay McDonald, who declared progress in negotiations between Great Britain and the United States for cutting back on naval weaponry. He planned to cross the Atlantic to meet with President Hoover as part of ongoing efforts by the world's powers to avoid a relapse into another "Great War." Germany struggled to repay reparations from World War I, and France, the strongest nation on the Continent, occupied the Rhineland. Japan had yet to invade Manchuria, much less China. And Adolf Hitler was a name that would not ring any bells, even for the most astute student of world affairs: in 1929, he was merely a failed architect and little-known leader of a small, but noisy group of German brown shirts.

Most Americans were paying more attention to Bobby Jones's golfing exploits or news about the travel potential of dirigibles such as Germany's *Graf Zeppelin*. After seeing its round-the-world journey, some building designers, including those who engineered the Empire State Building, pondered installing mooring masts for the ships of the sky. The future seemed bright indeed, from the potential of coast-to-coast airlines to a stock market with a seemingly endless upward trajectory.

Though most Americans did not notice the growing turmoil from Germany to Japan, some military planners knew that the fragile peace—just like the soaring stock market—could not last. Among the most visionary of these strategists was Earl H. Ellis, who had the foresight as early as 1912 to begin what Lt. Gen. Victor H. Krulak would call "a messianic exploration" of the inevitable clash in the Pacific between American and Japanese forces. "He predicted that the Japanese would initiate hostilities and that the United States would have to fight its way back across the Pacific in a series of hard amphibious assaults."[1]

Even as the Marine Corps began developing an amphibious assault doctrine, the men who would fill the boats and landing crafts and be put to the ultimate test at Tarawa endured early initiations into life's hardships after the stock market crash of 1929. Norm Hatch, for his part, developed a unique talent for staying upbeat and finding a way to be in the right place at the right time. He was an energetic youth with vast curiosity, courage, and physical stamina. He had enjoyed the halcyon days of Model Ts, jazz, flappers, Babe Ruth, and the *Spirit of St. Louis*. But when Wall Street crumbled and the economy tanked, his late childhood and teen years were tempered by his father's search for steady work and his mother's struggle to provide food and shelter.

His father, Irving Norman Hatch, started out in the auto business, working as an engineer for Marmon Automobile, whose founder, Frank Marmon, was known for perfecting the V-8 and later V-16 engines for pricey models that sold for $5,000. Hatch had moved on to Stutz Automobile, which sold more affordable two-door coupes. And in 1927, he was transferred to Chicago to solve some dangerous problems facing the car company in Capone's town.

A former boxer, the tall, square-jawed Irving Hatch had worked as a strike-breaker for the Pinkerton Detective Agency in his youth. His physical stature, integrity, and engineering prowess made him a natural choice to take over Stutz's Chicago franchise in the age of Prohibition and organized crime. The city was rife with corruption and violence, and Irving Hatch's son took it all in.

"They sent my father to Chicago from Indianapolis because they were having a lot of trouble at the Stutz agency at the 2400 block of

South Michigan," Hatch recalled. As the dealership became a popular car lot for bootleggers, it also led to two holdups of his father. As a result, the dealership was losing money. Yet the Hatches, including Irving's wife, Ruth Francis Colby, knew from personal experience that some bootleggers—even members of the notorious Capone Gang—weren't so bad.

"When we moved to Chicago, we moved into Capone's hotel, where he owned the top three floors. I was six years old. My father said, 'Now look, be careful going up and down in the elevator because you don't want to antagonize these people.'"

Capone would become Public Enemy Number One, but the man Hatch remembers from his childhood was a generous and friendly figure in his apartment hallway, always sporting a big white hat. "The interesting thing was that all the Italians liked children. They'd be nice to me and give me quarters. My father said, 'You can't take that!'" To which the wide-eyed boy replied, "I can't say no!"

Sirens blared across the city night, and Hatch stared out his bedroom window, wondering what was going on outside. Occasionally, he heard the sputtering cracks of Tommy gun fire, the first sounds of violence in his young life. His father bought some collapsible steel gates to protect the back windows of the family's bungalow at the corner of 87th Street and Harper Avenue. Years later, as he built his own bunkers and command posts across the Pacific, Hatch sometimes remembered his father's defensive measures in Chicago.

Irving Hatch finally worked out a truce with Capone's comrades, displaying a knack for personal diplomacy that would serve as another life lesson for his son to emulate. "My father made friends with one of the Capone guys and said, 'Hey, look, I've been held up three times in this place, and it's all mob-oriented. Is there anything you can do about it?'" Stutz was selling custom-built, armor-plated vehicles to various mobsters, including Capone and his cohorts.

One of the gang members reassured the auto dealer, "Yeah, we'll take care of it." The robberies screeched to a halt.

Along with his automotive interests, Irving Hatch was a big fan of radio and spent his evenings assembling them in a basement shop. In those days, radios were not built in one piece, but rather had to have their components installed in a wooden box. Irving Hatch would purchase the cases, build the radios, and sell them at a profit.

One night he called his son downstairs and said, "Norm, there's something I want you to hear." He turned the dial, and they both listened to a distant voice coming through the crackling airwaves. "It's San Francisco!" his father exclaimed. "Can you imagine that?"

Norm Hatch belonged to the YMCA, where he learned to shoot a rifle at an NRA range. He also took swimming lessons from a master, Johnny Weissmuller, winner of five Olympic gold medals and holder of countless world records. Weissmuller, who lived near the Y, went on to star in twelve Tarzan films and became known for his jungle-piercing yell as he swung from vine to vine.

The Depression was hard for everyone—criminals, car dealers, and actors. So in 1931, Irving Hatch packed up his family and drove them back to their native Boston, where he got a job with a Lincoln dealer. Norm, meanwhile, found a job on a soap opera broadcast in nearby Brookline. "They told me how to get rid of the pages so I wouldn't make a noise. I'd slide them off and drop them to the floor."

His father struggled to make ends meet, bouncing from one car company or dealership to another. Irving Hatch probably could have made more money, but his conscience sometimes got in the way as he refused to go along with crooked bosses who wanted to cook the books. His son took note of his insistence on doing the right thing rather than pocketing ill-gotten gains. Life for him "was black and white," Norm recalled. "You were right, or you were wrong—no if's, and's, or but's." After Irving Hatch quit one lucrative auto dealership, "My mother was so mad at him. The guy was paying him pretty good money. But he said, 'I'm not going to work for a crook.'"

Like millions of their countrymen, the Hatches struggled to stay afloat while maintaining their dignity and values. As her husband struggled to find work, Ruth Hatch persuaded her mother, Lucretia Colby, to help her buy a four-story brownstone on Marlborough Street in Boston, where she opened a rooming house on the banks of the Charles River. They took in students from the Massachusetts Institute of Technology, which was right across the river, and soon had a thriving enterprise. Norm Hatch enjoyed being around a variety of people, even more so when his mother moved to a more upscale neighborhood on Boston's Bay State Road. That rooming house became known as the home-away-from-home for baseball and hockey players on the Boston Red Sox and Boston Bruins. His mother became known as "Mother Hatch, of the Red Sox and the Bruins."

Finally, Norm moved to another family home on the coast in Gloucester, Massachusetts, to finish high school and try to earn some money on the side. Living in a cottage on Rocky Neck, an island in the middle of Gloucester Harbor, the strapping young man enjoyed life in the seaside fishing village, an experience that would prepare him for the seafaring life of a U.S. Marine. Gloucester was teeming with fishermen and lobstermen and also hosted a thriving artists' colony. As he made his way around town, Hatch got to know some of the painters and sculptors of the day, including Leonard Kraske, whose statue, "The Man at the Wheel," was commissioned as part of the seaport's 300th anniversary. Unveiled in 1925, the statue paid tribute to the thousands of Gloucester fishermen who lost their lives pursuing the ancient profession that inspired another local boy, Herman Melville, to write of the sights and sounds at sea which "language cannot paint, and mariner had never seen . . . dread Leviathan. . . . Whales, sharks, and monsters, arm'd in front or jaw. With swords, saws, spiral horns, or hooked fangs."

For his seafaring tribute, Kraske stuck to the the 107th Psalm: "They that went down to the sea in ships." The kindly sculptor took Hatch under wing, paying him to care for his sailboat. It was one of many jobs Hatch drummed up around the seaport, including twenty-five-cent-an-hour labor at Booth Fisheries. Even though many fishermen were out of work, they refused to clean out the bowels of the ships. Hatch, always the opportunist and entrepreneur, gladly took on the work. He wore rubber boots and sloshed through the stench to clean out dead fish and clear fishing nets of crawfish.

Norm held another job at a restaurant, where he was paid a dollar a day to wash dishes and peel potatoes. It was worth it, though, because he could eat all he wanted at the café. But the restaurateur warned Hatch to make sure he wasn't spotted by federal labor authorities. At age sixteen, he was well under the minimum age of eighteen that had been set by the New Deal legislation as a way of giving grown men the first crack at even the most menial of jobs.

When he wasn't scraping barnacles or washing dishes, Norm Hatch managed to meet many of the colorful—and sometimes wealthy—characters who came in off the ocean into the harbor. This included a stint during his senior year of high school aboard a ship, the *Sachem*, that had been owned by William S. McCoy, a local ship captain and boat builder known for running shipments of bootlegged rum in the 1920s and early 1930s. While other rum-runners diluted their booze to increase profits, Bill McCoy took pride in delivering only quality booze. This dedication to authenticity led to a popular nickname that stuck as surely as thick rum: "the Real McCoy."

Hatch seemed to make friends as easily as Tom Sawyer. One hot summer day, as he was cooling off by diving from a pier into the harbor, he noticed a newly arrived sailor caulking a boat.

"Hi, there," Norm said, striding up to him. "I'm Norm Hatch."

"I'm Sterling Hayden," said the tall, blond seaman who looked to be in his early twenties, but was actually only a year older than Hatch. Hayden had run away to sea at age seventeen and, at nineteen, took a schooner from Gloucester to Tahiti. Though an acting career in Hollywood would come soon enough, when Hatch met Hayden, he was "as bashful as a man could possibly be." This was true even though he quickly became the envy of all of the girls in Gloucester, "a blond god hanging off the yard arm."

While his summers were filled with adventures and colorful characters, winters on the New England coast could be harsh. Tempera-
tures dipped to twenty degrees below zero, freezing the harbor. Hatch
took a short cut to school by walking across the ice floes. When the
tide went out, the ice would break from hitting the rocks. "The trick
was to run fast enough to keep one foot on the ice floe until you got
to solid ice. I was forbidden from doing that, but I did it anyway."

His antics nearly took a tragic twist one day when he climbed
down the side of a ship in the harbor to cross over to his house. He had
forgotten that the warmth created by the ship would soften the adja-
cent ice. He promptly slid down to his chest in the frigid water, barely
managing to pull himself out before hypothermia set in. Once he
pulled himself up onto the frozen surface, it was all he could do to
knock the ice off his trousers and move his legs. From then on, he
never forgot the deadly power of the sea.

At Gloucester High School, he spent three years in the ROTC
program, a requirement in those days. He also took a weekly class in
military science, where he studied World War I–era tactics, as well as
the care and feeding of an '03 .30-caliber Springfield rifle. So began a
lifelong infatuation with the military.

"It was a very fine rifle," Hatch said of the single-shot weapon
adopted by the armed services in 1903. Semi-automatic M1s would
replace it, but decades later, Hatch would fondly recall, "With the '03,
you had to aim and shoot."

Hatch studied the Army field manual, practiced marching, and
learned about military organization. Another seed was planted for the
future combat cameraman when he joined the photography club at
Gloucester High. He started shooting with a Kodak camera that had a
simple development process, requiring only sunlight and no chemicals
to turn a negative into a print (chemicals were needed only to preserve
the positive image). As his camera work improved, he spent $12 on a
35-millimeter Argus, a compact German camera equipped with a
range-finder that allowed for longer shots. It was an exciting time to

be a cub photographer, and he decided to venture over to Boston to visit an old burlesque house with some buddies. Cameras were prohibited, but Hatch managed to sneak in his Argus.

The lighting was dim in the strip joint, though, so his first investigative photojournalism was something of a bust. But the mere prospect of photographing scantily clad ladies was enough to whet his appetite for future attempts. It was the age of the "candid camera"; even in the depths of the Depression, camera sales soared.

In the spring of 1938, as he was close to completing his senior year and graduating from Gloucester High, Hatch got an offer to sail around the world. "I wanted to go with them, but my mother said, 'No, you're not. You're going to finish high school.'" By now, Norm had already attended thirteen schools. Ruth Hatch wasn't about to let him stop this close to the finish line.

After graduating at age seventeen—a year younger than most of his contemporaries—the Depression was still grinding away. Job prospects were dim. Norm had dreamed of applying to Harvard University, where he had watched Saturday football games. But when Ruth Hatch asked her son what he wanted to study there, Norm was honest and said, "I don't have the slightest idea."

"Well," she replied, "If you don't know, I'm not about to find the money for you to go."

So Norm went to work, first as a messenger boy for Metropolitan Life, then as a self-employed handyman around Boston. He bought a Ford dump truck for $75, using its hand-cranked rear bed to pick up loam and deliver the rich earth to gardeners around town. It wasn't long before he tired of delivering dirt and visited the federal office building in Boston to enlist in the U.S. Navy. His father, an engineer, saw it as a pragmatic move, telling Norm, "Look, I think the only thing for you to do is join the service, because it will give you room and board and give you an education. Of all of them, I suggest you join the Navy because you get aboard a capital ship and you've got everything a city's got" in terms of learning a professional trade—plumbing, electrical work, or carpentry. "So you're bound to learn a trade," his father concluded, "and when you get out at the end of four years, you'll at least know how to do something other than fire a gun."

That made sense to Norm, so he took a mental and physical exam to join the Navy, which he passed. He had high hopes for shipping out fairly soon, especially after the Boston recruiting office sent a chief petty officer to visit his house to check out his home life and family. "That was because of the Depression. The services were all filled up with people who were looking for a paycheck and a place to hang their hats and get something to eat."

The recruiters advised him to be patient, since it could take at least four months to accept him for the First District, which included all of New England. The Navy was accepting only about a dozen young men each month. Months passed, and Hatch kept dumping his loads of loam around town. As 1939 began, Norm returned to the recruiting office to see where he stood. Again, he was told to be patient. He kept asking, even after he turned eighteen on March 2, 1939. The answer was always the same: because the peacetime Navy had reduced its recruiting quota, he would just have to wait.

Hatch managed to hold on for more than a year after graduation. Finally, in June 1939, he walked into the Navy recruiting office and was told that his enlistment date had been delayed again, probably for another four or five months.

Frustrated and fed up, Hatch walked out, but on his way to the elevator, he dropped by the Marine Corps recruiting station on a whim. "Sergeant, if I was to say today I want to join the Marine Corps, how long would it be before you take me?"

The recruiting sergeant looked up from his desk and said, "When do you want to go? Friday or two weeks from Friday?"

Hatch tried not to show he was stunned. "Not this Friday," he replied. "That's too soon. But how about two weeks from Friday?"

When he went home to announce his momentous decision, his mother did not object, though his grandmother let it be known she had never approved of Marines ever since Ruth had dated one during World War I. His father was traveling, working for an old friend at Marmon Harrington in Indianapolis. The farm-equipment manufacturer made small tanks for The Netherlands' and, coincidentally, for the U.S. Marine Corps. Because Irving Hatch sensed that war with Japan was inevitable, when he did learn of his son's enlistment, he didn't try to stop him.

Before he could second-guess himself, Norm Hatch revisited the Marine recruiting office, raised his right hand, and, on July 7, 1939, swore to preserve and protect the government and Constitution of the United States. With that, he was given a train ticket to travel, along with a few other Boston youths, to the recruit training depot located somewhere in the swamps of South Carolina at a place called Parris Island.

CHAPTER THREE

Carpe Diem at P.I.

The transformation of floundering youth with flaccid muscles and soft souls into steely soldiers, sailors, airmen, or Marines is a quintessential American rite of passage. But the U.S. Marine Corps has always prided itself on setting a high bar for reshaping the bodies, minds, and possibly even the souls of its recruits. This military alchemy was made all the more mysterious by the location of its training laboratory in the swamps of coastal Carolina. By the time Hatch boarded a southbound train in Boston—his first trip below the Mason-Dixon line—he could hardly hazard a guess about what awaited him.

Like other youths of his day, Hatch's view of the Marines was slightly idyllic, shaped by the post–World War I plays and books that tended to glamorize the rakish Leatherneck. Broadway plays like *What Price Glory?*—written by World War I Marines Maxwell Anderson and Lawrence T. Stallings—reflected the battlefield exploits of the men who bravely battled the Germans at Belleau Wood. The 1926 book *Fix Bayonets!* by Capt. John W. Thomason Jr. of the 5th Marines also helped etch into the American consciousness the enduring image of what historian Edwin H. Simmons calls "the tough, wise-cracking, hard-as-nails, heart-of-gold Marine sergeant." This role would be played in film by such actors as Wallace Beery, Edmund Lowe, and Victor McLaglen, who shaped the public image of the Marine as "lean, sunburnt, in faded khakis and rakish field hat, rattling through some jungle banana republic," Simmons writes, with "an '03 rifle in one hand and a bottle in the other." Or if he was serving in France, this mythical Marine would be "shouldering arms and starting down a shell-rutted road for the Western Front murky with gray-green fog, turning to grin and wave good-by to Mademoiselle, the innkeeper's gallant if naughty daughter."[1]

There were no naughty daughters waiting for the recruits, only a tiring train ride down the eastern seaboard, with glimpses of Independence Hall in Philadelphia, the docks of Baltimore, and the Capitol dome and Washington Monument. Then the train left civilization as Hatch had known it, rocking through the rolling farmland of Virginia, the pine forests of North Carolina, and the pine tar shacks—where children in overalls ran out bare-footed—along the tracks in South Carolina. Hatch gazed in wonder at the passing panorama.

But for all the strange sights and his natural insecurity about leaving home, Hatch had an intuitive sense that he was heading down the right path. "You've often heard about the effect the Depression had on people who lived through it," he reflected later. "We didn't suffer in a sense the way many people did. We always had a place to live and food to eat. But I think it pretty much established my credo for how I was going to live. It was looking for the next thing, never standing still and waiting for something to come to you. You had to go out and look for it."

As the first man sworn in at the Boston recruiting office, he had been made the senior recruit on the trip, with orders to try to keep the five other men together after the train pulled up at Port Royal, South Carolina. The small group was met by a Marine drill instructor who was direct but didn't start shouting at them, at least not then and there.

"Shape up, men, and just do what I tell you to do, and you won't have any problem." With that admonition, the D.I. loaded them into a boat that crossed Archer's Creek to the nearby training base.

Established in 1915 to prepare enlisted Marines who were shipping out to fight the Germans in France, Parris Island consisted of more than 8,000 acres of salt marsh, with less than half inhabitable by humankind. Most of the island was a breeding ground for alligators, water moccasins, hammerhead sharks, mosquitoes, and other insects and beasts—all guaranteed to test the mettle of city boys and farm boys alike.

With its tin Quonset huts and double-deck wooden barracks from the Great War, its wood-hewn obstacle courses and sandy hand-grenade pits, Recruit Training Depot Parris Island had a Spartan simplicity that was rooted in the Corps' DNA. As one gunnery sergeant put it in 1935, "They started right out telling everybody how great they were. Pretty soon they got to believing it themselves. And they have been busy ever since proving they were right."[2]

Yet when Norm Hatch stepped off the boat at Parris Island, the proud Corps was still operating as a small branch of the Department of the Navy. The Marines were seen by Navy and Army leaders as little more than a security unit for American vessels. There was historical precedent for this view, since the Continental Congress created the Marine Corps on November 10, 1775, to help protect George Washington's naval forces.

The Corps' first two battalions—led by one colonel, two lieutenant colonels, and two majors—distinguished themselves in the Revolutionary War, joining the Navy's John Paul Jones on the sloop-of-war *Ranger* in overpowering British warships and supply vessels. But for all its colorful history, by June 30, 1939, when Norm Hatch joined the Corps, there were only 18,052 active-duty Marines—about the same size as the New York City Police Department.[3]

Now Hatch was a "boot," a Marine in name only until he completed the rigorous nine weeks of training. After an uneventful arrival, he followed the D.I. to the sick bay with the other new arrivals. They were ordered to strip down to their shorts and given a physical and dental exam. Though Hatch was in good shape thanks to his sailing and swimming, his teeth were rotten, requiring fourteen fillings.

Adding to his modest start to his military career, Hatch learned the Corps was running short of uniforms, so the recruits were forced to wear their civilian clothes for about a week—in his case, white flannel trousers, blue jacket, and loafers.

His D.I. was a short, bandy-legged sergeant named Johnny Watkins, an old-school China Marine and "field music"—as Corps musicians were known at the time—who could blow a horn. Sergeant Watkins was also known for blowing his top at the slightest provocation. "He carried a golf stick without the driver on the bottom of it. You'd hear this thing whistling through the air to your back side if you did anything wrong. And if he had a notion that your drill was not going correctly and you were the cause of it, he might wait until you had faced away from him . . . and he would run at you full speed, and then leap into the air and with his elbows and knees hit you in the small of your back. You'd go sprawling, and if you were in the rear rank, you'd take down two or three guys with you."

Watkins seemed to enjoy the recruits' fear and loathing, hollering, "Well, that ought to teach you a lesson." The D.I. had other disciplinary techniques that Hatch charitably called "quite innovative." Once, when someone snickered during formations, the sergeant yelled, "All right! You want to laugh, go ahead and laugh."

The stunned recruit couldn't laugh, of course, but others foolishly did. "All right," the D.I. announced, "if that's the way you like it, we'll *all* laugh." With that, he promptly lined up the entire platoon at the wooden wash racks in the middle of the barracks. The racks were V-shaped with water piping and faucets in between. Sergeant Watkins ordered the recruits to mount the wooden racks on their knees, forming two lines, rear to rear.

In this absurd pose, he forced them to grasp their Springfield rifles, each weighing more than eight pounds, and hold them out over the edge of the racks. Then he ordered them to put their wide-brimmed field hats in their mouths and hold them with their teeth.

"Now try to laugh!"

The recruits who failed to laugh loud enough to please the sergeant were kicked in the rear and knocked down to the concrete floor.

Hatch could deal with the silly hazing rituals, but the confirmed New Englander found it hardest to adjust to running, marching, and crawling in the oppressive heat and humidity of South Carolina's low country. Nonetheless, Hatch managed to distinguish himself in his platoon. His high-school ROTC training helped him achieve sharpshooter status on the rifle range, and he was named a platoon squad leader. While this was an honor, it was not without its hazards.

"We had a young fellow from the Georgia hills who looked and acted like he was permanently tied to a plow. He was a big fellow who had long arms and they always looked like they were holding onto the plow handle. . . . He could not make a timely facing movement [during close-order drills], so the D.I. took people in each position around him and said, 'Every time you face him on a facing move, you *kick him* until he learns to run and move in the right sequence.'"

As it happened, Private Hatch was the first one to face him, and when the Georgia boy failed to make the correct move, Sergeant Watkins hit Hatch in the back and yelled, "I told you to kick him no matter which way he faces, no matter how he faces, or when he faces." The message sunk in: every time the errant recruit turned, his fellow recruits kicked him over and over. The Georgia boy suffered such a beating that he could not sit down for more than two days, but the harsh training must have served its purpose because the farm boy eventually learned the lesson and went on to win the distinction of "most improved" recruit.

Before the end of the nine-week-long regimen, Hatch remembered some of the rare cerebral advice given by his drill instructor: always read the barracks bulletin board. That way, you could follow what was going across the wider Marine Corps. One day, something caught his eye: a notice that the Marine Corps Institute in Washington, D.C., had an opening for an English teacher. "Hell," he thought, "I never had any problem with English in high school, so I'll apply for it."

He wrote the Institute, which he knew nothing about, and promptly forgot about it. As one of the top graduates at boot camp— with good height, looks, and bearing—Hatch was picked to attend Sea School in Portsmouth, Virginia, where he would receive advanced training to stand guard aboard ship. "Even though I liked the idea of going aboard ship, I'd been aboard ship in Gloucester, and I knew what it was like." After trudging through the swamp and mire of Parris Island, he was also having second thoughts about serving as a regular infantryman or "gravel cruncher." Teaching in Washington sounded like an interesting alternative.

Two days before graduation in September, Hatch heard the ominous sound of Sergeant Watkins's boots pounding the wooden floor of the barracks. His sense of dread deepened when he saw the sergeant waving a letter above his head. Norm had formed a grudging friendship with the diminutive D.I., who even had trusted him to mail a letter to a "Mrs. Watkins" in Shanghai, China. Hatch knew darn well that Watkins already had a wife in the nearby town of Beaufort, South Carolina, but he also knew that such long-distance bigamy was not unusual among "Old Corps" Marines.

"Norm," the agitated D.I. exclaimed, "what in the goddamn hell have you been doing?"

"I haven't the slightest idea, sergeant," he replied. "What have I been doing?"

Watkins handed him the letter from Washington. "I've got orders to transfer you to Washington immediately to the Marine Corps Institute's English department." He shook his head and said in disgust, "What the hell kind of a job is that for a Marine?"

Hatch couldn't help but grin. "I don't know, sergeant, but I'm sure I will find out."

On a crisp Sunday morning in late September 1939, Pvt. Norman Hatch stepped off the train at Union Station in Washington, D.C. Striding across the marble floor, he gazed up at the high ceiling, triumphal archways, and classical statues and felt like a million bucks. He was in the nation's capital, off on his own while the rest of his graduating class was bound for Portsmouth for Sea School or to Quantico for advanced training with the Amphibious Corps. At eighteen years of age, Hatch felt independent and was eager to experience the next chapter of his new life in the Marine Corps.

In those days, servicemen carried their weapons while they traveled. Norm shouldered his Springfield rifle, hoisted his sea bag, and set out for Marine Barracks, about a mile away. As he passed the taxi stands, he scanned the headlines on the Washington papers—the *Post*, the *Evening Star*, the *Times-Herald*. Hitler was menacing Poland, which his troops had invaded on the first day of the month in their vaunted *blitzkrieg*, and Russian Premier Stalin was trying to defend the ten-year "non-aggression pact" he had signed with the German Führer. Britain and France were mobilizing troops. War was in the air.

Yet on this pristine day, Hatch took time to marvel at the sights and sounds around him: the U.S. Capitol dome and, at the other end of Constitution Avenue, the Washington Monument looming over the stately government offices. He strolled along the shady streets east of the Capitol, idly thinking how some of the brownstone homes reminded him of his mother's boarding house back in Boston.

After a long hike from the train station through the Victorian neighborhoods of southeast Washington, he approached a gate at Eighth and I Streets. Hatch stopped to admire the brick-walled complex of the Marine Barracks, which covered two city blocks. He noticed the mansard roof of the Commandant's House, which, according to legend, survived the attack by the British in 1814 when they burned most of the other public buildings in Washington.

Walking up to the front gate, he explained his orders to the guard and was sent to the Marine Corps Institute housed inside. He found

2nd Lt. Hugh Elwood, who was in charge of the Corp's educational branch. He assigned his newest teacher to a bunk up in a tower that rose above the brick barracks like some kind of medieval castle.

Once he went to work grading papers, though, Washington's magic quickly wore off. Hatch grew bored with the routine at the Institute, which provided a correspondence course for Marines stationed around the world. He read English lessons and letters sent from the field and corrected grammar, punctuation, spelling, and any writing mistakes he spotted among the far-flung students, some of whom were naturalized Americans simply trying to master the basics of English. It was tedious work, so he was happy to receive orders to travel to Warm Springs, Georgia. There he would join the Marine Guard for a two-week stint at President Franklin D. Roosevelt's famed rural retreat.

Hatch smiled to think of FDR, whom he had seen on the campaign trail back in 1932 during Roosevelt's first run for office. Ruth Hatch, eager to see this man who she trusted would cure the nation's economic woes, drove her eleven-year-old son from Gloucester to nearby Ipswich, Massachusetts, and found a viewing point on the city's main street. They stood on the running board of their car, waving and hollering at the official entourage as it approached. As luck would have it, FDR stopped and motioned for Ruth and her son to come over to his car. Perhaps flirting a bit, he said to Mrs. Hatch, "I have always liked red hair, and you resemble the movie star Jeannette McDonald." Then he patted Norm on the head and said, "Be a good boy and make your mother proud!" Enchanted, Ruth Hatch became a staunch Democrat and voted for FDR each time he ran for reelection.

By the time Norm Hatch arrived for his guard duty in Georgia, the president was making one of his periodic forays to Warm Springs to exercise his polio-weakened body in the mineral water and escape the crush of New Deal politics in Washington. Hatch was walking as a guard on post behind the Roosevelt's cottage with his Springfield rifle on his shoulder when he saw a stunning sight: the president himself was motioning him to come closer—the second time in his life that FDR had beckoned him over. But Hatch assumed the president simply wanted him to walk closer to the cottage, so he did.

FDR had other ideas, though, and kept waving for him to come closer, a visual cue that put Hatch in something of a bind. For his orders strictly prohibited him from any close contact with the president while he was on duty. When he respectfully told this to the president, Roosevelt informed him that Hatch should remember that he was the commander-in-chief and thus could modify or change any military order.

"Where are you from, son?" FDR asked.

Hatch told him the story of the 1932 campaign stop in Ipswich. Roosevelt flashed his trademark smile and said he did indeed remember the visit. He told Hatch he greatly admired Gloucester's fishing fleet and nautical history. Then he suggested Hatch return to walking his post, assuring him their conversation would remain a secret between them.[4]

Soon enough, Hatch learned that the president was quite the prankster. The sentries were under order any time they sighted him driving in his Ford Phaeton convertible past the main gate to shout, "Turn out the guard for the President of the United States!" At this order, everyone was supposed to hurry out of the barracks and stand at attention for their commander-in-chief. So when the sentry yelled, "Turn out the guard," all thirty men who had been sleeping, writing letters, or relaxing scrambled to get into their guard uniforms and grab their weapons to present arms to the president. Only about two thirds of the men had turned out when FDR disappeared down a logging road, grinning broadly and waving to the confused formation of Marines.

Then he repeated the prank, passing the gate, smiling once more, and waving his cigarette holder. He kept driving by, only to pass by the gate for a third time. This time around, the Marines had managed a nearly complete formation.

So when Hatch spotted the president's car for a fourth time, slowly inching its way past the officers' tents and creeping toward the parade ground, he cried out again, "Turn out the guard for the President of the United States." Only this time, no one believed him because the Ford was nowhere to be seen. In the wake of Roosevelt's prank, Hatch wryly observed, "If a strong noncommissioned officer hadn't prevailed, I probably would have been stomped into the ground."[5]

Meanwhile, FDR was enjoying his prank, sneaking into the middle of the Marine encampment without being detected until Hatch caught him. Unfortunately, the joke was on the officer-of-the-day, who was crossing the parade ground headed for the showers clothed only in his wooden clogs and a wraparound towel.

That spring, Hatch drew a second assignment to Warm Springs. This time around, he volunteered to be the quartermaster's assistant, which excluded him from guard duty. Instead, he went to Georgia a week ahead of the troops, riding in the back of a truck filled with supplies and tents.

Once the camp was set up, Hatch spent his free time riding horses that lived in a stable used by patients of the Warm Springs Foundation. Since few of the polio patients could ride, the Marines were encouraged to exercise the horses. Norm was an experienced horseman, so he selected a large mustang to ride through the Georgia woods.

The best part of the ride was when the mustang made a stretch run for the barn, "a full-out canter which allowed you to sit back in the saddle and enjoy life," as Hatch would describe it decades later in *Leatherneck* magazine.

"On one of those rides heading for the barn, I nearly maimed the First Lady," he continued. "I was about to round the corner near the main gate of the camp when Mrs. Roosevelt and Missy LeHand, the president's secretary, were in the middle of the old logging road. When I came upon them, they couldn't have been more than fifteen feet in front of me.

"My horse was in full canter and had a real head of steam! The startled look on the faces of the two women was one of abject fear.

There were trees on each side of this small roadway which precluded me from trying to change the horse's direction. . . . I took the gamble that the horse would do its best to stop, so I pulled hard back on the reins, and the animal sent straight up on its hind legs. I fell off, still holding the reins, and when I got up, the horse was shaking and quivering from fright. I immediately looked for the two women and found that each had jumped sideways into the rutted ditch nearest them."

Firmly grasping the mustang's bridle, he rushed to the First Lady to help her out of the ditch. All the while, he was quite sure that "my Marine Corps future had just gone down the proverbial drain. As I was helping her to her feet, I was apologizing just about as fast as I could, when she interrupted me and said, 'Son, please do not be concerned. It was our fault for not getting out of your way. We could hear you coming, but did not realize how close you were.'"

With that, she left Hatch, who led the shaking horse back to the barn.[6]

After six months of tedium teaching the English correspondence courses, Hatch learned of an opening at *Leatherneck*, the official magazine of the Marine Corps. The publication began in 1917 as the *Quantico Leatherneck*, a newspaper published by off-duty Marines. ("Leatherneck" is one of the Marines' various nicknames, derived from the leather-lined collar worn by the first Marines.) In 1920, Commandant John A. Lejeune made *Leatherneck* the Corps' official newspaper; in 1925, it became a magazine.

Hatch applied for the job and was accepted by the editor, Lt. Joe Butcher, who laughed, "At least you can put a sentence together." Hatch became a jack-of-all-trades, but his main job was to edit a column called "Sound Off," which answered questions from Marines stationed around the world on a wide array of topics, from uniform changes and pay to complaints about food.

The magazine touted the accomplishments of former Marines and provided a mix of history, opinion, lore, and scuttlebutt. Under the heading, "Marine Oddities," for instance, the November 1939 issue announced that "Peter Berger, a Marine flyer in the World War, is now boss of the mechanics for United Airlines." A sketch of Berger showed him jauntily wearing his United cap. Another item noted the close connection between the Marines and the Secret Service in protecting the president, including "such occasions as President Roosevelt's visits to Warm Springs, Ga. or at his home in Hyde Park, New York."

The December 1939 issue marked Pvt. N. T. Hatch's first appearance on the masthead. The cover showed a sketch of a rosy-cheeked, blue-eyed Marine in dress blues with a champagne glass in hand and the headline, "A Merry Christmas!" Notwithstanding the cheeriness, the Christmas editorial took a somber tone: "To thinking persons, this Christmas will be the saddest day of the year. Nearly two thousand years ago, in the humble town of Bethlehem, there was born a babe destined to teach the world a new philosophy—a doctrine of peace and love. . . . Yet celebrations this year will come to many merely as an interlude between bombardments. Peace does not reign this year, and men are showing little good will toward one another."

Hatch enjoyed his half-year tenure on the magazine, which allowed him to do more writing, including wry commentary on one fan letter: "An eminent member of the Art Department is now receiving 'fan mail.' . . . We only hope it was the staff member's talent as an artist, and not merely personal magnetism, that brought forth those effusive expressions of admiration from a certain feminine reader."

Hatch's dry wit seems evident throughout "Sound Off." In one item headlined "Warm Springs," the anonymous columnist wrote, "We understand that those members of the Marine Detachment who visited Camp Roosevelt for the first time over Thanksgiving holidays consider WARM Springs a masterpiece of misstatement." In another, he wrote, "We heard over the radio the other day that Rear Admiral Byrd had six pet penguins which he wanted to dispose of before leaving on his expedition to the Antarctic. Which reminds us that there is nothing so serious and dignified as a penguin, unless it is a newly-minted corporal."

Hatch took advantage of the opportunity to learn magazine design and move about the military circles in Washington. Part of his monthly routine was a visit to a printing business operated by a former Marine where he used an "address-o-graph" machine to mail out copies of *Leatherneck*.

After about six months of this routine, Hatch, always on the lookout for new opportunities, started talking with one of his bunkmates who worked in the Office of Navy Information at the Main Navy Building on Constitution Avenue, right in the heart of the federal government. The Marine was unhappy with his work there and proposed trading jobs with Hatch. The switch was approved by a sergeant major; as Hatch explained, "I'd like to see what's up there and see what I can find out."

His on-the-job education continued in downtown Washington. At age nineteen, barely a year into his Marine career, Hatch reported to the Office of Navy Public Relations. He worked Monday through noon on Saturday and enjoyed the bustling office just inside the Main Navy. "We ran the mimeograph machine, we ran all the press releases, we sharpened pencils." And he delivered press releases all over town— his first exposure to Washington's press corps. He could never have imagined this relationship would continue for the next seventy years.

The Navy PR office provided photographs of Navy ships taken at docks and from airplanes around the world, including the proud 7th Fleet based at Pearl Harbor in Hawaii. Hatch savored the feeling of walking around town to deliver press releases and pictures to the newspaper offices—the *Post, Star*, and *Herald-Examiner*—and to the National Press Club. His favorite destination, though, was the studio of Arthur Godfrey, the popular morning radio personality at WJSV, a CBS affiliate in Washington. Godfrey's Navy roots were deep: he had lied about his age to join at age seventeen and became a radio operator on a destroyer. After a stint in the Coast Guard, he got to know President Roosevelt, who gave him a commission in the U.S. Naval Reserve. Hatch loved chatting with Godfrey and enjoyed listening to his morning wakeup call—playing "Anchors Aweigh," the fight song of the U.S. Naval Academy, to rouse the midshipmen at nearby Annapolis.

Though it was a splendid time to be in Washington, enlisted Marines like Hatch often were not held in high repute. This first became apparent when he visited a quality men's clothing store, Raleigh's, to buy some suits and shoes. He put down $20, about half of the purchase price, and started to fill out a form to start a credit line with the store, a standard practice of the day. But when the sales clerk learned Hatch was in the Marine Corps, he turned him down, explaining that was store policy.

Hatch found that strange, so he tried other downtown stores, such as Woodward & Lothrop and the Hecht Co., and was told the same thing. He had avoided going to the cheapest clothier, 7 11 Lucky Regal's on 7th Street, which filled the airwaves with ads promising, "No money down and we'll chase you for the rest."

Hatch discovered that his fellow enlisted men often ran up debt at Lucky Regal's because they had no choice but to do business at the bottom of Washington's retail totem pole. Stumped for a while, Hatch noticed a nattily attired sergeant in the barracks who wore the latest grey herringbone coats, dark trousers, and cordovan shoes. He even had a set of tails in his locker. The NCO, Hatch learned, was living a double life—a tough Marine sergeant by day and an elegant bridge player by night. Such cultured and educated enlisted men were called "gentlemen rankers."

Hatch approached the suave sergeant and told him about the brush off he had gotten at Raleigh's. "How in the hell can I go buy clothes?"

"Well, I buy at The Mode," he explained. The exclusive store was across from Woodward & Lothrop at the corner of 11th and F. The sergeant helped Hatch meet the credit manager, who found him trustworthy and sold him a sport coat and shoes. But though he was better dressed than most of his young peers, Hatch still bristled at the anti-Marine bias. When he met a young lady named Lois Rousseau, he simply didn't tell her at first about his military profession or even where he lived. "I just live over in Southwest Washington," he said vaguely, hoping she wouldn't see through his subterfuge.

Hatch remained alert to notices on the bulletin board at work. One in particular fascinated him: *The March of Time*, the major newsreel series based in New York City, was training military motion-picture cameramen in photojournalism. "Experience not a factor. Anyone can apply," it read.

The March of Time was known as a first-rate operation founded in 1935 by Time, Inc., executive Roy E. Larsen. It was produced and written by brothers Louis and Richard de Rochemont, whose twenty-minute films—which combined filmed news with interviews and dramatizations—were shown weekly between feature presentations in more than 500 theaters nationwide.

Hatch jumped at the chance to become an apprentice at this state-of-the-art media venture. This time, however, his luck did not seem to hold: he soon received a rejection letter for the six-month program in New York City. He applied again, but with the same result. He likely would have given up if he had not worked closely with a lieutenant named Allen Brown, a reserve officer in Navy public relations. Though it was unusual for enlisted men to share meals with officers, Hatch asked Lieutenant Brown if they could have lunch at Main Navy. Then he poured out his story of rejection and said he was ready to give up. Brown, who had been a director for *The March of Time*, told him to persevere and keep him apprised.

After his third rejection in late September 1941, Hatch received an unexpected phone call from Brown. "The producer of *The March of Time*, Louis de Rochemont, is coming to Washington tomorrow, and I've told him your story," he said. "I have to give him some film from stuff we've been releasing that he's going to use in a production, so why don't you take it up to the hotel?"

For once, Hatch was speechless.

The next morning, he picked up the Navy film and hustled to a downtown hotel, where de Rochemont was meeting with some cameramen from the Norwegian Air Force. The journalist-soldiers had escaped the German invasion of Norway by skiing to Sweden and then into Russia. They shipped out to South America and eventually Canada, where they were doing a picture on their escape. De Rochemont was offering some pointers.

When it was Hatch's turn to deliver his film, he managed to tell his tale of rejection, his repeatedly rebuffed efforts to get into the training school. "What do you know about motion pictures?" a dubious de Rochemont asked.

"I don't know much of anything," Hatch replied, "but I've been doing photographic work and have a pretty good understanding of that."

De Rochemont remained noncommittal during the brief meeting. Heading back to Main Navy, Hatch was sure he would be writing press releases for a very long time. But just two days later, his boss came by his desk, uttering something that was becoming a kind of mantra for the young Marine. "Hatch, what the hell have you been doing? I've got orders to transfer you immediately to *The March of Time*."

Hatch grinned broadly. Once again, he had been in the right place at the right time. Though he wasn't a particularly religious man, he was starting to sense that something—or someone—was helping him move on to another rich opportunity. Only later would Lieutenant Brown tell him what happened. Louis de Rochemont had served in the Navy during the First World War, where he had befriended a number of lieutenants who had since climbed up the service's chain of command. One of his old Navy chums was the department's personnel director. De Rochemont had called him and asked for a favor, asking to add a man to the normal complement in the training program so that Hatch could attend. The Navy's personnel chief then called his counterpart in the Marine Corps, who promptly agreed and cut the orders for New York City.

Before he left Washington, Hatch had a chance encounter with the commandant of the Marine Corps, Maj. Gen. Thomas Holcomb.

"How do you like the Marine Corps?" Holcomb asked, standing at the next urinal at Main Navy.

What could he say to the highest-ranking Marine and his ultimate boss? "Sir, I like it very much."

Holcomb asked the nervous private where he worked, then inquired, "Well, do you plan to stay in the Marine Corps?"

"Well," Hatch replied, "at this stage of the game I'm thinking about it seriously."

Washing up, the top Marine offered some advice: "You be good to the Corps, and it will be good to you."

"Yes, sir," Hatch said, pondering the general's wisdom. It would be many years before he realized just how right he was.

In New York in October 1941, the newspapers were blazing with cautionary headlines about the dangers of war with Germany, creating a sense of urgency in the bustling city. Hatch busied himself at the newsreel school, learning mostly by osmosis from such motion-picture pros as George Stoetzel, who had been booted out of Hollywood after telling off a prima donna actress. Stoetzel took the new student along with him on assignments, such as filming the first air-raid sirens installed in New York and attending a meeting of the German Bund, an organization sympathetic to Nazi Germany, with chapters springing up across the U.S. After Stoetzel heard about a Bund meeting in the Bronx, he decided to drop by with Hatch as his assistant cameraman. They set up their camera equipment in the rear of the meeting hall and started filming the proceeding as speakers began railing against Jews and praising Hitler. Suddenly, though, the audience turned and began shouting epithets at the cameramen, who had not been invited to cover the meeting. Amid full-throated cries of "Heil Hitler," the pair was marched out of the meeting, a chilling reminder of the hatred and bigotry that had spread like a cancer across the Atlantic.

There was little time for reflection, though, as Hatch peppered Stoetzel with questions about camera angles, lighting, and cinematic storytelling. The cameraman liked to get out into the field, including a foray to North Carolina to visit a recently opened training base named for John J. Lejeune, the legendary hero of campaigns from the Spanish-American War to the "devil dogs" who scared the Germans fighting in France during World War I. Camp Lejeune would become one of the Corps' major training and education bases, but in late 1941, it was little more than a tent camp in the pine forests and bogs of eastern North Carolina. Hatch served as a go-fer setting up lights and sound equipment as Stoetzel chronicled the 1st Marine Division's training for overseas deployment.

On December 7, 1941, Hatch was sleeping soundly in his room on Lexington Avenue after staying out late the night before. He drifted off to sleep listening to the radio. Then he heard something which, at first, his mind simply refused to believe. He wondered if it was a hoax like Orson Welles's broadcast of *The War of the Worlds*, which had sparked widespread panic with reports of martians tromping across New Jersey. But when he heard the radio announcer say, "All service men should report to their service installations," a chill went down his spine. This was no hoax. The Japanese really had attacked the United States at Pearl Harbor. Japanese aircraft carriers launched 366 aircraft in an early-morning assault on the U.S. Navy Pacific Fleet, sinking or damaging eight battleships and destroying or severely damaging another eleven warships. The sneak attack killed 2,400 Americans. Japan also attacked Malaya, the Philippines, and Hong Kong. Hitler and Mussolini, in a show of Axis solidarity, also declared war on the United States.

For Hatch, the very ground seemed to shift beneath his bare feet. He dialed up the sergeant major at the Brooklyn Navy Yard, where he could hear chaotic shouting in the background. "Do you want me to come down?"

"Jesus, no!" the sergeant major bellowed. "I'm so filled with people now I don't know what to do with them."

Soon Louis de Rochemont called. "Norm, I want you to come in the office and load up one of the Buicks with equipment. You drive it to Washington because you know your way around town." The plan was for him to bring all of the necessary camera gear, arriving that night in Washington, to meet the cameramen the next morning after they arrived by train.

De Rochemont explained the reason for the road trip: "The president is going to declare war."

The next morning, de Rochemont called again. "Wear your uniform. You'll probably be one of the only ones allowed to move anywhere around the Capitol."

It was sound advice. After picking up the veteran newsreel cameramen and delivering them to the Capitol, Hatch could see that the seat of American government was under unusually high security in the wake of the shocking attack on the Pacific Fleet and the deaths of a large number of sailors, soldiers, and Marines.

After *The March of Time* crew got its big camera set up in the House gallery, high above where Roosevelt would address a joint session of Congress, Hatch took one of the crew's handheld cameras. Just as de Rochemont predicted, since he was in his uniform, he was allowed to freely roam around the halls of Congress to shoot "cutaway shots"—extra scenes to help tell the story. Out in the hallways, he looked for important members of Congress and used the small camera to capture images of the nation's leaders: House Speaker Sam Rayburn, Senate Majority Leader Alben Barkley, and Vice President Henry Wallace, among others. As they waited to enter, they talked excitedly among themselves. Their faces showed the shock, anticipation, and anger they were experiencing at the death and destruction of America's Pacific foothold at Pearl Harbor.

Pumped up to cover the story of a lifetime, Hatch went outside to the special side entrance where FDR was to arrive. After the presidential limousine slid up to the curb, the commander-in-chief got out of the car and into a wheelchair. But following the protocol of the day, neither Hatch nor any of the other photographers on hand took pictures of their disabled president. Some things were better left unsaid or unshown—or so thought the journalists of the day.

Hatch stood out as the only man in uniform among the civilian press corps. Roosevelt nodded at him, flashing his ebullient smile and giving him a half wave, half salute. Hatch returned the salute. Then the president rose from his wheelchair and, aided by his son, James, a captain in the Marine Corps, he locked his leg braces and lurched toward the House chamber.

Hatch ran up to the upper gallery, where the buzz of anticipation among congressional staffers and visitors down on the floor was fast becoming a roar. *The March of Time*'s camera stood ready, alongside a battery of other newsreel makers—Fox Movietone News, Paramount News, MGM, Warner Brothers Hearst Metrotone News, and Universal Newsreel—along with a line of excited photographers for the wire services and major newspapers.

With everyone working knee to knee, there was no room to store boxes of extra film. And since each camera ran through about ninety feet of film per minute, the newsreel-makers faced the same problem: how to feed their cameras. Hatch agreed to serve as a runner, grabbing film as needed from the boxes stashed by each crew out in the hallway.

Shortly after noon, the senators, congressmen, and Supreme Court justices somberly filed into the House chamber. Hatch looked across the upper gallery and saw another familiar face, Mrs. Roosevelt. After their close call at Warm Springs, he felt a special kinship with the kindly First Lady who had spared his career. She looked worried as only a mother can be at such a critical juncture: four of her sons were of military age. Sitting nearby for moral support was another great lady, Mrs. Woodrow Wilson, the widow of another war president, who had come at FDR's request.[7]

Shortly before one o'clock, Speaker Rayburn rapped his gavel and silenced the restive chamber. "The President of the United States!"

Hatch stopped running for a moment and watched as FDR moved slowly on the arm of Captain Roosevelt. Then the president opened a loose-leaf notebook and began his speech: "Yesterday, December 7, 1941—a date which will live in infamy—the United States of America was suddenly and deliberately attacked by naval and air forces of the Empire of Japan."

Hatch didn't feel chills at that point as much as resignation and suspicion about what might happen next. The 7th Fleet, now battered and mostly sunk in the oily waters of Pearl Harbor, was supposed to form America's first line of defense against Japan's military aggression across the Pacific. The scuttlebutt among the reporters and cameramen was that America was now exposed to attack along the West Coast. Except for the Marine Corps' recruit training depot at San Diego and the nearby Navy base and the Army's small base at The Presidio in San Francisco, America had few ground, naval, or air forces to defend thousands of miles of Pacific coastline. Even now, the Japanese were rumored to be preparing an invasion force for the rocky crags and beaches of California, Oregon, and Washington.

But Roosevelt sounded strong and confident and not the least bit cowed. His short speech was frequently interrupted by bursts of applause as he concluded, "I ask that the Congress declare that since the unprovoked and dastardly attack by Japan on Sunday, December 7, 1941, a state of war has existed between the United States and the Japanese Empire."

Roosevelt closed his notebook, and Hatch dashed out for more film as Congress cascaded with cheers, claps, and rebel yells. The die was cast. The cameras needed to be fed.

CHAPTER FOUR

War on the Silver Screen

In early 1942, America was preparing to wage a two-front war, starting in North Africa with British forces in Operation Torch, that would stretch the Atlantic Fleet's new Amphibious Force to the limit. It would take months to coordinate the massive movement of more than 100,000 troops and equipment around German U-boats menacing the East Coast of the United States in predatory "wolfpacks." As America awoke from two decades of isolationism and began gearing up its manufacturing might to fight for its collective life, the country went through a period of doubt and despair as the Japanese Army rampaged across China and down into the Southwest Pacific, where it occupied Guadalcanal and the rest of the Solomon island chain.

During this period, all Norm Hatch could do was prepare for whatever lay ahead by honing his cinematic skills at *The March of Time*. Producer Louis de Rochemont was impressed by his drive and talent and received permission from the Corps to extend Hatch's apprenticeship for three months to help instruct other bright-eyed Marines. Among the trainees in his class was a native New Yorker, Johnny Ercole, with whom Hatch became fast friends. A street-smart kid with French and Italian roots, Ercole always had an interest in motion pictures and spent the last year of high school working a night job at *The March of Time*. After graduation, he worked as a still photographer for the *Daily Reporter* in White Plains, New York, before joining the Marines in 1940.

This intensive training for shutterbugs like Hatch and Ercole was one small part of the Marine Corps' wider effort to recruit, train, and deploy journalists and cameramen to document the unfolding epic. This was especially important in the area of recruitment since the Corps—historically the stepchild of the U.S. Navy—was being reconfigured as a much larger, division-size military force. Only by such rapid expansion would the Marines stand a chance of defeating the Japanese on the dozens of heavily defended coral islands that were strung like barbed-wire across the western Pacific. The Japanese took advantage of both natural and man-made obstacles to stop American forces from exacting revenge for the attack on Pearl Harbor.

The key player in the Corps' public transformation was Brig. Gen. Robert L. Denig, the head of the public-affairs office, who began plundering newsrooms for talented journalists. Denig and his staff recruited the likes of Sam Stavisky, then assistant city editor of the *Washington Post*, and *Post* reporters Al Lewis, Jack Gerrity, and Irv Schlossenberg. These hard-charging combat correspondents became known as "Denig's Demons."

Other top reporters and editors were lured away from the *Washington Times-Herald* and the *News*. Denig's best recruiter was a tall, handsome first sergeant, Walter J. Shipman, who cut an impressive figure as he strode into newsrooms wearing his dress blues. He was a real-life recruiting poster, according to journalists who signed up. "Shipman, to me, represented the Gung Ho, China Marine," said the *Post*'s Stavisky. "He did as good a selling job for the Marines as anybody."[1]

Shipman, however, denied he was the main motivator for reporters to join the Marines. Instead, it was his ability to give them "the complete assurance of their getting into combat."

The Marines felt that they had to hustle to keep up with the better staffed and funded recruiting efforts of the Army and Navy. In this regard, the Corps' leadership could see the importance of keeping the public, including President Roosevelt and Congress, informed about the long road ahead in the Pacific. An early clash with the Japanese at Wake Island on December 11, 1941, proved that when it came to getting frontline and front-page coverage, the Corps was woefully behind the Army and Navy. At Wake, 2,000 miles from Honolulu, the Marines had been attacked by Rear Adm. Sadmichi Kajioka's Wake Island Invasion Force consisting of a light cruiser, six destroyers, two transports, and a landing party of 560 infantry-trained sailors. The small garrison of Marines commanded by Maj. James Devereux mounted a courageous and "savage" defense, rebuffing the Japanese on the morning of December 11.[2]

Kajioka regrouped and, with 830 men, returned to Wake with a vengeance on December 23. Devereux had 250 Marines, 100 civilian volunteers, and no more than a few rounds of ammunition. The Americans valiantly fought until they had fired their last bullet. But after nearly two weeks of resistance, Devereux was forced to walk out of his battered command post "with a white rag on a swab handle and surrender to a Japanese officer." The officer spoke fluent English and offered Devereux a cigarette, informing him that he had attended the San Francisco Fair in 1939.[3]

The Marines at Wake Island served in the best tradition of the Corps, but back home, most of Devereux's countrymen knew little or nothing about it. "There was a story on Wake to be written but there was no one there to write it," Marine historian Benis M. Frank explains. "All that arrived in Washington were dry, dispassionate, routine messages which had to be converted into communiqués for general release." The Corps was failing to tell its story, both in words and in pictures. Denig and his boss, Commandant Thomas Holcomb, realized they needed cameramen, too, including motion-picture professionals. Wallace Nelson, a young officer with friends in Hollywood, was called on to start the first photographic-services branch. Nelson had experience making training films on amphibious operations in San Diego and hobnobbed with animators at the Walt Disney Studios in Los Angeles.

Shortly after the attack on Pearl Harbor, Nelson arrived at Quantico and started from scratch with a two-man staff (a private and a corporal) and little camera gear. One of his first decisions was to arrange with Louis de Rochemont to send more enlisted men to join Hatch for training at *The March of Time*. Then he went to New York to visit Time, Inc., and other media outlets to learn more about the latest motion-picture innovations.

Nelson was ordered by Commandant Holcomb "to get a recruiting film made by a major studio in Hollywood as a quid pro quo for cooperation that we had routinely given in the production of service-oriented feature films." Twentieth Century Fox Studios had recently finished a film at Marine Corps Base San Diego, so Nelson decided to start there.[4]

"The studio was most cooperative," Nelson wrote, "assigning one of their top screen writers, Lamar Trotti, to prepare a narration, and providing the narrator (an anonymous Robert Taylor)." Nelson never met Fox studio czar Darryl Zanuck, but his underlings helped produce a two-reel film "which was very effective in our recruiting effort."

Nelson also was wined and dined at the Ambassador Hotel in Los Angeles, mostly through the good graces of Louis Hayward, the British actor who before the war had starred in many adventures and dramas, such as *Anthony Adverse*, *The Man in the Iron Mask*, and *The Duke of West Point*. Shortly after the Japanese attack on Pearl Harbor, Hayward, a South African by birth, became a naturalized U.S. citizen and was commissioned in the Marines. He helped roll out the red carpet for the visiting Nelson and introduced him to a number of luminaries, such as Joan Fontaine.

Later, Nelson attended a top-secret conference headed by a Royal Navy captain and Douglas Fairbanks Jr., the son of the swashbuckling star of *The Mark of Zorro* and *Robin Hood.* The younger Fairbanks had established his own acting career (*Little Caesar, Gunga Din*, and *The Prisoner of Zenda*, among others) before his commissioning as a lieutenant in the U.S. Naval Reserve. He was assigned to Lord Mountbatten's commando staff in England, and upon his return to the United States, he became an innovative strategist, especially in the art of deception.

Fairbanks arranged a joint conference, attended by Nelson, that was held at sea aboard a motor yacht berthed at Governor's Island in New York Harbor. "It was a luxurious vessel with several staterooms, dining and living areas, gold-plated fixtures in the bathrooms, and a small crew complete with a bartender," Nelson recalled. "We cruised at sea for several days, close in because of the submarine threat," he wrote. "We carried out some exercises with a specially equipped plane," all in an effort to plan "combat-deception activities." Later, Fairbanks would help plan and execute a program, called Beach Jumpers, to create diversionary feints for the U.S. forces making amphibious landings in the Mediterranean.

Nelson also was summoned to Denig's office to meet with David O. Selznick, the producer of the biggest blockbuster of the 1930s, *Gone with the Wind.* Selznick was lobbying to head up one of the service's photography branches, preferably with the rank of admiral or general. Such a request wasn't as audacious as it might sound: a number of his contemporaries, including directors John Ford, Frank Capra, and John Huston, had been commissioned into the Army or Navy and would later go on to produce some of the most important documentary accounts of the war. As a studio mogul, Selznick assumed he would start at the top of any military film organization.

Hollywood had a long symbiotic—and some might say overly cozy—relationship with the armed services. The Army, Navy, and Marine Corps donated planes, tanks, rifles, and personnel—as well as access to military bases and training areas—in exchange for friendly accounts of the services. For the Marines, this relationship dated back to the 1918 film *The Star Spangled Banner* and MGM's 1926 picture *Tell It to the Marines*, featuring Lon Chaney as the archetypal Marine. The tough-guy sergeant, much like the hard-nosed but lovable private eye or cop, quickly became a stock character.

The Marines had plenty of competition for winning America's hearts and minds on the silver screen. In 1927, *Wings* became the first major film about the Army Air Corps and "received virtually unlimited assistance from the War Department," wrote film historian Lawrence Suid. The assistance paid off as *Wings* won the first Academy Award for best picture.[5] In 1928, Frank Capra directed *Submarine*, and a number of films based at the U.S. Naval Academy in Annapolis followed, including *Submarine D-1* in 1937 and *Dive Bomber* in 1941.

According to Suid, "The Navy provides a superb case study of the manner in which the armed forces formed a symbiotic relationship with Hollywood to sell themselves to the American people."[6] Indeed, Suid notes that the Navy's close ties with the film industry predated World War I and became "part of the service's public affairs apparatus." But the coziness came with an unintended consequence. The Navy's attempt to use Hollywood to boost its image and create near-mythical defenders "may have succeeded too well. Before World War II, the many preparedness films had assured the nation the military was defending it against attack. Pearl Harbor exposed the falseness of that promise."[7]

Sometimes, the Navy and Marines teamed up for joint exercises on film. In 1935, Jimmy Cagney and Pat O'Brien starred in *Devil Dogs in the Air*, which the Marines aided with planes, personnel, and shooting locations. The Navy, not to be outdone, simulated a pre-assault bombardment supporting a Marine amphibious landing south of La Jolla, California. *Devil Dogs in the Air* provided a glimpse of things to come in the war with Japan. It was the first film to show Marines flying from an aircraft carrier as part of a naval aviation force.[8]

A *Washington Herald* reviewer noted the "favorable publicity value" of *Devil Dogs* and predicted it might have an impact in improving what were then limited defense appropriations by an isolationist Congress in 1935. "Congressmen and governors of the states seeing this picture will take pride in the marvelous efficiency of the American flier and will be humiliated by the knowledge that among the world's important nations, we stand last in airplane defense."

A *New York Times* reviewer, marveling at the film's aerial stunts and photography, observed, "Even the most determined of the anti-militarists is likely to find his principles rolling under the seat when the photo play is in the air."[9]

When Selznick arrived in Washington, "he was impressive and articulate," despite the fact that he "looked as if he had been up all night and could stay up another," according to Nelson's account.[10] In the end, General Denig passed on the offer since, Nelson wrote, "the Marine Corps might not afford sufficient scope for his talents—without considerable disruption of other activities, the war itself not excepted."

Denig faced more basic problems, such as staffing and training his growing ranks of writers, photographers, and filmmakers. But the Marine Corps was still playing catch-up with its sister service, the Navy, and with the Army and its Army Air Corps, all of which, according to Hatch, "had already been to Hollywood and scarfed up a number of people." Indeed, the other services had the foresight to "look far ahead and had gotten a lot of them into the Reserves several years prior to the outbreak of the war, so they could bring people very quickly to active duty," Hatch said.

Among the men in this talent pool of actors and directors was Eddie Albert, another budding star with a penchant for sailing. Albert's path into naval service read a bit like the script of a *film noir* thriller circa 1940. Sailing off the coast of southern Mexico before the war, Albert learned there was a German Bund meeting taking place. Curious about the Nazi front-group's intentions, Albert took it on himself to investigate. Armed with a movie camera, he infiltrated the gathering and discreetly took some footage. Upon his return to Los

Angeles, he went straight to the office of Naval Intelligence. The intelligence analysts were grateful for the rare footage and were particularly interested in the boasting by Bund members about Germany's intentions to invade southern California. Later, Albert was offered a commission in the Navy. He served with distinction at Tarawa, where, under heavy fire, he evacuated wounded Marines off the beach.

Hatch continued to hone his craft, mastering the more sophisticated cameras and film being created at Eastman Kodak in Rochester, New York, and in Hollywood itself. *The March of Time* also continued to contribute to the war effort. A 1942 newsreel provides an example of the kind of patriotic messages that Henry Luce's film series was producing. It starts with Marines boarding ships bound for upcoming operations in the Pacific. "We're trained, we're ready to fight," intones a baritone-voiced narrator, describing the troop carriers as "transports lined at the pier like carriers of fate." As wenches haul tanks in cargo holds, the narrator observes, "There's no feeling in the world quite like the sight of weapons." Martial music swells in the background as he says of the Marines in long coats and duffel bags boarding ship: "With us goes the best our country can give."

The film is full of such unabashed support of the war effort, with no hints of the carnage to come. It is also filled enough purple prose to make even a romance writer blush: "This ocean is new to us, more bright and blue, more vast than anything we've ever known."

Standing on deck, one well-groomed young man asks another, "Where do you think we're heading—Alaska?"

"No," says his tow-headed buddy, "we're going to the South Seas."

"South Seas," the first Marine replies, "where's that?"

A map of Guadalcanal flashes onscreen, and the film cuts to Navy and Marine officers planning an attack on the Japanese-controlled island, even as a Filipino steward fills their coffee cups. (Such scenes seem to have come from stock footage, as, indeed, much of the report appears to be a reenactment of what must have led up to the Marines' landing in the Solomons, drawn from training films rather than actual combat. There is no disclaimer or explanation of what was staged and what was actual war footage.) Planes rise from below the decks of an aircraft carrier and take off. Heavily laden Marines slowly descend cargo nets. The film seems as stiff and staged as B-grade movies of the day, especially when one Marine (or reenactor) says to another, "Hey, Mac, this is it!" "Pipe down back there!" his stern sergeant barks.

Actual combat footage appears to have been spliced in amid the chatter of machine-gun fire. "This is the far Pacific," the narrator concludes, "on islands the Japanese had seized at so little cost, the U.S. Marines delivered our first solid punch. . . . On the road to Tokyo, no one could guess how long, how bitter, and how bloody was the road that lay before them. There is no turning back . . . perilous and heartbreaking as the road may be, it is still the road of the Marines . . . fighting and slugging, island by island, until they went at last to the farthest islands of all—the island of the infamous, condemned Japan." With that, the newsreel closes with riflemen hiking along a dusty trail singing the Marines' Hymn.

In June 1942, some three months before the Marines landed at Guadalcanal, Hatch began his own trek from *The March of Time* back to Quantico, home of the newly formed photographic-services section. Before catching a southbound train, he received a telephone call from the chief signal officer of the Marine Corps, Lt. Col. Wally Wachtler. "We need some camera equipment in Quantico very badly, some motion-picture equipment," he told Hatch. "Will you go around to the second-hand stores, the camera hock shops in New York, and see if you can find some 35-millimeter equipment that we could buy?"

Sure, Hatch said, but he asked for some guidance. "If I go into a place and say, 'Hey, I'd like this,' what am I going to do? They are not going to hold anything longer than about five minutes on just my say-so."

Wachtler instructed Hatch to call him from the store, and he would issue a purchase order and check for a down payment to the merchant to cover all expenses. So began the first of many government-sponsored buying sprees by Hatch to help equip the Marines' fledgling film and photo operations. But as he visited camera stores and hock shops around Manhattan, he could see he had been beaten to the punch by the other services, which already purchased most of the best cameras. Still, Hatch persevered and found a number of motion-picture cameras; others he bought for spare parts. A used 35-millimeter Bell & Howell Eyemo—the workhorse motion-picture camera of the day— usually went for $60, but with a catch: it lacked the camera's triple lens. Hatch had to buy those separately.

He also looked for a big 35-millimeter sound camera so the Marines could join their more sophisticated Army and Navy brethren in making talkies. A fully equipped sound camera usually sold for $800 to $900. Hatch's impromptu shopping-scavenging experience showed "the extent of unpreparedness" of the Marine Corps at the start of the war. "We just did not have the equipment," he recalled. Making matters worse, the camera manufacturers, especially leader Bell & Howell, had not geared up for the war effort. As a result, their supplies were dwindling as fast as nylon stockings as the services searched and scrounged for whatever they could send out to the fields of battle from North Africa to the South Pacific.

Regular cameras, by contrast, were not hard to come by. The workhorse for newspaper and magazine photographers was the four-by-five Speed Graphic; plenty of those were on the market. "You could go in the stores and buy the boxes and the lenses and necessary gear to go with it. Nobody used 35 [millimeter] in those days. The format was just not considered a professional format. It was an amateur format."

Over time, the combat cameramen would acquire the Rolleiflex, made by the German camera company Rollei. These sturdy dual-lens models were favored by professionals because they were light and compact, with excellent lenses. They were hard to find, though, because of a ban on German imports.

Eventually, American camera-makers began to fill the void left by the Germans. Eastman Kodak in Rochester, New York, came out with two new models, a 35-millimeter camera and the Kodak Medalist, a "a very big and bulky camera" with "big knobs to turn things with so that you weren't fiddling with little, tiny dials," according to Hatch. He liked the Medalist, but truly loved the Combat Graphic made by Rochester-based Folmer Graflex.

To make a more durable, combat-ready camera, Folmer Graflex adapted its Speed Graphic, which was essentially a wooden box with a leatherette covering and a bellows. "You'd have to extend the lens out with a bellows, which was very prone to damage from anything from dirt to puncturing holes in it."

The Combat Graphic, by contrast, had a box made from water-resistant plywood and painted with a drab, olive-green, scratch-resistant paint. "You could hardly damage it," said Hatch. "You could take the damned thing and drop it, and nothing would happen to it—short of dropping it twenty feet on concrete." It also came with a flap on the front to cover the lens, protecting it from sand or dirt.

Hatch, though specializing in motion pictures, carried 35-millimeter and 16-millimeter color cameras throughout the war. Improvisation was the order of the day as many of his colleagues rigged their cameras with rifle stocks to steady them when the shooting started.

Before he took the camera cache down to Quantico, Hatch was given a final Marine-related assignment for *The March of Time* in the summer of 1942. The 1st Marine Division was preparing to ship out for the Pacific to a destination unknown. Louis de Rochemont, as part of a monthly series that ran in theaters around the country, wanted to shoot a feature film on the Leathernecks' training in eastern North Carolina.

Hatch traveled with old pro George Stoetzel and other trainees to a tent camp at Camp Lejeune, then under construction. The experience "was a big eye-opener for me because it really gave me my first good training and doing some coverage of the Marine Corps," Hatch said.

The March of Time crew began setting up to shoot in the pine woods and swamp. Director Jack Glenn "was known as a wild man [who] liked realism," Hatch recalled, and ordered demolition charges to be set in abandoned homes left by local sharecroppers. The hyper-realism backfired: when the charges exploded, one house caught fire. The blaze quickly spread to some tinder-dry pine trees in the summer heat. It was a Saturday, so the base was deserted—with no chance of alerting the fire department. The cameramen raced to find some water, then poured it on the flames and put out the blaze. It was a close call. "We could have lost a good portion of that base that day, and I could picture my career as a PFC going down the drain but fast." It was not the last time Hatch would see his promising career on the brink of disaster.

Quantico in the hot summer of 1942 was no picnic. Hatch sweated through the heat and humidity of the wooded training base on the Potomac River south of Washington. He studiously edited training films and was promoted to corporal. He was itching to see action, though, and wondered when he would finally put his newfound film prowess to work against the Japanese.

In his off hours, Hatch was not a drinker or hell-raiser, especially compared with other young Marines. His time in New York and his earlier experiences in Washington gave him a sense of professional maturity, though he was only twenty-one. Love was in the air, though, and he was still dating Lois Rousseau up in Washington. Sometimes, it was hard to balance the call of the Corps and the call of the heart. After standing guard duty one Friday night and then working all of

Saturday, he unwisely tried to cram too much fun into his weekend liberty: driving Lois several hours to the Eastern Shore of Maryland and back. By the time he tried driving back to Quantico early Monday morning, he fell asleep at the wheel, ramming into a bridge railing at a high speed. The one-car collision demolished the front end of his Ford, and the engine was thrust into the passenger's seat, barely missing Hatch. He also tore up a bridge on Route One, whose supports fell into the creek about twenty-five feet below.

When he awoke, Hatch smelled gasoline. Disoriented in the dark, he tried to escape, but the door would not budge. As he fell in and out of consciousness, he finally managed to kick his way through the rotting cloth roof of his car. On his way out, he had the presence of mind to grab his barracks cap since failing to wear it would mean he was out of uniform. Even in this disoriented state, the little things about being a Marine stayed with him. In this injured and bleeding condition, he started a long, painful trek back to Quantico.

A light shone in the darkness, and Hatch flagged down a Greyhound bus. When the driver swung open the door and saw the bleeding Marine stumbling toward him, he asked, "What the hell happened to you?"

After Hatch explained the mishap, the Greyhound driver gave him a towel to soak up the blood from his head wound. Then he asked him to sit down on the front steps to avoid bleeding on the seats, not to mention scaring any of the passengers staring in disbelief at the sketchy-looking man.

When they arrived at the base's front gate, Hatch thanked the driver and climbed off to a nearby taxi stand. "Take me to the sick bay," he told a taxi driver, before passing out the back of his cab.

But when he awakened, he glanced up and could still see the front gate. "Why haven't you driven me in yet?" he mumbled.

"I'm waiting for a full cab," the driver said nonchalantly.

The next morning, Hatch awoke in bed at the base dispensary with a pounding headache, aching legs, and sore mouth. He seemed to have taken a bite out of the steering wheel, broke a front tooth, and injured both knees. When a state trooper found him, Hatch learned his one-car accident had sparked a jurisdictional dispute between two counties, Prince William and Stafford, along Route One. He had hit the bridge so hard that it caused damage in both localities. But when the trooper discovered he had not been drinking and had just fallen asleep at the wheel, Hatch was absolved of any blame. Once again, he survived another mistake that could have gotten him discharged from the Corps before he had shot a single frame of combat footage.

On September 19, 1942, Norm and Lois were married before a Virginia justice of the peace. There was no time for a honeymoon. Later that day, he boarded a train at the Quantico train depot while Lois forlornly waved good-bye. He was off to San Diego, California, to join the 2nd Marine Division.

As Hatch began his westward trek—accompanied by Johnny Ercole, his best friend from *The March of Time*—parts of the 2nd Marine Division were joined by the 1st Marine Division and the Marine Raider Battalion at Guadalcanal in America's first offensive battle against the Japanese. The campaign was dubbed Operation Shoestring because the Navy and Marines had to scramble to launch the operation on short notice and with minimal supplies. Most of America's war effort was going in the other direction—to war zones in Europe and the Middle East. Besides suffering shortages of equipment and weaponry, most of the ships that had brought the Marines into battle with field rations, weapons, ammunition, and fuel had not been loaded in a way that allowed for effective unloading under combat conditions.

After surveying the chaos on the docks of Wellington, New Zealand, which were littered with debris like cereal, food, and cigarette cartons bloated from the heavy rains of July, the 1st Marine Division's commander, Maj. Gen. Alexander A. Vandegrift, said that only materials "actually required to live and to fight" were to be stowed on the ships bound for Guadalcanal. He ordered the ammunition supply cut by a third, plus a drastic cut in the typical ninety-day supply of food and fuel. Later, Vandegrift wryly observed that he could have listed "a hundred reasons why this operation would fail."[11]

Arriving near San Diego at Camp Elliot—"a godforsaken, wind-blown miserable spot" on the southern California coast—Hatch found a photographic unit that could have cited its own reasons for failure. The photo officer, Chief Warrant Officer John "Pappy" Leopold, was a good man, but Hatch quickly determined that the former taxi driver from Washington, D.C., lacked the professional training and experience that he and Ercole had acquired in New York. They soon clashed over photographic techniques—professional differences that would have unintended consequences after the Marines went into battle at Tarawa.

Leopold fixated on trying to shoot three-dimensional photography, a tricky process in the best of times, since it required refrigeration in the lab and other precise preparations. In the dust of the California coast, the enlisted men dutifully followed Leopold's orders, but the 3D photography was a flop, since the emulsion of the film fell off like dandruff in the overheated dark room. Ercole and Hatch would emerge from the lab laughing together while Leopold fumed.

They tried to keep on his good side, though, because they knew they needed his approval to secure equipment before they left for the war. Ercole, the savvy New Yorker, figured out the way to play Leopold to get what they wanted: appeal to his vanity. The Navy had just released director John Ford's much-acclaimed color documentary *The Battle of Midway*, and Leopold could not stop talking about the release, which had set a high bar for military filmmakers everywhere. "Ford pretty much had the option of selecting his own crew from the whole industry," Hatch recalled, with sound men and directors entering the Navy as officers or high-ranking enlisted men. They marveled at the shots Ford captured from a tower on a nearby island as the Navy pilots fought the famed Japanese Zeroes for control over Midway. (Ford was wounded by shrapnel during a Japanese bombing run.[12])

The 2nd Marine Division's photo unit looked pretty puny by comparison as it prepared to ship out in September to New Zealand for pre-combat training. With so many new Marines entering the Corps, it would take time to re-form the division into a cohesive fighting force. How could a handful of new filmmakers have a chance of replicating Ford's feat?

Hatch and Ercole were sure of one thing: they needed better cameras just to be in the same ballpark. So they conspired to travel to Hollywood to buy new 16-millimeter cameras and perhaps get some training from the film-studio pros.

If we do this, Ercole told Leopold, maybe *you* can become the next John Ford! With visions of an Oscar dancing in his head, the warrant officer told them to get off to Hollywood. Their first stop was Technicolor, the manufacturer that was producing an innovative 35-millimeter color film called monopack, a name derived from a revolutionary design that used just one roll of film. Previously, Technicolor film was a labor-intensive process that required properly aligning three pieces of film, each with its own color dye. Those three color strips had to be matched to create a final print that would run as Technicolor film through a movie projector. It was a time-consuming, mistake-prone process. Technicolor's engineers had worked for years to create something better, a single piece of color film. When they succeeded, Technicolor's engineers had created the film equivalent of Kodak's Kodachrome for still photography, simplifying and improving the production process.

Arriving at Technicolor's offices, Hatch was fascinated to see the cutting-edge process from the inside. And he delighted when the company's technicians presented him with 1,000 feet of film, along with instructions in how to use it under field conditions. The Technicolor crew had only one request, asking Hatch and Ercole to slate every scene—that is, put a "lilly" color spectrum along with the scene number each time they began shooting. Hatch had to be honest with the film innovators: "Look, I'm going into combat," he told them, "and I've never been in combat before. I'll take it with me, and let's see what happens."

The Marine cameramen also visited Twentieth Century Fox, where they were well-received by the head of the camera department. He gave some pointers on making movies far from the sets where stars like Bogart, Bacall, and Gable worked every day. Hatch and Ercole were impressed to be in same orbit as these celebrities, but they stuck to their craft, eagerly absorbing tips and tricks from these camera masters. The Marines had learned three basic principles during their *March of Time* apprenticeship: start with a long shot; move in to your subject for a medium shot; and then go for a close-up. By following this simple but effective formula, any well-trained cameraman could tell a good story with film.

The Twentieth Century Fox cinematographers gave them a crash course in more sophisticated techniques, such as varying the long shot before moving into the medium distance or watching for film direction (if everyone is running one way, don't all of a sudden have someone run the other way). There were plenty of other tips that helped the combat cameramen improve their sense of visual narrative.

Now they needed more cameras to capture whatever battles awaited them. As they began their buying spree, they put out a call over Los Angeles radio stations that the 2nd Marine Division was looking for donated 16-millimeter cameras and/or projectors with sound capability. The public's response was overwhelming, and they were deluged with offers of free equipment. Ercole and Hatch also scoured the Los Angeles camera stores and purchased about a dozen 16-millimeter Bell & Howell Auto Load Master cameras, along with a few Eastman Kodaks. They loaded up on 16-millimeter film, emptying store after store.

Fully stocked, they rejoined the 2nd Marine Division, which was getting ready to deploy in a Navy convoy docked at San Diego. They boarded a ship called *Bobo Spooner* (*Bobo* was the ship's code name, *Spooner* its destination). The relatively small 300-foot-long vessel was a former cruise ship that had been converted to a troop vessel—and jam-packed with Marines, plus their gear, weapons, food, and supplies. Hatch faced four weeks at sea as the Navy convoy made the treacherous voyage—on the lookout for Japanese submarines—some 6,700 miles to Wellington, New Zealand. The first couple of days at sea confirmed Hatch's distaste for life below deck as he lay in his bunk in poorly ventilated, packed quarters.

Fed up, Hatch cooked up a scheme that he presented to the ship's executive officer. "Look, I've got twenty photographers on this ship, and they're going to need some training. Can I have access to the flying bridge? I'd guess you call it the funnel deck on a cruise ship. Can I have access to that for training?"

The executive officer was a recent cruise line employee who had been ushered into the Navy, so he granted Hatch's unusual request. This allowed Hatch to spend his days on the flying bridge, enjoying the ocean breeze and sunshine and surveying the white caps and waves while looking for signs of enemy periscopes or scout planes. If they were attacked by the Japanese, he reasoned, his position outdoors would allow him to photograph the action and direct coverage by his crew of newly minted combat cameramen who were assigned other positions on deck. In the course of roaming about the vessel, the Marines made a remarkable discovery: a large storage area in the tail of the cruise ship which came equipped with triple bunks. After schmoozing the Navy's chief boatswain assigned to that area, Hatch managed to move his entire crew out of their cramped quarters to this more comfortable setting.

He made other discoveries as well, such as the better meals enjoyed by a nearby Navy gun crew and some civilian sailors. So Norm cooked up another deal: in return for washing dishes, his men would get to grab some of the better chow and eat in their own quarters. It made the long voyage pass by a little faster.

CHAPTER FIVE

Shooting Down Under

After sailing into Wellington harbor in late September 1942, the Marines were greeted warmly by the people of New Zealand—a citizenry, Hatch noticed, that had more than its share of lovely ladies, since many of its young men had gone off to fight with their British allies in North Africa. He took an immediate liking to the warm people of this chilly place, which was still experiencing wintry conditions in the Southern Hemisphere. Right off, he was amazed to see the islanders had built them a nice little camp. "They believed in doing things in style," he said of the New Zealanders. The wooden huts were equipped for eight men, with four sets of two-man bunks and a pot-bellied stove in the middle.

Division headquarters was in downtown Wellington, with the rest of the more than 18,000-man force spread over a wide expanse of the North Island, the larger of the two main islands that comprise New Zealand. The camps were named for the indigenous Maori, such as Titahi Bay, Paraparamu Beach, and Pahatanui.

The photo-section offices and laboratory were on the first floor of the Windsor Hotel. This prime location gave the young Marines easy access to the street and the city.[1] It also gave them a great view of the capital's attractive women, many of whom had been left behind by husbands and boyfriends fighting in Anzac units in North Africa and elsewhere. The remaining New Zealanders viewed the Americans as protectors who had blocked the Japanese advance on their homeland by winning the day at Guadalcanal.

New Zealand, a nation that spans 1,000 miles north to south and is slightly larger than Great Britain, reminded Hatch of films he had seen about America's Old West. There were sides of beef hanging in the windows of butcher shops that lacked refrigeration, and European-style shops for bread, dairy, and wine. One entrepreneur seized upon the Americans' love of milkshakes and burgers, opening The Haisty Taisty Hamburger Shop next to the Windsor Hotel. The Russian storeowner had a mouthful of metal teeth that glittered as he grinned at the Marines, who freely advised him on how to make a real American shake.

It didn't take long for the men to develop a taste for other kinds of local sweets. One of Hatch's colleagues, Pvt. William F. "Kelly" Kelliher, began dating a member of New Zealand's Women's Air Force. Kelliher was a clean-cut twenty-year-old private from Kansas City, Missouri, and he was soon invited to his girlfriend's hometown of Gisborne, on the island's eastern coast. The sojourn developed its own zany plot line when Hatch, who was Kelliher's immediate supervisor, would not approve his request for leave; he could only go, Hatch suggested, if the three other Marines in the movie section could tag along. The order was meant as a joke, but Kelliher, being a good Midwestern lad, took it seriously. He got his date's mother to make room for the other Marines—Hatch, Ercole, and Pvt. Robert Opper—to stay in separate homes. It would be a kind of cultural exchange as the New Zealanders were getting their first looks at the Yanks in Gisborne, a city known for being near Captain Cook's first landing in 1769.

The plot thickened as Hatch was told that the entire photo section could not leave the office for nearly two weeks. They would have to come up with a legitimate reason for such a long road trip, so they told their bosses that they had a story fit for photos, motion pictures, and print: the U.S. Navy had taken over a local hospital, Silverstream, to treat American Marines and sailors who had suffered wounds, malaria, dengue fever, hookworm, and dysentery during the extended fighting at Guadalcanal. (The division reported 13,000 confirmed cases of malaria alone.)

With the help of the mother of Kelliher's date and the approval of the division's commanding general, "Gentleman" John Marston, they lined up sixty or more homes as well as a special rail car on the New Zealand Railway to bring them up for Christmas. Hatch later wrote about the good cheer of these Marines on their last adventure before combat: "On a late December day in 1942 the men left the Wellington railroad station for the trip to Gisborne. The hilarious trip was completed with singing, storytelling, card playing, the joy of being free from military control and the anticipation of what the next 10 days would bring."

Along the way, the train stopped at several stations where they were "cheerfully greeted by the local inhabitants who had prepared tea and cakes and entertainment." At Napier, one of the larger cities, they were treated to an elegant luncheon where "Mrs. Oakden's attention to detail and planning was very touching and deeply appreciated by all."[2]

After the day-long trip, they were greeted by the host families who filled the station "eager to see what Marines were," Hatch recalled. Gisborne's Mayor Bull, fully adorned in official regalia, greeted them and expressed appreciation to the Marines and U.S. Navy sailors for providing a defense against the Japanese.

Ercole and Hatch were glad to be assigned to a home right on the beach. Since Christmas takes place at midsummer in the Southern Hemisphere, they rolled out of bed each morning, put on their swim trunks, and swam in the rolling surf. There were picnics and Maori dance parties. The Marines also visited a sheep ranch, where they learned the hard skill of shearing wool.

The day after Christmas was Boxing Day, celebrated in the British Commonwealth to give presents to the needy. Gisborne's residents also

liked to hold Boxing Day horse races. Naturally, with sailors and
Marines feeling their oats, there was plenty of betting—and eventually
the horse owners arranged a challenge race for the Marines and the
sailors. Some of the riders, with scant equestrian skills, held on for dear
life. Hatch came in third in a wild stretch run.

After this respite, the Marines looked for another reason to escape
the routine back at division headquarters in Wellington. They saw their
chance when they heard that some sailors and Marines had left the
hospital to spend time in the countryside, working on farms and eating
good food to help restore their health—just the stuff for a human-
interest story with pictures for the papers back home.

They traveled around Rotorua, a mountainous area of geothermal
activity, geysers, bubbling mud pools, and snow-capped peaks. It was
the land of the native Maoris. Hatch, always the goodwill ambassador,
got to know some of the tribal singers, who were led by a woman
named Minnie, chieftess of the village of Whakarewara. He marveled
at the wise woman's cooking methods, which included boiling water
in the hot spring bubbling up outside her kitchen window.

They also enjoyed a dip in a pool formed by a series of rock falls
that cooled the water. His pale white skin elicited surprised giggles
from Minnie and her minions. This was followed by a three-day cele-
bration, or "Hui," to honor a lieutenant from the Maori Battalion
who died fighting the Germans in North Africa. The young man was
awarded Great Britain's highest wartime medal, the Victoria Cross, for
scaling a cliff with his troops to attack German machine-gun nests.
When they ran out of ammunition, they threw rocks and fought
hand-to-hand, finally taking out the enemy emplacements. It was the
first Victoria Cross given to a Maori warrior during World War II, a
milestone to be celebrated with three days of singing, dancing, eating,
and drinking.

Amid the festivities, Hatch conversed with the chieftess's daughter,
who was upset over some recent letters from her husband, who was

serving in the Maori Battalion. His praises of the local Egyptian girls were making her jealous. Hatch made a mental note to avoid making the same mistake when he wrote to Lois back home.

The 2nd Marine Division spent most of 1943 in New Zealand preparing for the next major clash—putting into practice the lessons of Guadalcanal and trying to prepare for what naval intelligence showed was a growing fortification of the steppingstone islands to Japan. Years of planning, doctrinal development, and angry debates with counterparts in the Army and Navy would now be put to the test.

"Until the 1920s, there was no real institutional dedication in the Corps to the idea of an assault landing attack against organized defenses," wrote Lt. Gen. Victor H. Krulak.[3] Most military experts had viewed the disastrous British landing against the Turks at Gallipoli in 1915 as a textbook case of frontal amphibious assaults. But as Krulak noted, "the British violated so many basic principles" at Gallipoli—resulting in the slaughter of more than 40,000 British, Australian, and French soldiers—"that the test was deceptive."

"Only a few . . . visionaries were willing to attack the formidable tactical and material problems associated with the modern amphibious assault landing: how to get heavy equipment and weapons ashore through surf and across reefs; how to exercise command authority," Krulak wrote, and on and on, from avoiding mines to getting supplies ashore. Among those visionaries was John A. Lejeune, the pioneering officer for whom the camp was named. While earlier Marine leaders had been willing to settle for a limited combat role—essentially serving as a police force aboard ships and naval bases—Lejeune "saw the Navy's need for advanced bases for coal and other logistical purposes as a cardinal factor in preparing to face the challenge of an imperialist Japan, and he was determined to get the Marines involved."

According to Krulak, Lejeune "realized that somebody might have the unenviable task of capturing those logistic bases from a well-prepared enemy. . . . What would be a more logical organization to do the job than the Marines, with their traditional maritime orientation?"[4]

To fulfill that mission, though, the Marine Corps needed a better vehicle to move the troops from ship to shore. The solution came from an unlikely source: Andrew Jackson Higgins, a rakish, hard-driving New Orleans boat builder. He was the designer of the workhorse landing craft that provided an alternative to other experimental amphibious vehicles that, more often than not, became death traps for unsuspecting Marines. These included a plodding, top-heavy craft called the "beetle boat," whose steel canopy, designed to protect troops from small-arms fire, often caused it to sink like a stone during practice landings. With little money for innovations in the 1920s or 1930s, neither the Navy nor the Marine Corps did much in the way of innovation.[5]

That is, until Higgins came to the attention of the Corps' leadership. As prewar intelligence showed the Japanese had outpaced the U.S. Navy in landing craft design, "Howlin' Mad" Smith pushed for a better, more reliable way to ferry the Marines from ship to shore. Higgins originally designed a shallow draft boat for rum-runners who dodged federal agents in the Mississippi Delta during Prohibition in the mid-1920s.[6] The Marines could put these stealthy boats to good use, continuing a tradition of consorting with criminals that began in the early nineteenth-century clashes with the Barbary pirates of North Africa.

By 1941, Higgins developed a larger, lighter ramp-bow craft capable of carrying an eighteen-ton tank. After more tinkering, Higgins was hired to build boats not only for the Marines, but for the U.S. Army as part of its planning to launch amphibious landings in North Africa. (Krulak, who as a young officer became a vocal proponent of the Higgins boat, noted the irony of this turn of events: "As late as 1945 General Eisenhower, in testimony before the Senate Military Affairs Committee, complained that 'before World War II it was hard to get anyone interested in the design and production of landing craft,' ignoring the fact that the Army was aware, at every step, of what the Navy and Marines were doing in this area. . . . The truth is, the Army was not interested."[7])

"Howlin' Mad" Smith—like Earl Ellis, a Marine visionary with a legendary temper—helped ratchet up the quality and scope of amphibious doctrines and training exercises. Among those training in eastern North Carolina was a quiet, unassuming fifty-eight-year-old veteran officer, Julian C. Smith. In May 1943, after leading division-size training for Marine and Army units, Smith was transferred to take over the 2nd Marine Division in New Zealand. He assumed command from its rather aloof leader, Maj. Gen. "Gentleman John" Marston.

Almost overnight, there was "a tremendous change of attitude" among the troops, Hatch said, because Smith "was out there with the troops while they maneuvered, and he wanted to see what they were doing, whether it was good, bad, or indifferent."

Some said Julian Smith lacked command experience, and others complained that his voice was too soft and his bearing too dreamy for a Marine general. But one of his battalion commanders, Lt. Col. Ray Murray, dismissed such pickiness, calling the division commander "a fine old gentleman of high moral fiber; you'd fight for him."[8]

Smith was an excellent marksman and former rifle team coach. And as a native of Maryland's Eastern Shore, he also knew a thing or two about sailing on the Chesapeake Bay. His expertise, especially in reading tides, would soon come in handy. A veteran of more than thirty years in the Corps, Smith had fought in the "banana wars" of Nicaragua, where he was awarded the Navy Cross, as well as Panama, Mexico, Cuba, Haiti, and Santo Domingo. But the newly formed 2nd Marine Division was now facing its first operational assignment, one that would take the measure of every bit of Smith's wisdom, experience, and instincts. When he took command on May 1, 1943, the division had three infantry regiments (the 2nd, 6th, and 8th Marines), an artillery regiment (the 10th Marines), a composite engineer regiment (the 18th Marines, including engineers and Navy Seabees), and various special and service battalions.

Elements had joined the fighting on Guadalcanal, but the entire division would not coalesce as a fighting unit until shortly before Smith took charge. Much of the force had been depleted by the tough Guadalcanal fighting, and as Hatch discovered, many men were recovering from the debilitating illnesses of the tropics. Thus, Smith's challenges were formidable, especially given the relative lack of knowledge of amphibious warfare tactics and logistics on his division staff. To plug this talent gap, he reached out to the commandant and requested him to assign Col. Merritt "Red Mike" Edson to serve as his chief of staff.

Edson was already a legend. He had received his second Navy Cross for his command of the 1st Raider Battalion at Tulagi and the Medal of Honor for commanding a composite force of raiders and paratroopers at "Edson's Ridge" on Guadalcanal. "Tough, competent and visionary, thoroughly professional (he single-handedly wrote the USMC Small War Manual in 1940) and combat savvy, Edson did not suffer fools," historian Col. Joseph H. Alexander wrote. "He was the perfect counterpoint to Julian Smith's easygoing, paternalistic leadership style."[9]

Smith also promoted a thirty-eight-year-old operations officer from an Indiana farm who worked hard in New Zealand even as some more senior officers enjoyed the local sights—and ladies—a bit too much. David Monroe Shoup was a detail man who burned the midnight oil as he tried to come up with more options for his men to wage war against the dug-in defenders.

In August, Vice Adm. Raymond A. Spruance came to Wellington to disclose the time and target for the division's top-secret mission: in late November, they would attack the Tarawa Atoll. Spruance, the victor of the Battle of Midway, was hand-picked by Adm. Chester Nimitz to head the just-formed Central Pacific Force. It was part of Nimitz's broader plan to counterattack Japan with a "sea-going blitzkrieg," and Operation Galvanic, the campaign to seize the Gilbert Islands, was the first step in this strategy. Unlike earlier landings, which had relatively short distances between launches and target objectives, Galvanic would present the Navy-Marine task force with a host of daunting challenges, from tactics to logistics to the difficult terrain. As they discussed the problem of getting over the reef, Shoup suggested using the tracked vehicles used on the beach at Guadalcanal. The LVT-2, known as the Water Buffalo, was an improvement on the earlier tracked vehicle (the LVT-1), with a redesigned suspension system, rubber-tired road wheels, and torsion springs for better stability. It had more power and could carry 1,500 pounds more cargo than the original model, according to Alexander.[10]

But neither Spruance nor Rear Admiral Turner, the naval commander of the amphibious force, had been willing to commit to the request. In an earlier meeting in Honolulu, this had sparked a heated argument as the Marines' advocate, "Howlin' Mad" Smith, lived up to his nickname, shouting, "No amtracs, no operation!"[11]

In a solomonic decision, Turner split the difference: half of the 100 new LVT-2s would go to the Marines at Tarawa, the other half to the Army's 27th Infantry Division attacking nearby Makin. Adding to the Corps' heartburn, the shipment of the vehicles from southern California was delayed. They would not be ready for pre-invasion maneuvers and would have to go into Tarawa cold.

As the headquarters staff scrambled to prepare for the coming invasion, Hatch took the opportunity to get away from Wellington to cover a variety of other stories, such as a visit from First Lady Eleanor

Roosevelt and filming Japanese POWs. Hatch had last seen Mrs. Roosevelt—at least up close—some three years ago during the close call with the mustang back at Warm Springs, Georgia. Would she remember him? She was part of a group of visiting American Red Cross luminaries, and he filmed her meeting sick servicemen and pressing the flesh with the islanders, including a ceremonial rubbing of noses with "Rangi, the senior greeter/hoster of the Maori nation."[12]

After spotting him filming her every move, Mrs. Roosevelt stopped and asked the Marine cameraman why he was being so persistent. "If I didn't," he responded, "I'd probably be court-martialed." Hatch did not think she recognized him and kept a polite distance.

On the last day of her visit, the First Lady—clad in a dark overcoat with an orchid corsage and a low-brimmed hat—posed with a group of Marines, including Hatch, who squatted beside her. As she prepared to leave for the airport, Mrs. Roosevelt called him over to chat. Flashing her trademark toothy smile, she asked, "Do you still like to ride fast horses?"

A tougher assignment came from the U.S. Office of War Information soon after Hatch arrived in New Zealand. The government wanted to counter Japanese and German propaganda on the alleged mishandling of Axis prisoners of war. So along with Johnny Ercole and a couple of other men in the photo unit, Hatch drove in a jeep from Wellington up into the mountains. They climbed to about 3,000 feet in the Rimutaka Range, where they were buffeted by high winds, then descended on the switchback roads into the flatlands below. Spread across empty farmland was a POW camp operated by the New Zealand Army—or what was left of the army since most able-bodied men were fighting the Nazis. These were mostly fresh-faced kids standing guard inside the barbed-wire front gate.

The prison camp held a group of more than 300 Japanese sailors and a handful of officers, taken prisoner when their ships were sunk by the U.S. Navy in the Battle of Midway and other early naval battles. The photo assignment was to do stills and motion pictures to document that the camp was meeting the rules of the Geneva Convention (the treatment of prisoners upon arrival, clothing and bedding, recreation, decent food, and so on).

The Marine photographers were given free rein to walk the camp without guards, so Hatch enjoyed meeting the enemy for the first time. Remarkably, he found most of the young Japanese sailors to be polite, respectful, and, in many cases, quite artistic. As to their treatment, most of the prisoners seemed content with their conditions and more than happy to be fed, clothed, and sheltered in the clean tents. With the picturesque mountains all around them, the camp actually had a certain charm. Still, he sensed a lingering tension among a group of senior enlisted men. These sailors, he learned, resented their seven officers for seeming to enjoy the Americans' largesse. Why had they not done the honorable thing and committed *hara-kiri*? Hatch had learned this while filming some of the officers, who told him in English that hey had attended college in California or Washington state. These men "saw no reason to kill themselves," Hatch said. "They were thankful to get dragged out of the water."

When the camp authorities became aware of trouble brewing, they separated the officers into another building for their own protection. While Ercole recorded them with a Wahl sound camera, he allowed some of the curious Japanese to peer through the lens finder. Hatch captured the moment on his Speed Graphic: an enemy officer grinning broadly as he gets a turn at the Wahl.

Other pictures showed the humanity of the prisoners as they tried on clothes and demonstrated wood carving. Hatch paid one prisoner two packs of cigarettes for an eight-by-ten-inch carving based on a New Zealander's cap insignia. (He brought home seven plaques that he hung in his offices at Headquarters Marine Corps and the Pentagon. Years later, they were donated to the New Zealand Embassy in Washington, D.C., and sent back to a museum in Featherston.)

The Japanese had been resourceful artists, recovering nails left on the ground during the camp's construction and turning them into chisels for wood carving and sculpting. Somehow, they squeezed out homemade paint by wringing dyes out of the Red Cross towels.

Hatch, Ercole, and their colleagues were filming a morning roll call when the camp's simmering tensions boiled over. Tempers flared when one of the young guards fired a shot out on the edge of the camp, apparently sensing a prisoner escape. Yet another nervous guard fired his rifle. Suddenly, it dawned on Hatch that he was surrounded by several hundred agitated enemy sailors who started running around the compound, confused by the gunshots and seemingly on the verge of escape. Glancing at the senior enlisted man nearby—a British Army sergeant major named Les Godfrey—he asked, "What do we do now?"

Godfrey grinned slightly and muttered, "Stand fast."

The prisoners finally calmed down, but barely a month later, a junior lieutenant POW balked at being part of forced work parties. This sparked a riot that left forty-eight Japanese dead, with many more wounded. One New Zealand soldier died in the fracas. When he heard about it later, a chill went down Hatch's spine. It had been a close call.

While Hatch's luck continued to hold, some of his counterparts on the print side struggled to get their accounts sent back to the States. Marine Corps public relations was still a new, and fairly foreign, notion for many of the old-guard officers who viewed reporters and photographers either with suspicion or derision, sometimes both. "Most senior officers laughed at and disparaged the efforts of the [public relations] section, and moreover, refused to cooperate," according to historian Benis Frank. Adding insult to their injured egos, the print reporters watched in horror as their dispatches about the 2nd Division's training were held up by jealous Army censors who were only too happy to throw a wrench into anything that smacked of favorable publicity for the Marines. There was a lingering feeling among the Army commanders that the Marine devil dogs had gotten more than their share of praise for their contributions during the fighting in France during World War I. (That resentment would later stoke the fires burning in Washington among those, including Harry Truman, who served with the Army in France and became bent on humbling, and even dismantling, the Marine Corps.)

Besides the interservice rivalry, the Marines also had themselves to blame for the early struggles of their battlefield reporters. It would take until 1943—nearly a year after the Corps launched its combat correspondents program—before Commandant Holcomb finally got around to issuing a directive explaining their role to field commanders.

Yet General Denig, the public-relations chief, never missed a trick in promoting the Corps. On a trip to St. Louis in July 1942, he found he was the only member of the armed forces addressing a convention of department-store window dressers. He so charmed the gathering that the retailers let the general pick any week, and they would gladly feature the Marines in their store displays across the country. Denig gladly accepted the invitation, and by the next month, millions of shoppers across the nation, including those passing Macy's in New York, were treated to a display of cardboard-cutout Marines. Little did they know that within a few days, the real men of the 1st Marine Division would land on Guadalcanal, mounting the United States' first offensive operation in the Pacific.

Slowly, the bureaucratic barriers that had stopped correspondents from getting their copy back home came down, and news and features, known as "Joe Blow" stories, started popping up in the *Washington Star*, *New York Times*, and other papers across the country, including the thousands of local newspapers eager for news of their men in combat. "As soon as the men in the field began receiving hometown news clippings sent by their families, they and their officers realized that those . . . unknown quantities—the unit [combat correspondents]—were doing something after all," Frank writes.

Indeed, the Corps managed to get a bigger bang for its promotional buck as district recruiting officers contacted local newspaper editors telling them they were free to run the combat correspondent accounts for special coverage of men in their area, creating "enormous good will for the Marine Corps," according to Frank. "Almost every local editor responded and soon the country was covered with Marine Corps 'Joe Blow' stories." The Army, which was fighting bravely from North Africa to Europe, was probably too busy to notice—except in Washington, where jousting for position and political gain never ends, even during wartime.

Before departing New Zealand, Hatch found time to hone another kind of shooting skill—this time, a handgun. Normally, only officers were assigned pistols, but since the cameramen were loaded down with equipment and supplies, they lobbied for lighter, small-caliber weapons. Finally, the division photographic officer, Capt. Bill Halpern, agreed to help.

Halpern was another Hollywood veteran lured into the Marines with promises of colorful combat. An assistant director for Selznick on *Gone with the Wind*, Halpern brought a convivial and entrepreneurial spirit to the unit as it went on maneuvers in the hills of New Zealand. He managed to secure dozens of .45-caliber pistols and ammunition for his cameramen and then arranged for target practice up in the hills. Their mentor was a former Louisiana state trooper, a Sergeant Diet, who had gone through the FBI school of pistol marksmanship. He not only helped them improve their shooting proficiency, but also shared some tricks of the G-Man's trade, such as firing through the holster in order to get the drop on an adversary.

The eager cameramen began firing away—so enthusiastically that some had to replace the barrels in the pistols "because we had just about blasted them out," said Hatch. The pistol practice probably saved many lives because it gave them an option other than a bulky rifle against any enemy soldiers they might encounter. "By the time we got ready to move out and get into combat, why, we were pretty well versed in our weaponry, and I think everybody was confident that if they ran into something, they could take care of themselves." And if they did not like using handguns, they could always take cold comfort in the conventional wisdom that they likely would find a rifle on the ground somewhere as Marines lay dying.

The division's shutterbugs also became more proficient with aerial photography as they crouched in low-flying aircraft above the cragged coastline of New Zealand with the bulky K-20 camera. They took montage shots of the shorelines and hoped to put their newfound skills to use for intelligence gathering. Mostly, though, they did what Marines did best: attack from the sea, bobbing along in Higgins boats and LVT-1 amphibious tractors, trying to protect their cameras from the saltwater as the vehicles rocked through the surf. Indeed, some of the coastal training proved treacherous to the infantrymen since the LVT-1 amtracs had a tendency to turn over in the waves, leaving Marines gasping for air and often swimming for their lives. Hatch witnessed a number of training accidents, including one in which a Marine had stepped off a boat's ramp before the Navy coxswain was ready to stop. The boat ran over him and caught him in its prop. "When we dragged him out from behind, he was in pieces . . . dying fast."

In the fall of 1943, as D-Day for Tarawa loomed near, Halpern was replaced by a well-known actor of the day, Louis Hayward. After helping the Corps form its early photographic unit, the star of *The Man in the Iron Mask* and the recently released *Ladies in Retirement* was taking a break from the movie sets to serve with the 2nd Marine Division. This caused a great deal of consternation among Hatch's colleagues, who were concerned that the strong-willed assistant photo chief, "Pappy" Leopold, might be too much for an effete actor to handle. "But Louie came out, and he was accepted fairly well, and he managed to hold his own," Hatch said.

No matter how much he tried to blend in, though, Hayward never entirely lost his star quality. As he walked around Wellington, fans spotted him and girls squealed, "It's Louie Hayward!" He grudgingly signed autographs, but otherwise, he shunned the spotlight. Much to his chagrin, Hayward also suffered from asthma, a condition that was exacerbated by New Zealand's cool, moist nights. When the division surgeon noticed his wheezing, he said he might have to order him back to the States for medical reasons.

Hayward pleaded to let him stay since, as he told Hatch, it would be humiliating for the star of so many swashbuckling films "to be sent out of a war zone because I have asthma." The issue of Hayward's health went up the line to Gen. Julian Smith, who ruled he could stay as long as he fully recovered before going into battle. So Hatch and the other photo boys began devising their own home remedy. From sick bay, they obtained Mentholatum to soothe bronchial passages. Then they found an inhaler, which they placed on the stove inside his cabin. They made the cabin air tight, then made Hayward stay there until his tubes cleared and he could breathe again normally. The treatment worked, and Hayward was soon feeling like a leading man again. But he could go out only to eat or to relieve himself until the division surgeon approved him for combat.

On the morning of All Saints Day, November 1, 1943, the 2nd Marine Division sailed from Wellington in sixteen amphibious ships, leaving in its wake plenty of broken-hearted young ladies, and, according to rumor, some 600 new brides of the unsaintly Americans. Hatch had stayed true to his beloved Lois back in Washington, though, and once again began angling for a prime spot above the deck of his transport ship. Ostensibly, this was just another training exercise at nearby Hawkes Bay. Indeed, Gen. Julian Smith briefed New Zealand's air force command on the part they would play in the exercise and made arrangements with the railroad to transport the division's heavy equipment back to Wellington. It was a ruse created to avoid the public relations–intelligence nightmare that occurred the previous year when the 1st Marine Division set sail from Wellington. The local newspapers ran banner headlines about the impending attack on Tulagi, reports that provided fodder on the radio for "Tokyo Rose," the UCLA zoology graduate of Japanese descent who had been visiting a sick aunt in Japan at the outset of the war. Iva Ikuko Toguri, who agreed to do propaganda broadcasting to stay out of work in a munitions factory, became a staple of Japan's attempts to get under the skin of Marines and GIs tuning in before and after battle.

The earlier security breach led to a tight lid on the 2nd Marine Division's true mission this time around. The entire division was aboard ship before Smith and his operations officer, Shoup, hailed a cab and headed to the Government House. Soon they broke the news to Sir Cyril Newall, Governor General of New Zealand. The 2nd Marine Division would not return, and he was the only person in the nation who knew it. Sir Cyril took Smith's hand and wished him luck on the new mission, "wherever it takes you and your splendid lads."[13]

The night before they steamed out of Wellington Harbor, Hatch had boarded his ship and, once again, tracked down its executive officer to get his favorite spot on the flying bridge. He maneuvered to set the stage for smooth sailing and keep an eye out for enemy subs. He carried his camera equipment and a large bottle of thick rum purchased from a non-drinking New Zealand sailor. Duly impressed by the prospect of a daily toddy, a chief petty officer found Hatch a suitable place on the funnel deck for the Marines. He and Kelliher spread their bedrolls, and through the good graces of a boatswain, they found a supply of Coca Cola and lemons. They worked out a deal where they could store their stash of booze and condiments in an outside boat. And so "we cruised our way across the Pacific, sitting there with the beautiful sunset drinking the rum."

There was occasional work to do, of course, including shooting some training exercises at Efate in the New Hebrides Islands northeast of Australia. The joint Navy-Marine exercise did not bode well for the tough combat ahead. The fleet's aircraft carriers and air wings were elsewhere, busy attacking targets in the Solomons for General MacArthur's forces. Medium-size Sherman tanks had yet to offload, and the coveted LVT-2s were still in transit. Naval gunfire ships bombarded Erradaka Island, far from the Marines coming ashore at Mele Bay. It was a near-total flop.

Yet Hayward was proud of his photo team's performance as they took turns loading and unloading 100-foot rolls of film. "I know all of us are fed up with hearing about the 'marvelous' photography coming out of the European war. This time," he exhorted the men, "let's really give 'em something to talk about—from the Marines in the Pacific."[14]

Maj. William K. Jones, commanding Landing Team 1/6, used the Efate exercise to marshal his troops onto rubber rafts, since the first battalion in each regiment was dubbed "the rubber boat battalion." This mini-flotilla inspired catcalls, and Jones become known as the "Admiral of the Condom Fleet."

Hatch took advantage of this final rehearsal to try out the 35-millimeter monopack from Technicolor. He took time to create the markers requested back in Hollywood, the lilies of color spectrums and the slates showing the scene number. He shot about 1,000 feet of film and sent it back to the film wizards in California. This footage, at least as far as Hatch ever heard, was never seen again. But there would be much more to shoot in a very short while.

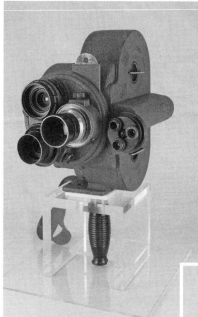

Hatch discovered that a used Bell & Howell 35-millimeter Eyemo camera could be purchased—without a lens—for $60 at secondhand camera stores and hock shops around New York City. He used an Eyemo to shoot his classic footage at *Tarawa*. BENJAMIN KRISTY, NATIONAL MUSEUM OF THE MARINE CORPS

The bulky Fairchild K-20 aerial camera, manufactured by Folmer Graflex of Rochester, New York. It was used by the air services of the Army and Navy. BENJAMIN KRISTY, NATIONAL MUSEUM OF THE MARINE CORPS

The Combat Graphic, also known as the Graflex Combat 45, was a sturdy 4x5 camera made by Folmer Graflex. "You could hardly damage it," Hatch said of this custom-built camera, with its water-resistant plywood box and olive-drab scratch-resistant paint. It became the workhorse for newspaper and magazine cameramen, as well as for Navy and Marine combat photographers. BENJAMIN KRISTY, NATIONAL MUSEUM OF THE MARINE CORPS

S/Sgt. John F. Ercole behind Wahl 35-millimeter sound camera in New Zealand. The
2nd Marine Division's photo officer, Capt. William A. Halpern, is on the right, with
Pvt. Bill Kelliher, who would become Hatch's able assistant cameraman at Tarawa,
smiling in the back.

Sergeant Hatch with 35-millimeter
Bell & Howell Eyemo filming
training exercises in New Zealand.

Happy staff sergeant. A portrait
taken of Hatch right before he left
New Zealand for Tarawa.

Hatch checks his 2nd Division photographers covering a practice amphibious landing in New Zealand.

Marines crowd on shore of Betio Island on D-Day, November 20, 1943. An outhouse on stilts over the water (left) suggests the only available sanitation facilities the Japanese had at Tarawa.

Hatch (foreground) sits against a log seawall on the beach at Betio as he clasps film canisters.

Marines carry a wounded comrade to safety over the seawall amid the carnage of D-Day at Tarawa.

Marine riflemen of the 6th Regiment come ashore at Green Beach after the first two days of battle. The division reserves would be tested in fierce, hand-to-hand combat.

The Japanese used British-made Vickers 8-inch rifles to pick off the incoming Higgins boats and amtracs. These weapons were purchased by the Japanese during the Russo-Japanese War of 1904–5, but they were not used in combat until nearly four decades later at Tarawa.

Hatch, always a sucker for animals, gives water to a kitten that he heard mewing under an abandoned Japanese tank.

Warrant Officer John "Pappy" Leopold, assistant photo officer, offloading equipment from a Higgins boat to S/Sgt. Carlos P. Steele.

One foot at a time. Marines crawling on sand at Betio, moving inland. The coconut trees were splintered by the American naval bombardment.

Bloody baptism by fire. Marines wade ashore at Tarawa as Higgins boats and amtracs ferry in men who face fierce enemy defenses.

The wages of war. A damaged amtrac dangles over the coconut seawall as corpses float nearby.

Eye of the battle. Hatch (center) stands tall with his Eyemo, filming the attack on the Japanese blockhouse.

The blockhouse attack continues as Marines swarm the Japanese, who have a periscope atop the protected structure to alert them to intruders. Hatch (right) returns from shooting what may be the only motion-picture footage capturing Americans and Japanese in a fighting stance in the same frames.

The 2nd Marine Division's photo section hammed it up for this group shot. First row (left to right): S/Sgt. Carlos P. Steele, PFC Jack E. Ely, PFC Fermen Dixon, S/Sgt. John F. Ercole, Cpl. Obie E. Newcomb, Sgt. Ernest J. Diet. Second row: Cpl. Christopher Demo, Sgt. Forest A. Owens, PFC James Orton, Cpl. Raymond A. Matjasic. Third row: S/Sgt. Roy Olund, Capt. Louis Hayward, Warrant Officer John Leopold, S/Sgt. Norman T. Hatch. Hatch's assistant, PFC William Kelliher, was among five Marines not pictured.

Dark humor. One spelling-challenged wag posted a skull with the caption, "Tarawa Recruitin Office."

At Camp Pendleton in late 1944, before leaving for Hawaii, Hatch peers into the viewfinder of a Bell & Howell Eyemo Model Q.

Warrant Officer Hatch behind a Bell & Howell Eyemo Model Q at Camp Tarawa at Hilo, Hawaii, in December 1944. Hatch was the photo officer of the 5th Marine Division as it completed its training to attack the Japanese fortress at Iwo Jima.

LEFT: *Joe Rosenthal's iconic photograph of the second flag raising at Iwo Jima.*
RIGHT: *PFC Bob Campbell (left) shot still photos while S/Sgt. Bill Genaust shot motion pictures at the second flag raising at Iwo Jima. The photos and film helped chronicle the controversial sequence of events atop Mount Suribachi. Genaust was shot and killed in a cave; his remains have yet to be found.*

Boxes of blood marked in a supply shed at Iwo Jima. Sadly, the Marines shed a warehouse's worth of blood to wrest the critical island away from a tough, intractable foe.

LEFT: *Before Joe Rosenthal made it to the mountaintop, T/Sgt. Lou Lowery of* Leatherneck *shot this picture of the first flag raising. A Marine keeps a lookout in the foreground while, behind him, Marines work hard to plant a flagpole into the rock-hard summit.*

RIGHT: *Marines take down the first flag raised over Suribachi while another group holds a pole for the replacement flag. The debris littering the mountaintop was cropped out of Joe Rosenthal's photo, creating a cleaner, vertical image of the historic scene. This photograph was taken by PFC Robert Campbell.*

In a cave at Iwo Jima, two corpsmen treat Marines wounded in battle.

Hatch (left) on Iwo Jima with elbows on a D-2 (intelligence) box talking to 1st Lt. Herbert Schlosberg, the photo officer of the 4th Marine Division.

As the Japanese rain artillery and mortar fire down from Mount Suribachi, a lone Marine ducks for cover.

*Warrant Office Obie
Newcombe (left) next
to Hatch in the photo
section's command
post at Iwo Jima.
Newcombe was the
5th Marine Division's
assistant photo officer.*

Marine flamethrowers at work attacking a blockhouse on Iwo Jima.

After the landing at Iwo Jima on February 19, 1945, the Marines dig in for cover. The U.S. Navy armada can be seen off the coast of the "Sulphur Island."

A Marine wrapped in a blanket tries to stay warm on Iwo's cold, rocky ground.

Hi, folks! Joe Rosenthal did take a posed shot of Marines on Mount Suribachi—a standard wire photo for the folks back home. This picture brought together the two groups of Marines who raised the flags to signal early American success against the Japanese, even though the battle for Iwo Jima would rage for weeks.

Joe Rosenthal's close-up of Marines celebrating after the second flag raising. The mixture of photos—staged and unstaged—later created confusion over the AP photographer's work at Iwo Jima.

A combat engineer with a flamethrower dashes across Iwo's rocky ground—hazardous duty since the charged canisters would blow up if it hit by an enemy bullet.

Joe Rosenthal (left) and Marine photographer Robert Campbell.

After the bomb. Nagasaki was in ruins when the 2nd Marine Division arrived in late 1945. The only buildings left standing had reinforced concrete.

A dual-barrelled 100-millimeter gun destroyed with explosives by 2nd Division Marines at Omura, near Nagasaki.

Light Japanese tanks, part of the weapons cache captured on film by Norm Hatch's 2nd Marine photo unit in Nagasaki.

CHAPTER SIX

"Look! The Sons of Bitches Can't Hit Me!"

As the American armada steamed toward Tarawa, a letter was read over the public-address system to the men dozing, reading, or shooting the bull in the bunks below deck of the transport ships:

A great offensive to destroy the enemy in the Central Pacific has begun. Our Navy screens our operation and will support our attack tomorrow with the greatest concentration of aerial bombardment and naval gunfire in the history of warfare. It will remain with us until our objective is secured. . . . Garrison troops are already en route to relieve us as soon as we have completed this job. . . . This division was especially chosen by the high command for the assault on Tarawa because of its battle experience and its combat efficiency. Their confidence in us will not be betrayed. We are the first American troops to attack a defended atoll. . . . Our people back home are eagerly awaiting news of our victories.

I know that you are well-trained and fit for the tasks assigned to you. You will quickly overrun the Japanese forces; you will decisively defeat and destroy the treacherous enemies of our country. Your success will add new laurels to the glorious tradition of our Corps.

Good luck and God bless you all.

Julian C. Smith, Major General,

U.S. Marine Corps Commanding

Within hours, the pre-dawn darkness of Betio Island was shattered by direct hits from the 14-inch guns of the battleships *Maryland* and *Colorado*. A bull's-eye on one of the enemy's 8-inch shore batteries sent up billowing balloons of fire and smoke. Occasionally, some of the enemy's formidable arsenal fired back. Indeed, the Japanese actually began the Battle of Tarawa at 5:07 A.M. on D-Day with shots from their coastal defense guns. These opening salvos created waterspouts and screamed over the heads of the Marines crouching in Higgins boats and LVTs on their way to the line of departure at the entrance to Betio's northern lagoon. The traditional pre-battle breakfast of steak and eggs made many men seasick as they see-sawed through the water.

Standing by Maj. Jim Crowe, Hatch was finding it hard to make much sense of the chaos on the shoreline, much less film it. The morning battle had a mesmerizing effect as he realized this was the moment of truth not only for him, but for the entire 2nd Marine Division. Yet after all of the beach-assault training of the past year, the combined task force seemed perilously close to flunking its final exam.

One of the first obstacles they faced was that morning's tide. Julian Smith's planners had to take their best guesses on the level of the twice-monthly "neap tide" caused by the moon being in its first or last quarter. According to historian Alexander, "Smith and [Admiral] Hill had little choice but to hope for the best and prepare for the worst."[1]

The landing force never saw the necessary four feet of water needed for a clear passage over the reef because of what became known in the wake of the battle as "the tide that failed." The neap tide was actually a predictable event, but it left thousands of Marines with no choice but to get out of their landing boats and wade up to 1,000 yards—or more than half a mile—to shore. The Marines wading through water, under heavy machine-gun and shore-gun fire, quickly became the dominant image of the first news reports from correspondents who themselves were caught in the thick of the carnage. But like most news reports, the early images—though they lasted for years—were not always accurate. As Alexander has documented, the real picture of Betio that fateful morning was more complex than it first appeared. If the tide had been higher, it might have hidden more of Japan's offshore defenses, including submerged concrete tetrahedron blocks with iron rails thrusting outward, and caught the Higgins boats like fish on so many hooks. This, in turn, would have left even more Marines trapped within easy range of the shore artillery. Furthermore, Alexander notes, a higher tide would have washed over the seawall that gave the first wave of Marines at least a small measure of protection from the pill-boxes raking the beach and lagoon with machine-gun fire. As it was, the D-Day tide actually was within six inches of its average depth of 3.3 feet.[2]

The Higgins boat carrying Major Crowe and Hatch followed the first few waves of LVTs bearing the assault waves of the 2nd Battalion, 8th Marines. These amtracs were under heavy fire and soon got bunched up along the long pier that divided the target beach, which, for planning purposes, was sliced into three sections: Red Beach One, Red Beach Two, and Red Beach Three. As the Higgins boat slowly sliced through the surf, Crowe could see the confusion along the pier which jutted some 600 feet over the reef.

The long pier may have provided some shelter from the withering fire, but it also became a kind of dangerous magnet, drawing far too many boats together. The troops were not doing any good if they were still huddled offshore, so when he saw this confusion, Crowe—back in the fourth wave of assault boats—ordered his coxswain to put his boat in at the reef. This was what leaders did: they took over when others' nerves seemed to fail.

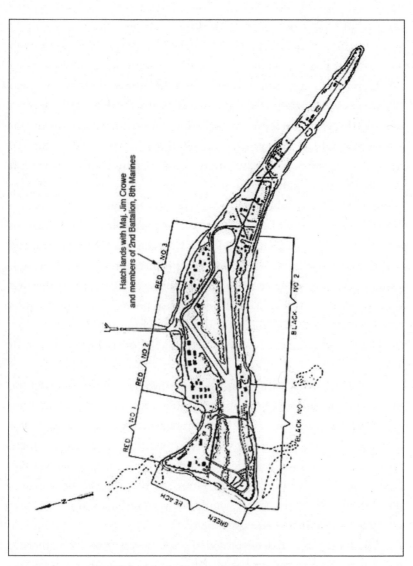

Betio Island in the Tarawa Atoll. U.S. MARINE CORPS

But when the other two sailors on board tried to drop the ramp to release the impatient commander, along with Hatch and the other Marines, it wouldn't budge. Perhaps it was the jarring of the reef, or maybe it was due to some other damage from the rough passage, but despite their best efforts, the sailors just couldn't get the ramp to drop. Swearing, the fiery Crowe clambered over the side and began wading to the beach from 500 yards offshore.

Hatch glanced at his assistant, "Kelly" Kelliher, and let him know to wait. With so much gear to carry—about 200 pounds in all—they would wait until the other thirty-one Marines left the boat.

Fortunately, the cameramen had taken some creative steps to lug their heavy Bell & Howell Eyemos and film canisters. With help from a New Zealand shoemaker, they had fashioned a big leather belt with pouches to carry up to five cans of film. Each man bore 1,500 feet of film along with their 35-millimeter Eyemo handheld movie cameras with three-lens spider turrets and the smaller 16-millimeter Bell & Howells. The cameras were protected in pockets, similar to holsters, that were woven into the customized carrying belts.

The division had only two fully trained motion-picture men, Ercole and Hatch. But while in New Zealand, they had taken time to cross-train eight of their fourteen still photographers to double as motion-picture cameramen using the equipment they had purchased back in Los Angeles. Besides the 35-millimeter Eyemos, their gear consisted of eight Bell & Howell 16-millimeter autoload motion-picture cameras, which shot color film and were favored more by the Marine Corps than any other service branch; the 35-millimeter Wahl sound camera, which had been a favorite of the Japanese POWs on New Zealand; and, for the still photographers, a number of the sturdy four-by-five Speed Graphics. They brought along chemicals, paper, and other supplies.

After all of the infantrymen had splashed into the water, Hatch pulled himself over the side of the Higgins boat with help from one of the sailors. He was already weighed down by his pack, pistol, ammunition, and the 100 pounds or so of camera gear which the sailor lifted onto Hatch's broad shoulders. Then he lashed the Eyemo around his wrist and, dropping into the lagoon, struggled to keep it above the chest-high water. Kelliher, also heavily laden with gear and his own Eyemo, followed suit as a sailor loaded him like a pack mule.

"If you fall down and get the camera wet," Hatch joked above the din, "I'm gonna kill you." At that moment, his idle threat must have seemed preferable to what the Japanese had in store. Yet Kelliher took his boss seriously because the saltwater could ruin their precious lenses.

With that admonition, they started wading to shore. The surf was fairly calm at this point, so most of the Marines ahead of them were ducking as low as they could get, often on their hands and knees, scurrying through the water to present as small a target as possible to the unseen pillboxes. With their helmets bobbing just above the water line, the Marines resembled a legion of amphibious turtles.

Nobody wanted to stand up and walk through the death tide, but the two combat cameramen, both six feet tall, knew they had no choice: either stand tall or ruin their equipment. And the equipment, which had taken so many months to scavenge from Los Angeles to Wellington, had to take priority over their personal safety. For without it, they would never fulfill their mission.

The pace of staccato rifle and rattling machine-gun fire quickened. Over by the pier, Hatch could see some Japanese snipers were having a field day picking off the invaders. With their heavy loads, Hatch and Kelliher were like slow-moving mules and could do nothing but keep moving. Their pistols were tucked out of reach, so they were essentially defenseless. But they were heartened to see a lieutenant colonel from the newly formed 4th Marine Division who had come along as an observer keep his wits about him and stop every so often to expertly fire his M-1 rifle. Several snipers splashed into the surf from their hiding places under the pier.

The slog to shore seemed to take forever. Hatch and Kelliher were increasingly weighed down with water in their boots, trousers, and other gear, but they managed to keep their cameras and film dry. After about fifteen minutes, they scrambled up on the sandy beach and collapsed into a shell hole, totally exhausted.

They couldn't have known it at the time, but Admiral Hill's decision to abort naval gunfire for twenty-five minutes earlier that morning had given the Japanese time to shift forces from the southern and western beaches to reinforce the north side of Betio and open fire on the Marines. Entire units were chewed up, especially on Red Beach One, due west of Hatch's position, and next to them on Red Beach Two. Crowe's troops fared slightly better, as many of the amtracs managed to rumble over the four-foot-high coconut seawall. Hatch heard someone crying and peered up from his shell hole to see his first wounded man close up, a Marine whose buttock appeared to be nearly torn off. The young man was writhing on the sand several feet away, his flesh exposed, bleeding badly, in total agony. "Corpsman! Corpsman!" several Marines cried.

As Hatch watched the corpsmen scamper across the sand, he shook off his initial thought—*That could be me*—and made himself get to work. "We've got to find some place to stash the camera gear and some of this packed crap so we can go ahead and start to do some picture taking," he said to Kelliher. His assistant nodded. Kelliher's job was to load the camera, hand it to Hatch, and record what he had shot on the roll. They worked out a system for slating each roll ahead of time, freeing Hatch to shoot without worrying about writing caption material. Kelliher was a superb assistant, and he fastidiously wrote on each canister the cinematographer's name, S/Sgt. Norman T. Hatch.

They stayed in the shell hole for a time as Hatch, shooting from a prone position, captured the images of Marines pinned down on the beach even as Major Crowe stood in the background, exhorting his men to keep moving.

The Navy's big guns occasionally struck gold, such as a direct hit on a munitions dump that exploded dangerously near the camera crew (another cameraman caught this blast in living color from offshore, a harrowing image that would soon excite movie audiences back home). The munitions dump burst into flames, sending black plumes of smoke heavenward and blotting out the bright blue sky. "Damn," Hatch cursed. The sudden darkness forced him to pause his shooting to lower the F-stop on his Eyemo and open the lens to let more light penetrate the fog of war.

Despite the damage inflicted by the destroyers and battleships, the American bombardment did not inflict the knockout punch that the Navy commanders had promised. Hatch and Kelliher could see an alarming number of unexploded shells lying impotently on the sand. They appeared to have hit the island, then skittered harmlessly over the pillboxes. This early failure—magnified by Admiral Hill's decision to abort the naval gunfire—meant the fortified positions would have to be taken by the Marines one pillbox at a time.

As they prepared to move out, Hatch and Kelliher got a harrowing close-up on ship-to-shore fire: a U.S. Navy submarine torpedo shot over the seawall and raced toward them. Hatch held his breath, expecting it to explode. But it was a dud.

Spared an early demise, the cameramen hustled along the beach to join Major Crowe at his command post beside a stalled amtrac. First, Hatch found a place to stash his extra cans of film and other supplies in a nook behind the wall. Now he could start filming again, starting with Crowe, who was dramatically pacing back and forth, repeating his courageous performance from Guadalcanal. He led by example, exhorting any of his reluctant men to stop crawling along the shore where they were ducking bullets and simply get over the barrier wall. "Look!" he hollered defiantly as bullets buzzed by his head like so many bumblebees. "The sons of bitches can't hit me! Get up and over that wall."

While unacceptable from a commander's point of view, his men's reluctance was surely understandable. The sniping made the pier and beach area a killing zone. Japan's 3rd Base Special Force earned its stripes in subterfuge and marksmanship, filling the thin strand of Red

Beach Three with increasing numbers of killed and wounded Americans. At times, some 2/8 Marines hardly lived up to their storied past or met General Smith's high expectations to "decisively defeat and destroy the treacherous enemies of our country." A few men, after losing their weapons, were decisive only in scampering under the pier to hide.

Crowe was outraged by such cowardice. The major, who by now had taken off his helmet to further show his disdain for the enemy, angrily clenched his cigar as his face turned as red as his mustache. He ordered a lieutenant to order the laggards to grab a weapon and reorganize into squads since many of their units ceased to exit. The reluctant warriors followed orders and returned to the fray only because they feared Crowe more than they feared the enemy. Gradually, over the course of the day, his Marines started to move out over the seawall and take positions that ensured they would gain at least a foothold on Red Beach Three.

But the pummeling of the next assault wave of Marines in the lagoon continued. The Japanese may have lost their vaunted 8-inch rapid-fire Vickers guns early in the battle, but there was plenty more firepower where that came from. The enemy's 13-millimeter machine guns could easily penetrate the thin skins of the LVTs, and the dual-purpose 75-millimeter antiaircraft guns also fired with deadly accuracy from their protected positions. Hatch could only watch in horror as a bloody scene repeated itself like a nightmare: a ramp would drop down from a Higgins boat, the Marines would begin to make a surge to come out, but a shell would explode in their faces, killing everyone on board. Hatch saw this repeated at least a dozen times and was sickened to see limbs and other body parts floating aimlessly across the lagoon.

All he could do was keep busy with Kelly, chronicling the routine and the extraordinary sights all around them (his Eyemo did not record sound): men digging in; patrols rushing over seawalls to take out the pillboxes; corpsmen treating the fallen; firefights and air strikes. Throughout the furious action, he worried more about his cameras than about himself. The intense heat, dampness, and sand were taking a toll.

The Eyemos were protected, but in the heat of battle, he put one down. Picking it up, he could see its shutter release was malfunctioning. *Jesus*, he thought, *I hope I don't have a dead camera.* If he did, they would be down to one Eyemo. As he worked the problem, he decided to open the camera door, despite the risk of exposing film. Then he saw what had happened: when he put the camera on the ground, the metal heated up in the intense sunlight, causing the film's emulsion (its coating) to melt. That, in turn, gummed up the inner mechanism.

By now, though, Hatch was an expert in camera maintenance, and even in the heat of battle, he managed to clean out the Eyemo and start filming again. But he had learned a lesson: store your camera in the shade when you're not shooting.

It was a good thing Hatch kept his camera rolling that first day at Betio. Only later did he learn that he was the division's only motion-picture cameraman to make it to shore on D-Day, along with Kelliher and still photographer Obie Newcomb. Others had been stranded off-shore, including "Pappy" Leopold, who was in a boat with Don Senick of Twentieth Century Fox Movietone News, the only civilian newsreel cameraman at Tarawa.[3] They never landed that day as a shell sent shrapnel through their vessel, nearly capsizing it. Somehow, Leopold managed to hold on to his dual 16-millimeter cameras and keep filming offshore. Unit chief Capt. Louis Hayward and cinematographer Ercole, among others, were among the frustrated combat cameramen that day as their Higgins boat couldn't get past the barrage in the lagoon.

The shore gunners also pummeled the mechanized amtracs, often sending Marines "jumping out like torches."[4] This forced Shoup to scuttle plans to use the LVTs to bring in men from the Higgins boats. If they did not go up in smoke, other LVTs simply ran out of gas after five hours spent plowing through the waves. The water also played havoc with most radio equipment, leaving Julian Smith and the rest of the commanders out on the flagship awaiting any shred of solid news. Major Crowe, for his part, kept his radio working but also pressed into service as runners two visiting lieutenant colonels from the 4th Marine Division. Crowe also had telephone wires strung between his command post behind the stalled amtrac and his forward positions, where riflemen were hunkered down in shell holes.

As much as any officer that day, Crowe used his communications options to good effect, according to historian Alexander. Crowe's shore fire control party established links with two destroyers, the *Ringgold* and *Dashiell*, which earlier in the day had bravely taken on the enemy shore batteries. The *Ringgold* had been battered by two shells, one at the waterline of its engine room on the starboard side, the other on its forward torpedo mount, where it had cut through the deckhouse and sick bay. Neither round exploded. Free to fight, the destroyer joined the *Dashiell* in delivering some serious damage to the shore batteries and helped dampen the enemy's major-caliber fire.

Now Crowe's men called for more fire missions, and the *Ringgold* fired 100 rounds over a twenty-minute period. The destroyer, led by the intrepid Cmdr. John B. McLean, swung into the lagoon and crept so close to the land that one Japanese officer would recount, "With the naked eye we could clearly see the American sailors on the destroyers' decks."[5] Asked how they were shooting, Crowe's executive officer, William Chamberlin reported back, "Fine, but don't get any closer."[6] The last shell landed only twenty-five yards in front of their line— dangerously close fire support indeed.

And yet many of the incoming Higgins boats and amtracs remained sitting ducks, as did hundreds of men pinned down from pier to shore. It was at this point on D-Day at Betio that some men exhibited uncommon valor that spurred their comrades to move on and attack. One of the valiant Marines was S/Sgt. William Bordelon, a combat engineer assigned to Landing Team 2/2, who managed to rally the survivors in his disabled LVT and then go on a rampage, personally knocking out two enemy positions. After getting hit by machine-gun fire, he declined a corpsman's assistance and waded back into the water to rescue a comrade calling for help. "As intense fire opened up from yet another nearby enemy stronghold," wrote Alexander, "the staff sergeant prepared one last demolition packaged and charged the position frontally. Bordelon's luck ran out." He was shot and killed, later becoming the first man in the division to be awarded the Medal of Honor.[7] The acts of courage multiplied, but so did the death toll as 217 sergeants alone were killed in what would become a seventy-six-hour-long battle.

One captain on Red Beach Three who had been shot through both arms and legs sent a message to Major Crowe, apologizing for "letting you down." In another case of timely valor, a group of Marines salvaged two 37-millimeter guns from a sunken landing craft, "manhandled them several hundred yards ashore under nightmarish enemy fire, and hustled them across the beach to the seawall," Alexander writes. As a pair of enemy tanks approached, the Marines realized the guns were too low to fire over the wall, so they hoisted them over and, in the nick of time, knocked out one tank and chased off the other.[8]

Time correspondent Robert Sherrod, already a veteran of several early battles in the Pacific War, knew he was witnessing a new level of death and destruction for American forces. As he followed Landing Team 2/2, he witnessed it getting torn apart. Under fire from a half dozen machine guns, he followed the battalion's "painfully slow" wade through the deep water for 700 yards marching into the teeth of machine-gun fire. "I was scared," Sherrod admitted, "as I had never been scared before. But my head was clear. I was extremely alert, as though my brain were dictating that I live these last minutes for all they were worth."[9]

Sherrod shadowed Major Crowe and his staff most of that afternoon, "watching the drama of life and death being enacted around me. Men were being killed and wounded every minute." He admired the courage of the Navy medical corpsmen who "bore their poncho-covered cargo in streams along the beach. Almost any man will go through greater danger to save a friend's life than he will endure in killing the enemy who is the cause of that danger."[10] Out of twenty-nine corpsman, he heard later, some twenty-six were killed or wounded in the fierce fighting.

For all of the gallantry, Hatch later observed, "If we had really known how bad off we were, I doubt if we would have stayed on the damned island. I think we probably would have pulled out of there that night if we could have done it, because if the Japanese had been able to mount a force, if their communications hadn't been so badly debilitated, they could have pushed us right off the beach. I don't think there's anything we could have done about it because we didn't have enough people ashore."

Colonel Shoup made the same point to Sherrod, saying, "We're in a tight spot. We've got to have more men."[11]

Gains on the beach were measured not by the mile, but by the yard. United Press correspondent Richard Johnson wrote, "In those hellish hours, the heroism of the Marines, officers, and enlisted men alike was beyond belief. Time after time, they unflinchingly charged Japanese positions, ignoring the deadly fire and refusing to halt until wounded beyond human ability to carry on."[12]

By 1 P.M. on that first day of fighting, the Marines began the grim business of burying their dead at sea. One of the LVTs, "with a gashed hole in its side, like something alive but mortally hurt," drifted by a transport ship. The sailors lowered a boom and retrieved the damaged vessel. "Sprawled on its deck were the bodies of two Marines and a Navy doctor. The shell that had killed them had also wounded ten other men who had been taken off by another ship, but the tractor had drifted away before the three men could be discharged."[13]

As pallbearers gathered in the blazing sun, Marines and sailors removed their steel helmets while Chaplain Harry R. Boer of Holland, Michigan, read the last rites. The three bodies were tied into white sheets and placed under an American flag.

"We are in the presence of the last great enemy, Death."

Thunder from the shelling rolled across the water and mixed with the melancholic music from a portable organ. A few stray bullets whizzed overhead, punctuating the music with high notes from the ubiquitous enemy.

"We did not know these men, but God knows them, as we commit them to Him Who is the righteous judge of all the earth," Boer declared. "It is for us, the living, in the presence of these dead, to devote ourselves seriously to the task ahead."

More booms from the enemy's antiboat guns added a poignant counterpoint to his sermon. "I am the Resurrection and the Life, sayeth the Lord, and he that believeth in Me, though he were dead, yet shall he live."

The trio of shrouded Marines then slid under the colors and dropped into the sea with a splash, disappearing into the deep. "Men with set expressions lined the rails and watched the place where the white-sheeted figures had boiled the blue water."[14]

Offshore on the *Maryland*, Julian Smith was deeply concerned about the mounting losses and the thin strand of territory gained. By day's end, three-quarters of Tarawa was still in Japanese hands, and despite their own severe toll of dead and wounded, the Japanese probably had as many men on the tiny atoll as the Americans. The Marines held less than a quarter of a square mile of sand and coral. Given the tenuous situation, Smith reported up the chain of command to Nimitz: "Issue remains in doubt."[15]

But the Japanese, despite their enormous courage and fierce determination, failed to seize their inherent advantage against the Marines. Admiral Shibasaki, who had lost his communications from the Americans' offshore bombardment, could not get his troops to mount a counteroffensive. Soon his fate was in doubt. Without their intrepid leader and with their telephone lines shredded by naval gunfire, the Japanese failed to press their tactical advantage. After all, out of about 5,000 Marines who stormed ashore that day, about a third—1,500— were either dead, wounded, or missing. Shoup would describe the beachhead that night as a zigzag line, "a stock market graph." A concerted Japanese counterattack that night "would probably have been disastrous," Colonel Edson would later say. "There were certainly 500 to 600 Japs under good control east of our left flank."[16]

A few Japanese would infiltrate the Marines' lines, including swimming out to disabled amtracs and tanks floundering in the lagoon, but as night fell, no counterattack came.

Major Crowe passed the word down the line, and Hatch listened closely to the hushed orders: "No one move on the beach. If you have to go to the head, stay where you are and, if necessary, just piss in your pants. Otherwise, we're going to be shooting at each other. If you know for sure some Jap has crawled into your foxhole, don't use your pistols or your rifles. Use your knives. I do not want to hear a single weapon fired on this beach."

A Navy chaplain, one Father Lumpkin, came by Hatch's temporary command post, near his equipment cache in the coconut seawall. "Norm," he said, apologetically, "I'm so busy, but would you dig the foxhole for me?"

Normally, Hatch would have rejected a request to do another man's digging, especially since he was completely worn out. But this was not just another man. He had met the good chaplain aboard ship, when Lumpkin noticed a tiny gold cross hanging on Hatch's neck and asked, "Are you Catholic?"

"No, I'm an Episcopalian."

Lumpkin, it turned out, was also an Episcopalian.

"So why are you wearing a cross?"

"It's my wife's baby cross," Hatch replied. "See?" He held it up in the sunlight to show tiny dents on the gold left from Lois' teeth. "She gave it to me when I left."

They chatted about religion a bit. Hatch confided that he had stopped attending services in his teens after a priest needled him about failing to understand one Sunday school lesson. After this turnoff, young Hatch rarely darkened the red door of his Episcopal chapel or, for that matter, any church.

Yet in a twist on the old adage about foxholes and atheists, Hatch, despite his exhaustion, was happy to tell the pleasant priest, "Sure, I'll do it for you." Digging out the foxhole left him even more tired and thirsty. But when he sipped water from his canteen, he gagged at the acrid taste. Only later did he learn that it was contaminated with gasoline residue left in some of the containers when they shipped in water from Pearl Harbor. The Navy had washed out the cans and painted them with white paint. But neither the cleaning or the painting had done the trick, leading to a common joke at Tarawa: "If you belch near a flamethrower, you'll *become* a flamethrower."

Despite the acrid aftertaste, Hatch tried to get some shuteye. Part of his brain stayed awake, though, listening for any sign of a nighttime *banzai* attack. He managed to drift off to sleep until after midnight, when someone yelled, "There's a Jap in here, and he's killing people." Startled awake, Hatch frantically felt around for his knife, which he had left in his pistol holster. But by the time he found it, the intruder was dead. Somehow, the Japanese infiltrator had hidden among some captured Korean workers on the island and snuck away under the cover of darkness to kill Marines.

The night breeze caressed his sunburned face, and for a fleeting moment, he pictured lying on the beach beside Lois. He touched her cross with its tiny dents. Maybe someday they would have kids of their own. He tried to picture the future, but for now, all he could know was this tenuous present. And try as he might, there would be no sound sleeping tonight. The best he could expect was to get off his feet a while and not lug around the heavy gear.

And for all of his religious doubts, Hatch could take a small bit of comfort knowing that if anything did happen to him, Father Lumpkin would be close enough to administer last rites.

CHAPTER SEVEN

Tarawa, D–Day plus One and Two: "I Think We'd Better Get the Hell Out of Here"

The next morning, Hatch and Kelliher peered out of their fighting holes to see how everyone had held up through the restless night. Father Lumpkin was already gone, making his morning rounds along the beach. They all had been startled awake around 4 A.M. when some Japanese *Rikko* naval bombers began dropping bombs indiscriminately across the scorched atoll. The explosions did little damage except to further rattle the Marines' collective nerves.

As the cameramen prepared for another day of filming the battle, a rifleman collapsed to the ground with a bullet in his back.

"Where the hell did *that* come from?" Hatch whispered to Kelly. Death seemed to stalk the beachhead like some grim blackjack dealer, randomly handing out final cards to the unsuspecting players. Witnessing this first death of the second day of battle baffled the cameramen because of the Marine's proximity to what passed for enemy lines on Betio. He had been standing with his back to the water, which presumably was controlled by the Navy ships at the mouth of the lagoon. Had the Japs managed to sneak out to the coral reef under the cover of darkness? Had they found perches among the splintered Higgins boats, amtracs, and Sherman medium tanks? After the fierce fighting of D-Day, nothing would surprise them.

Faced with these random gunshots from the offshore wreckage, the Marines retaliated with mortar and naval fire. Still, the snipers and machine-gunners who had crept into disabled LVTs and boarded the sunken Japanese trader ship on the reef's edge—the *Nimonea*—kept shooting with deadly accuracy. The enemy rifles were joined by a chorus of booms from the dual-purpose antiaircraft guns which were still blowing up the arriving boats and LVTs in the lagoon. Faced with having to make snap choices of what to film, Hatch, on this second day of battle, found he could not stomach shooting some of the same disturbing images of D-Day. He could not stand to watch the sickly repetition of the carnage as the ramps went down on the Higgins boats and the Japanese took dead aim on his fellow Marines.

Shoup responded by calling for more naval gunfire to take out the enemy's effective gunnery positions. He also moved Marines into place to fire pack howitzers behind a sand berm created by the Seabees and their bulldozers the night before. They took aim at the enemy's protected blockhouses on the border of Red Beach One and Two. A flight of Navy F4F Wildcats joined in the counterattack by dropping bombs and strafing the pesky *Nimonea*.[1]

But the aviators' aim wasn't true, with some bombs missing by up to 200 yards and blowing up near the Marines plodding to shore. "Stop strafing!" Shoup screamed into his radio. "Bombing ship hitting own troops!"[2]

For all of America's naval and aerial power, the decisive factor in the battle proved to be the undying collective will of the Marines. Early on the second day of battle, Sherrod described this poignant persistence of the young troops: "One of the fresh battalions is coming in," he wrote. "Its Higgins boats are being hit before they pass the old hulk of a freighter seven hundred yards from shore. One boat blows up, then another. The survivors start swimming for shore, but machine gun bullets dot the water around them."

Yet the Marines who kept coming remained "calm, even disdainful of death," the correspondent wrote. "Having come this far, slowly, through the water, they show no disposition to hurry. They collect in pairs and walk up the beach, with snipers still shooting at them."[3]

Though some landing teams were decimated, Crowe's 2/8 and Maj. Robert Rudd's 3/8 were in fairly good shape with weapons and personnel on Red Beach Three. Nonetheless, their left flank was exposed to three large enemy bunkers that had tied together their defenses and seemed impossible to attack. Plus, the smaller Burns-Philip commercial pier was still being fought over.[4]

Hatch and Kelliher cautiously crept across the sand to hear the morning briefing at the battalion command post. Despite Crowe's admonitions to stay out of his way, Hatch was determined to keep abreast of the planning. He learned that the battalion faced three major obstacles: a steel pillbox near the pier; a coconut-log emplacement with a number of machine guns; and a sand-covered, seemingly impenetrable troop bunker.

Crowe was determined to clear out the enemy's entrenched resistance. But as he prepared his tired troops for the third day of battle, the former marksmanship coach began with a simple order: clean and field strip your rifles. Then he placed Maj. Bill Chamberlin in the center of the battalion's three attacking companies. The former economics professor at Northwestern University was nursing a shoulder wound from D-Day, but Hatch could see he relished the challenge.

"We're going to take the command post!" the slender, six-foot-tall major told his company and platoon leaders. But they would have to take out the enemy machine-gunners firing out of fortified positions that ringed the top of the sandy mound. These protected gunners had stymied the battalion's attempts to attack from the flanks, taking many lives along the way. Now it was time for the Marines to play their trump card. If they could divert the enemy machine-gunners, then they could get combat engineers on top to burn them out with flamethrowers or blow them up with thermite grenades tossed down the air vents. If nothing else, Chamberlin said, they should be able to flush them out into the daylight.

So far nothing else had worked—not mortars, not tanks, not pack howitzers—to penetrate the bunker's protections. Photographer Obie E. Newcomb Jr. was poised to shoot still photos of the attack, while Hatch would handle the motion pictures. Chamberlin, who was pumped up for the fight ahead, seemed glad to see them: "You ought to get a lot of good pictures. Want to come?"

"Sure, major," Hatch replied, appreciating an approach different from Crowe's.

Indeed, Chamberlin was almost the polar opposite of his blustery, hot-tempered boss. As Crowe's executive officer, he was the detail man, the second-in-command who handled the administrative and personnel matters that otherwise might be forgotten in the heat of battle. Unlike Crowe, who came from the Old Corps, Chamberlin was part of a new wave of officers who had joined through a new Reserve Officer Training Corps program that tapped into the talent on America's college campuses. This officer-recruitment drive began in 1921 when Commandant Lejeune arranged with the War Department to commission a dozen graduates of the U.S. Naval Academy. Lejeune's idea grew into the ROTC program, which created a much-needed pipeline for bright, young leaders who helped energize the Corps and get it through the long slog of World War II. Indeed, the Reserve program would attract a group of young leaders who would form the Corps' upper echelon for decades to come, among them Wallace M. Greene, Victor H. "Brute" Krulak, Lewis W. Walt, Raymond G. Davis, and William K. Jones.[5]

Chamberlin was even more cerebral than most of these ROTC boys. The Seattle native graduated with honors from Dartmouth College, where he was named a Phi Beta Kappa for academic distinction and went on to become an economics professor at Northwestern. After going on active duty, he joined the 6th Brigade in Iceland in 1940, where he found time to study for his doctorate.

His campus connections may have impressed his senior officers, but Chamberlin's degrees proved to be a dubious calling card with the everyday grunts. Chamberlin had joined the 2nd Battalion, 8th Marines, late in its training in New Zealand, and the combat-tested veterans of Guadalcanal first dismissed him as a lightweight—and a worry-wart to boot. They took umbrage when he admonished men lounging and sunbathing on deck, an activity that, while technically violating rules designed to avoid sunburn, was generally tolerated by other officers. Not Chamberlin, who fretted about the possible ill effects of men getting burned on their shoulders, which could cause the straps of their heavy backpacks to lacerate their skin. No matter their rank or experience, Chamberlin barked, "You put that skivvy shirt on."

When he was out of earshot, the old salts grumbled, "Jesus, what an old maid."

Now that they were in battle, the time had come for Chamberlin to shed whatever remained of his image as an egghead who wasn't a real Marine like Crowe. As the major wrapped up the briefing, Hatch cradled his Eyemo in anticipation. He knew this was going to be good.

"All right," Chamberlin told his NCOs and lieutenants, "I want you to know that we're going to jump off and we're going to take this place, and we're going to do it at 0900." There were 100 Japanese holed up in the bunker, maybe more. "We've either got to get them out or close them up," he declared. "We're going to go right over the top."

If anyone harbored doubts about his plan, they kept them to themselves. After synchronizing their watches, Chamberlin said, "When I give a signal, we're off and running."

Hatch told Kelliher to stay back to film the Marines from behind as they mounted up. Chamberlin stood up in his foxhole, announcing, "It's 0900. Follow me!"

Simultaneously, a mortar crew scored a direct hit, penetrating the bunker and detonating ammunition. A medium tank got close enough to the bunker's steel pillbox to penetrate it with direct 75-millimeter fire. Now it was up to the infantry to do the rest.

Hatch trailed the major through the sand, brush, and palm trees. Sometimes they crawled, sometimes they ran, avoiding angry bursts of machine-gun fire. The blockhouse rose like some ancient Buddhist burial mound some forty feet away. This clever combination of protection and elevation gave the Japanese a tactical advantage over anyone who dared to sneak up on them.

Apparently unseen by the guards, the Marines dashed up its back side to its precipice. Peering over the edge, Hatch was stunned to see they seemed to have gotten the drop on thirty Japanese soldiers standing idly by the bunker's entrance, with their rifles by their sides. The Japanese looked equally surprised to see the pair of Marines looking down on them.

But when Chamberlin and Hatch glanced behind them, they had another surprise: no other Marine had followed them up the sandy slope. And Hatch could not help noticing another big problem.

"Major," Hatch whispered, "where's your rifle?"

Chamberlin said he had loaned it to a Marine who lost their weapon in the landing.

"Major, where's your pistol?"

That, too, had been lost in the fighting.

Hatch gulped. His own pistol was jammed in the back of his belt, allowing his hands to protect his beloved Eyemo in its leather pouch. Not only were they vastly outmanned, they were completely outgunned. "I think," Hatch said, starting to back up, "we'd better get the hell out of here."

"I think you're right!" Chamberlin replied.

Feeling a little like the Keystone Kops, they dashed back down the hill over to the command post. After regaining his breath, Chamberlin gave everyone a royal tongue-lashing for failing to follow orders.

"This time we go!" Chamberlin roared. "No if's, and's, or but's."

As they mounted up for a second attack on the bunker—this time in full force—Hatch injected some humor into the situation. "You know, major, those were almost famous last words."

"What's that?" said Chamberlin, looking angry and embarrassed.

"*Follow me*," Hatch explained. "Those were almost your last words."

He was glad to see the major laugh a little. "Yeah, I know," he said. "I'm never going to say *that* again."

The stage for the infantry attack that followed had been set by the intrepid work of a group of combat engineers under the intrepid leadership of Lt. Alexander "Sandy" Bonnyman, a thirty-three-year-old mine owner from New Mexico whose industrial interests—deemed necessary for the war effort—could have kept him safe at home. Instead, he joined the Marines.[6] As Chamberlin's man laid down a base of fire, according to historian Alexander, "Bonnyman rolled over the seawall, darted for the shelter of a wooden fence perpendicular to the mound, and snaked his way to the edge."[7]

Cameraman Obie Newcomb "had experienced enough combat to realize he was in the presence of a most unusual Marine in Bonnyman," writes Alexander, and photographed his actions for posterity.[8] The combat engineers on what became known as "Bonnyman's Hill" followed him with flamethrowers that roasted enemy machine-gunners inside their pillboxes. The Marines' TNT blasts provided smoke and cover for other engineers to drop thermite grenades down the air shaft, creating enough death and havoc for the infantry charge.

"Go!" Chamberlin shouted. Hatch saw a periscope rotating atop the bunker. A pair of enemy infantry squads with six to eight men each rushed outside to blunt the attack.

"Here come the Japs!" someone yelled.

Hatch pivoted for what would become the defining moment of his life: filming the Japanese and Americans engaging in close combat, often shooting at point-blank range. It was a brief, bloody skirmish as dozens of Chamberlin's men mowed down the bunker's defenders. But though the clash was quick—less than a minute—it marked the first time that American and Japanese soldiers were caught in the same frames in fighting stances. Capturing such scenes on film proved to be elusive throughout the war because the Japanese were masters of camouflage, hiding in trees, caves, and tunnels. But Hatch stood tall during the Betio fighting to capture this epic moment for the Marine Corps.

Newcomb shot a still photo of his friend that shows the lone camera-man plying his trade in the thick of combat. Hatch's beloved Eyemo points forward from his helmet as smoke rises like a mist and the Marines charge up the debris-strewn bunker.

After the firefight, most of the Japanese defenders were either killed or wounded. The bunker was taken, allowing Crowe's men to start making inroads on the island's small interior. And Major Chamberlin dispelled any doubts about his courage or leadership ability (along with Crowe and a number of other Marines at Tarawa, he would be awarded the Navy Cross).

Bonnyman was shot and killed in the fighting. He was honored with a posthumous Medal of Honor, the third to go to a Marine on Tarawa and the second for a combat engineer (Sgt. William J. Bordelon was the other). "His sacrifice," Alexander wrote of Bonnyman, "almost single-handedly ended the stalemate on Red Beach Three." Word of Bonnyman's exploits spread like the tales of brave Ulysses around the Corps, sometimes portraying him as somewhat reckless in the charge on the bunker. Newcomb's photographs, while documenting his gallantry, also helped "belie the common myth of Bonnyman himself strapping on a flamethrower or single-handedly repelling the swarming Japanese counterattack," Alexander wrote. "Bonnyman's valor this day was not melodramatic, but intelligent, sensible, unselfish—and absolutely fearless."[9]

During a lull in the fighting, Hatch made an astounding discovery: fourteen cases of Kirin beer, a potent favorite brew of the Japanese, could be seen poking through the sand where they had been buried for cool safekeeping.

The discovery was timely, since clean drinking water had been in especially short supply on the island. With the snafu over the water cans and their gasoline residue, the discovery of Kirin beer seemed like manna from the emperor's heaven. Hatch carefully lifted the metal clip on one of the longneck bottles, knowing there was a possibility it was booby-trapped. But after spitting out the ghastly water in his canteen, he was willing to take his chances. When the bottle opened without incident, Hatch gratefully tilted it back and drank deeply. The enemy beer slid smoothly down his gullet. Now, slightly relaxed and refreshed, a plan bubbled up in his always-percolating brain. When he returned to the battle line, he took along half a dozen bottles on his pistol belt.

"Want a beer?" he casually asked the battle-worn Marines.

Some stared at him as though he were an alien: who was this guy offering beer as casually as if they were watching a ball game? But most accepted the beverage and its welcome relief from heat, fatigue, and fear. As more men slaked their thirst, word spread across the beach-head about this cameraman operating without a liquor license. He kept pulling bottles from their sandy stash, and before long, all fourteen cases had been distributed. "Everyone who had the opportunity to sample the Kirin beer went back to the battle refreshed," Hatch recalled. "I should have made a commercial."[10]

Then things seemed to start winding down, at least for Hatch and his assistant, Kelliher. Only later did they learn that the outcome of the battle was still very much in doubt. General Smith called in his reserve, Landing Team 1/6, the rubber-boat battalion derided as "the condom fleet." The Higgins boats towed four rubber boats at a time to the reef's edge, and the Marines, riding seven men to a boat, started paddling toward the shore some 1,000 yards away. It was dusk. Though he was called "the admiral," Maj. "Willie K." Jones paddled right alongside his men, hoping the Japanese gunners wouldn't open up on these floating ducks framed by the setting sun. Jones would later say the control he felt over his 150-raft "fleet" spread across the ocean's horizon was "nebulous at best."[11] They managed to land with minimal losses because Maj. Mike Ryan and his Love Company of Landing Team 3/2 had secured the beach by the time they landed in the dark.

Jones's only casualties came when a supply LVT that tried to come over the reef hit a mine, which turned it over and killed several Marines.

Other reserve forces had already been decimated. The Japanese inflicted grievous losses, which prompted comparisons to European charnel houses, the final resting places of bones and corpses. "A dreadful sight," one lieutenant observed, with "bodies drifting slowly in the water just off the beach" and the stench of rotting flesh filling the air. The air of decay drifted across the reef and continued out to sea, "a bad omen for the troops of 1st Battalion, 8th Marines, getting ready to start their run to the beach."[12]

Time correspondent Robert Sherrod reported the garish tableau on the beach: "A half dozen Marines lie exposed, now that the water has receded. They are hunched over, rifles in hand, just as they fell. They are already one-quarter covered by sand that the high tide left. . . . The smell of death, that sweetly sick odor of decaying human flesh, is already oppressive."[13]

Hatch kept recording search-and-destroy missions, cautioning Kelliher to be vigilant as they continued poking around the island. Danger lurked behind every tree—indeed, the trees themselves couldn't be trusted. At one point, as bullets whistled overhead, Hatch ordered his assistant to lie low. "Let's just wait and see what happens. Let's not make a move until we know where all this firing is coming from."

Scanning the palm trees and dunes, Hatch turned just in time to see a tree edging up toward Kelliher. Hatch quickly surmised that a well-camouflaged soldier had gotten the drop on them. There was no time to warn him, though. Hatch pulled out his .45-caliber pistol and fired a single shot. He knocked a branch off the enemy's helmet, distracting him long enough to give Kelly a chance to hit the dirt. A squad of nearby Marines saw the action and shot the stalker. He was left dead on the sand, buried beneath his own branches.

Catching his breath, Hatch thought back to his New Zealand training with the former FBI agent who taught them to always fire quickly to get the drop on an attacker. That tip was a lifesaver. It would be the only shot Hatch would fire in combat during the war.

Later, Kelliher had another close call when he crawled into a cave in search of souvenirs—a violation of battlefield regulations, but a common practice by victors on both sides of the shifting battle lines. Kelly's foray was short-lived as he screamed and wriggled out of the cave.

"What's the problem, Kelly?" asked Hatch. His assistant looked like he had seen a ghost. "There's somebody alive in there!" he said, pointing behind them. As he had crawled over the stinking pile of dead soldiers, who he assumed had all committed ritualistic *hara-kiri*, one of the bodies grunted, startling Kelly.

After reporting the incident, some nearby Marines stormed into the cave, found the Japanese Lazarus, and dragged him outside, where they shot him dead.

For Hatch, like most of the Marines at Tarawa, there were too many close calls to count. He was crossing with Newcomb what seemed like a fairly secure stretch of beach the second day of battle when a gunshot rang out, felling a nearby Marine who was shot through the head. Then it happened again: another rifle shot, another Marine dropping like a sandbag dead on the ground. So when an unsuspecting infantryman walked toward them, Hatch and Newcomb hollered in unison, "Hit the deck!" The Marine ducked a millisecond before another shot rang out. It pinged against the man's helmet, leaving him dazed, but otherwise unharmed. Hatch and Newcomb, running low along the beach as they hefted their cameras, ducked and dodged their way to him. When he started to get up, they both shouted, "Stay down!"

"What happened?" the Marine asked.

"You've just been shot in the head," Hatch explained. "Your helmet saved your life." Newcomb photographed the Marine, who couldn't have been a day over nineteen. He wore a jacket stenciled with "Pappy, the Iowa Kid."

Everyone froze, knowing that any sudden movement would give the sniper an easy target. Peering over the seawall, they spotted the turret of a Japanese light tank just twenty feet away. The damaged machine had been well-camouflaged and buried in the sand, creating the perfect cover for a sniper to wreak havoc. Somehow, in the confusion of combat, this hiding place had been missed by hundreds of Marines moving back and forth along the shoreline. Hatch figured the sniper either snuck in under the cover of darkness or managed to play possum during the day. Whatever his method, he was now a one-man killing machine, firing out of the turret's port, picking off any Marine in his rifle's sight.

Hatch, Newcomb, and the Iowa Kid froze, hoping the audacious shooter would show himself. When he finally popped off another shot, a joint cry erupted: "There he is!" A hail of gunfire struck the tank turret, but not before their nemesis dropped into his hole like a prairie dog. After more bullets bounced off the tank's armor, an engineer was called up to deliver a satchel charge. He tossed the explosives that rocked the turret. Then a team of combat engineers torched the tank with flamethrowers.

They finally got results as the hatch flew open and the sniper popped out, screaming in agony. He was on fire and desperately dashed toward the seawall to extinguish his flames in the water. But the burning man made it only a few steps before falling in front of Hatch and Newcomb, a nightmarish sight on the sand.

Normally, the cameramen would have done their jobs and filmed even this gruesome scene. But the sniper's ammunition pouch starting popping off, and everyone dove for cover. Finally, someone shot the burning sniper, putting him out of his misery.

The conflagration happened so quickly that it eluded Hatch's normally reliable trigger finger on his Eyemo. It was one scene at Tarawa that got away, yet so terrible that the image stayed scorched in his memory.

Finally, after two days of heavy losses on both sides, the Marines began to get the upper hand, and the Japanese were on the run. By evening on the second day, Shoup turned to *Time* correspondent Sherrod and wearily remarked, "Well, I think we're winning, but the bastards have a lot of bullets left. I think we'll clean up tomorrow."[14]

During another lull in the fighting, Hatch had a rare opportunity to show his life-long love of animals. As they were passing the wreckage of a tank, Hatch, Newcomb, and Kelliher heard a keening sound. Someone, or something, appeared to be trapped below.

"What the hell is that?" Hatch asked.

They suspected the Japanese were luring them into an elaborate trap. But as the high-pitched cry continued, Hatch's curiosity got the better of him. He pulled out a flashlight and peered past the tank treads to the machine's underbelly. Two almond-shaped eyes blinked back at him. "That's not anybody," Hatch exclaimed. "It's a cat!"

Try as he might, he couldn't entice the tiny kitten to leave its refuge in the tank treads. So Hatch found the lid to a coffee can and poured some water from his canteen. The kitten darted out and started sipping. Newcomb snapped a photo of Hatch on his knees in full battle gear, a canteen in his right hand while proffering water with his left. "I was prepared to tuck her in my pocket and carry her with me," Hatch said. But the kitten, no bigger than his hand, dashed back in the darkness to sit out the war.

Newcomb's picture was sent back to the States, where it was widely distributed. A photographer from the *Washington Star* stopped by the Hatch home and took a picture of Lois gazing at the picture. Even on the field of battle, she could see Norm was up to his old tricks.

CHAPTER EIGHT

"Methinks I Have Some Good Pictures"

B y the third day of fighting, Hatch hooked up with Johnny Ercole, who finally made it ashore. It was good to see the street-savvy New Yorker again, and they set out across the island, careful to watch out for any lingering pockets of resistance. By now, the Japanese were clearly fighting for pride and honor, with no chance of keeping the island. But before they committed suicide as part of their *bushido* code, most of the enemy soldiers were determined to take out as many Marines as possible.

The old friends settled into a workmanlike routine, filming whatever seemed interesting—a flag-raising ceremony here, a gun battle there. They finally reached the airfield, a prize possession that the Seabees were busy repairing. The runway would be a critical jumping-off point to attack the next line of the Japanese empire's defenses, the Marshall Islands, as the Navy-Marine juggernaut continued its push across the Central Pacific. Without Tarawa and the rest of the Gilbert Islands, "we held no positions close enough to the Marshalls to enable us to obtain the amount of photographic reconnaissance required," declared Adm. Raymond A. Spruance, commander of Central Pacific Force. Pictures taken from carrier-based aircraft during infrequent carrier strikes on the Japanese "were no substitutes for the almost daily reconnaissance work conducted by regularly-equipped photographic planes operating from a shore base in range of the objectives" several hundred miles to the north."[1]

The air base was also critical for attacking the enemy's fortified positions in the Marshalls and to learn the lessons of the Tarawa operation. That educational component was where the photos and film were worth their weight in yen. And there were more discoveries to come. Like archeologists discovering relics of Spartan and Persian spears along the Aegean, the cameramen marveled at the sight of the many unexploded shells from the Navy's big guns that had skittered across the sand. Hatch and Ercole gave wide berth to the duds and kept filming.

Even though Hatch thought things were slowing down, the Marine Corps still had its hands full on the third day of battle, including the morning attack on the command bunker led by Major Chamberlin. No one needed to be reminded of the dangers as hundreds of bodies continued to decompose on the hot white sand. The oppressive heat seemed to fuel the sickly sweet stench wafting across land and sea. Scores of Marines, exhausted and dehydrated from days of combat, collapsed from heat prostration and started throwing up.

Though the Japanese were beaten down, they were not yet beaten. By nightfall, they began to mount counterattacks. Contrary to the popular notion of the Japanese *banzai* attack mounted by drunken, suicidal, and poorly armed "fanatics seeking a quick and honorable death," the attacks on Betio "were intelligently planned and carefully executed," historian Alexander writes. Indeed, the thrusts were part of the Japanese doctrine to counterattack any penetration and reflected an assumption that "Japanese forces were superior night fighters, that darkness evened the tactical odds." Alexander notes a more primal reason why the *rikusentai* decided to charge the larger, better equipped Americans: "the natural preference of any fighting man to die moving forward rather than wait passively for the inevitable flamethrowers."[2]

Maj. "Willie K." Jones braced his forces for an attack from the east end of the island, which was still under Japanese control. He registered field artillery support to hit a mere seventy-five yards in front of his front lines to a point 500 yards beyond; after that, naval gunfire would dial in. The Japanese did not disappoint, making their first charge at 7:30 P.M. by sneaking through thick vegetation. But after two hours of close-in fighting, they were repulsed by Jones's backline personnel—his mortar platoon, headquarters cooks, bakers, and administrative personnel. Capt. Lyle "Spook" Specht helped call and adjust star shells from two destroyers offshore, the *Sigsbee* and *Schroeder*. Pack howitzers fired from the 1/10 and 2/10 also helped rebuff further enemy penetration.[3]

The Japanese were undeterred, though, returning to strike at 11 P.M. Only this time, they tried to play with the Marines' minds, clinking canteens against helmets and yelling in decent English, "Japanese drinking Marines' blood." While this noisy group attacked, another one made a silent rush. This, too, was repulsed, but the Marines had to use their machine guns, thus revealing their positions. Two more attacks followed at 3 and 4 A.M., when some 300 to 400 Japanese launched a last-ditch attack.

The Marines responded with a full array of machine-gun and artillery fire, but despite heavy casualties, the *banzai* charge continued, and the Japanese wielded *samurai* swords and impaled a number of Americans. The Marines fought back with their own weapons of choice: bayonets and rifle butts. It was combat at its most primitive, waged with knives, fists, and bare hands on throats.

"We're killing them as fast as they come at us, but we can't hold out much longer; we need reinforcements," 1st Lt. Norman K. Thomas pleaded by field phone.

"We haven't got them," Jones replied. "You've *got* to hold."[4]

On the Japanese side, Warrant Officer Kiyoshi Ota, the senior officer to survive Tarawa among the enemy forces, recalled the preparations for the *banzai* charge. "We disabled the safeties on our hand grenades. 'ATTACK!' We rushed all together, here and there. I completely forgot my wounded knee. The dark night was lighted as bright as day. There were heavy sounds of grenade explosions, the disordered

fire of rifles, the shrieks, yells, and roars. It was just like Hell." Almost
all of his force of 750 *rikusentai* perished, "but I was somehow still
alive."[5]

When dawn broke, Jones had lost 40 dead and 100 wounded.
Hundreds of Japanese lay across the battlefield, stabbed or shot to death
at close range or torn apart by artillery or naval gunfire. "Major Jones
had to blink back tears of pride and grief as he walked his lines at
dawn," Alexander writes. "Several of his Marines grabbed his arm and
muttered, 'They told us we had to hold, and by God, we held.'"[6]

Eager to file stories filled with courage and sacrifice, wire reporters
and combat correspondents set up a field newsroom in a wrecked
Japanese warehouse. Dubbed "The Tarawa Press Club," the scribes used
water cans for chairs and an enemy torpedo for a desk as they
"pounded away at their typewriters on a story that was to electrify
the nation."[7]

The stories were unabashedly patriotic, such as this November 24,
1943, dispatch from Robert Trumbull of the *New York Times*: "Tarawa
fell because every Marine who died had a shot at the Japs before he
went down, and more Marines kept coming and coming as the men in
front of them died, until finally so many Japs were dead too that the
Marines were able to get on the beach."

While such accounts became a source of pride for many Americans, the death toll shocked the country. An easing of press restrictions
by President Roosevelt was at least partially responsible for this reaction; photographs of dead Americans were prohibited until just before
the assault on Tarawa. One of the earliest examples of this more open
press policy occurred on September 20, 1943, when *Life* magazine ran
a picture of three dead soldiers killed on a beach in New Guinea, with
the editorial comment, "These are our boys, born of our women,

reared in our schools, bred to our horizons." The stark realism of the picture—perhaps fueled by the maudlin caption—drew a storm of protest, including one letter that accused *Life* of engaging in "morbid sensationalism."[8]

But Tarawa's carnage presented a much tougher test of FDR's "open door" press policy; the battle would push the door open further still once the motion-picture footage and still photos from the 2nd Marine Division made it back to the States. Initially, the public's emotions were inflamed by news reports that left the impression that the Marines had somehow underestimated their foe. One of the most attention-grabbing headlines was on the front page of the December 4, 1943, *New York Times*: "Grim Tarawa Defense a Surprise, Eyewitness of Battle Reveals; Marines Went in Chuckling, To Find Swift Death Instead of Easy Conquest." (Ironically, this account was written by a Marine combat correspondent, Master T/Sgt. James C. Lucas, prompting outrage from Colonel Shoup. However, as is so often the case, it was the headline more than the article that left the impression that the Marines may have taken their foe too lightly.) Other papers played up the enormous toll in human lives, with a typical headline reading, "The Bloody Beaches of Tarawa," or as the *Dallas Times-Herald* declared, "Tarawa Costly Conquest for Marine Corps."

The news coverage sparked a debate in Washington over the heavy losses (997 Marines and 30 sailors dead and 88 Marines missing and presumed dead, for a total of 3,407 American casualties). Gen. Douglas MacArthur, still simmering over losing the 2nd Marine Division from his Southwest Pacific Command, complained to the secretary of war that "these frontal attacks by the Navy, as at Tarawa, are a tragic and unnecessary massacre of American lives." Other officials jumped into the fray, and Congress proposed a special investigation.[9]

On the other hand, *Time* used Sherrod's hard-won firsthand reports to reach a far different conclusion. "Last week some two to three thousand U.S. Marines, most of them now dead or wounded, gave the nation a name to stand beside those of Concord Bridge, the

Bonhomme Richard, the Alamo, Little Big Horn and Belleau Wood. The name was Tarawa."

Whatever the historical parallels, reading the accounts of such grievous losses was simply too much for most Americans to stomach. Across the country, mothers and fathers of Marines and sailors pulled out atlases and encyclopedias and tried to find the specks of sand in the far-off Pacific. It was easier to find this place called Tarawa than to somehow comprehend the scope of the loss of life and limb. Yet Sherrod took a contrary point of view. In light of Japan's devastating attacks on Pearl Harbor and the Philippines, he rhetorically asked, "Why then did so many Americans throw up their hands at the heavy losses at Tarawa? Why did they not realize that there would be many other bigger and bloodier Tarawas?"

Too many Americans had been lulled into expecting an "easy war," Sherrod continued, "bolstered by comfort-inspiring yarns from the war theaters, they really had believed that this place or that place could be 'bombed out of the war.' . . . Despite airplanes and the best machines we could produce, the road to Tokyo would be lined with the grave of many a foot soldier."[10]

For the battlefield commanders who were still trying to get all of the corpses out of the water, Tarawa carried another message: the training and spirit of their men had allowed them to overcome a nearly impenetrable target. Now they would have to learn from the panoply of errors made during the joint operation. Naval and air support, communications, heavy arms, and logistics—the list of lessons learned was long indeed.

Yet in the end, Tarawa was ultimately a battle marked by the courage and perseverance of countless heroes who, each in his own way, provided true and enduring expression of the Corps' code of honor, *Semper Fidelis*. Surveying the awful sight of hundreds of Marines stacked on the beach or still in the water, Gen. "Howlin' Mad" Smith pointed out a fallen Marine leaning against the seawall with one arm still upright, clutching a blue and white flag. The

Marine had successfully pinned the flag on the beach as a navigational aid to let the Navy boat drivers know where to land. "How can men like that ever be defeated?" Smith rhetorically asked. "This Marine's duty was to plant that flag on top of the seawall. He did his duty, though it cost him his life."

Stark images of the clash continued to make their way back to the States, including after-action photos taken by Associated Press photographer Frank Filan, whose images were used in the December 13, 1943, issue of *Life*. (Filan ruined both of his cameras in the initial assault while helping a wounded Marine in the lagoon. He continued to rescue wounded men, earning a Navy Commendation for heroism and later a Pulitzer Prize for his combat photography.) The *Life* photo shows two Marines, one with a cigarette hanging from the corner of his mouth, pointing their rifles at a nearly naked Japanese soldier whose arms are raised in surrender. The soldier has what appears to be a bandage or bloodied cloth around one of his legs. "Marines march off one of the very few Jap prisoners taken at Tarawa," a caption explains. "He was stripped to prevent suicide."

Other photographs in the magazine spread were taken by unnamed Marine Corps combat photographers, which was normal practice in both the Pacific and European theaters. Combat photographers and their motion-picture counterparts were rarely singled out for their work. But whether in still or motion-picture format, they sent home many of the most arresting images from Tarawa, such as a bloated body being recovered by a Marine with a pole. Along with the images came the early, and ultimately unreliable, explanations of the unexpected losses on the American side—for example, "U.S. casualties in the sea were exceptionally heavy because a sudden wind lowered the water over the reefs, grounding the landing boats and forcing the Marines to wade the last 800 yards to the beach."[11]

Perhaps the most poignant aspect of the *Life* account was the images of Japanese and American bodies lying "side by side on the sandy soil while other Marines rest from the fight." Yet for all of their poignancy, the images apparently had not completely opened the still-sleepy American mind to what lay in store battling the determined Japanese. President Roosevelt had yet to fully unleash his secret weapon for stirring the public's imagination: the motion pictures taken during the seventy-six-hour-long fight.

Norm Hatch had no way of knowing anything about the controversy erupting back home. Indeed, once he sensed a slackening of the battle tempo, he eyed a nearby atoll and decided to pay a visit. After checking in with Captain Hayward, Hatch, Ercole, and another Marine strolled across the sparkling blue reef and were pleasantly surprised to find a family of Melanesians who spoke impeccable English. The islanders had worked for some time with New Zealanders, harvesting coconuts that were loaded onto ships at the commercial pier at Betio.

The three Marines, charmed by this touch of paradise, promptly decided to go skinny-dipping. As they romped in the surf, they could see some bare-breasted women giggling and pointing at the pale-skinned interlopers. After cooling off, they were invited into a family's home, which had a thatched roof, open sides, and a deck off the ground. It was a relief to get out of their stinky, dirty uniforms after several days of wear and tear. Hatch threw away his T-shirt, which had nearly rotted off from dirt and sweat, and found a stash of clothes left by the Imperial Navy. It took a while, but he finally found a shirt big enough to fit his broad shoulders. Ercole took a picture of his friend enjoying himself and looking like an admiral. (Later, when Gen. Julian Smith saw his troops dressed like the Imperial Japanese Navy, he didn't get the joke and roared, "Take those off!")

But it was a brief idyll with the friendly islanders. The Marines quickly got word that it was time to ship out. So they walked back at low tide and prepared to board a troop carrier bound for Hawaii. By then, Gen. Julian Smith had invited Admiral Hill to finally come on the island. He was still steaming about Hill's unilateral decision to cease fire support during those twenty critical minutes on the morning of D-Day. The usually reserved Marine general confided to Sherrod, "The Navy supported us well—gave us everything we asked for, but God-damnit, they didn't let us run the show as promised. They didn't know what we were up against. Hill came ashore and measured the cement fortifications—then went back. He still doesn't know."[12]

Hatch gathered his voluminous stock of film, a total of nearly 4,000 feet in 100-foot rolls of 35-millimeter and 16-millimeter film shot on the Bell & Howell cameras. He turned it over to "Pappy" Leopold, who boarded a twin-engine PBY flying boat bound for Washington. The Navy and Marine Corps brass was eager to see these first motion-picture records of the battle.

With his work on the island done, Hatch took time to scrawl a note back home to Lois on government-issued V-mail stationery:

Darling sweet stuff,

Well, I've been through it all and theres [*sic*] not so much as a scratch on me. I was in the first wave to land and methinks I have some good pictures. I covered one complete battle stand-ing right up in the Front lines and I think that I got some pic-tures of the "nips" in Battle. You've probably read all about the Division in the papers and what a time we had. I am on the Tarawa atoll in the Gilbert Islands and it is now in complete control of the Marines. Johnny came through okay also though he came in a different day. Boy I have so many things to tell you that it will take days. I can only get this one letter out so please wire Mom & Dad that their handsome son is all in one piece. I have a few trinkets that I picked up to give to the people back home. It shouldn't be too long before I see you—I hope. That's the way rumor has it and it sounds logical. So long darling for the time being.

Love, Norman

His prediction of an imminent homecoming proved prescient. In late November, he spent nearly a week on the transport ship steaming to the big island of Hawaii, where the 2nd Marine Division disembarked at a sparsely furnished tent camp at Camp Kamuela (later renamed Camp Tarawa) left behind by the Army. The Marines got to work building lean-tos and gearing up for their next training regimen and, ultimately, their next battle. But after about two days, Hatch received orders to fly immediately back to Washington with four other combat correspondents, photographers, and public-relations staff, ostensibly to prepare a book about the Battle of Tarawa.

This order flummoxed the normally self-confident Hatch. Had he messed up somehow? Had he overexposed the film in the shifting montage of sun and smoke? Anything could have happened in the confusion of battle, sand, shrapnel, and stress. Burdened by such doubts, he boarded a Pan American Clipper "flying ship" with the rest of the D.C.-bound public-affairs crew.

As the snub-nosed, four-engine seaplane banked over Waikiki, he began replaying his shots frame by frame. He was sure he had taken some decent footage on his Eyemo, especially Major Chamberlin's charge of the command bunker. He pictured the half dozen Japanese soldiers bolting out of the fortified building, racing to the left toward the Marines.

Because Kelliher had so ably handled most of the captions and film loading, Hatch had been able to keep his eye on the battle and focus on the fight. He thought it had paid off in rare footage of the Americans and Japanese fighting within a bayonet thrust of each other. But maybe he had been wrong. Maybe he had been too cocky about his camera work. He was, after all, trying to capture fleeting images on sheets of chemically treated film. Shadows and light, the visible and invisible—trying to tell stories on film was a far cry from more tangible enterprises, such as designing and selling cars and trucks like his father. Nor was it as real as rigging sailing ships back in Gloucester. He could see now that he was a middleman in a very tricky business that could be as elusive as the kitten that scooted back under the tank.

"I thought I was going to have my sword broken and my epaulets torn off because I hadn't done any good. Who knows? The first time you're doing something in combat, you can forget to change your stop . . . there could be sand in the gate that scratches the film—there are a number of things that could happen."

Still only twenty-two years old, Hatch, like so many of his peers fighting from the Marshall Islands to the shores of Sicily, had seen the worst—and best—that mankind had to offer, from the first wounded Marine with his buttocks blown off, stoically waiting for a corpsman to tend him, to the heroics of Major Crowe tromping up and down near the pier, imploring his Marines to keep moving, with his cigar clenched in his mouth and his death-defying boasts.

And he laughed to think of Major Chamberlin's first, lonely charge up the sand bunker. Yet he would not soon forget Sandy Bonnyman and all the other Marines who had perished in this crucial taking of the Japanese position. And try as he might, he would never completely extinguish from his memory the anguished cries of the enemy sniper flushed out by a flamethrower team and his brief, desperate dash toward the cooling water. He also pictured the camouflaged Japanese soldier taking deadly aim on Kelly and his lucky shot that beat him back.

For all his memories, Hatch tended not to dwell on the carnage or his feelings, preferring instead to focus on the job he had done. "My training was in the newsreel field to go and find out what was happening, and of course, whatever was the worst that was happening was the best to cover. . . . I knew whatever I was shooting would have an effect on public information, on training, on operations. This was something brand new with the Corps. . . . To quote an old adage, we were flying by the seat of our pants. . . . We were making it up as we went along, just using common sense."

Flying home, though, he questioned his good sense and wondered whether his aim had not been true with the camera. What kind of grilling awaited him back in Washington? Was the commandant himself, General Holcomb, ready to chew him out?

His questions were answered soon enough when the Pan Am Clipper touched down in San Francisco on December 15, 1943. The Marines were met by the local public-information officer, Lt. Col. Dan Bender, a World War I veteran and close friend of General Denig. He was an engaging personality with press connections across the country. Bender also employed the first woman driver—and the first woman Marine—Hatch had ever seen. She was only about five feet, four inches, and loaded their gear into a huge six-by-six truck.

"You're driving that?" Hatch asked.

Ignoring his pointed question, she took her place on a raised seat with special footpads to reach the pedals. She expertly wheeled the truck through the downtown traffic to Bender's office, where he informed them, "You guys are going on to Washington, and I'm just here to clean you up and get you somewhat presentable." Pulling Hatch aside, he added, "Norm, I want to show you something."

Soon the amiable officer was whisking him in his car down to Market Street, home of the city's movie palaces. Opening the car window, Bender pointed to movie titles on the glittering marquees. Hatch could hardly believe his eyes.

"See that marquee, and see that one?" the colonel asked.

All of the movie houses were promoting the same newsreel footage about "Marines Fighting at Tarawa." That would have been remarkable enough, considering the fact that the battle had taken place just a few weeks ago. But the marquees also gave credit to one lone cameraman, Staff Sergeant Norman Hatch.

As Hatch struggled to make sense of it all, the colonel explained what had happened. En route to Washington, "Pappy" Leopold had dropped off Hatch's film with Bender, taking the rest of the footage back to Washington. (There had always been some animosity between Leopold and Hatch, and the latter suspected his film was purposely left behind to languish in obscurity. Hatch said Leopold, who died several decades ago, later admitted this to him, but there is no record of the discussion.) If that was the warrant officer's plan, it backfired badly because Bender immediately recognized the public-relations value of the dramatic footage. He took it to a newsreel pool for processing while simultaneously seeking clearance from a Navy official in Washington to approve its release to the newsreel companies: Fox Movietone, Paramount, Pathe, Universal, and News of the Day. In a stroke of luck for Hatch, the Navy official happened to be Allen Brown, the same officer who had once worked at *The March of Time* and lent a sympathetic ear to Hatch at Main Navy, the same Allen Brown who set up a meeting between Hatch and Louis de Rochemont and eventually helped Hatch's transfer to train in New York.

"It says on the slate, 'Staff Sergeant Norman Hatch,'" Bender told Brown.

"If he shot it, it's OK," Brown replied. "Let it go."

The five newsreel companies jumped at the chance to use the Marine combat photographer's black-and-white footage of the carnage that had both captivated and repulsed the nation. Each of the newsreel makers used Hatch's film differently to fit other news of the day (usually the newsreels included two to four stories, so the Tarawa reporting came as part of a weekly news summary). But though the editing varied, each newsreel credited Hatch because of Kelliher's conscientious credits on each and every roll of film. (Other combat footage, from both the European and Pacific theaters, typically did not credit the military cameramen; as a result of Hatch's experience, the Navy quickly issued an order prohibiting the practice.)

For now, though, the spotlight shone on the cameraman whose good judgment—and streak of good luck—put him in the prime position at Tarawa to chronicle a crucial battle which soon gained epic proportions for the Marine Corps and country alike. When Hatch landed in Washington, he was stunned to find that he suddenly had drawn attention in some very high places. After reuniting with Lois, whom he had not seen in more than a year, Hatch was invited to a party honoring his work thrown by the news bureau chiefs. He was humbled to meet Maj. Gen. Alexander Archer Vandegrift, who had recently been awarded the Medal of Honor and Navy Cross for leading the 1st Marine Division to victory at Guadalcanal, Tulagi, and Gavutu in the Solomon Islands.

Then, along with Obie Newcomb, Hatch was sent to Quantico to speak to Marines gearing up for war coverage at the photographic services section. It was hard to believe how far the Corps had come in its training, equipment, and sense of mission for telling its story in the past few years. Now Hatch and Newcomb were sought out by eager cameramen—some older than they—eager to learn more about choosing cameras, film, and protecting gear in combat. They also wanted to learn the secret of gaining access to the right officers to get into position to cover the action.

Yet even as Hatch kept taking bows over his body of work at Betio, the controversy over "Bloody Tarawa" kept swirling around Washington. Some of the Corps' public-relations wounds were self-inflicted, such as "Howlin' Mad" Smith's comparison of the D-Day assault to Pickett's Charge at Gettysburg. Other forces came into play as well. Even after the victory at Tarawa, the 2nd Marine Division kept suppressing reports of the success of the amtracs, hoping to maintain the element of surprise in upcoming battles in the Marshalls and Marianas. The Marines did not know that Admiral Shibasaki already had sent a flash message on D-Day at Tarawa warning about more than 100 amphibious tanks, an alert that Imperial General Headquarters soon shared with other island commanders, according to historian Alexander.[13]

To counterbalance the bad press, the Corps brought home Col. Merritt "Red Mike" Edson, the 2nd Marine Division's chief of staff. Edson, already a legend for his exploits with the 1st Raider Battalion, held the Washington press corps in thrall and tried to set the record straight.

Meanwhile, Louis Hayward was summoned to Washington and started working on a documentary film that would blend the black-and-white scenes captured by Hatch with the 16-millimeter color film shot by the rest of the division's photo team. Frank Capra, the popular Hollywood director, also worked on the project and other Tarawa-related reports.

Hatch met Capra, now an Army major, in early 1944, and learned about the director's early dismay when he first received orders from the Joint Staff in Washington to produce a film to go across the globe to U.S. troops. All Capra could find was routine color footage of Navy guns firing offshore on Betio and distant shots of the amphibious landing. There was none of the close-up footage he had expected, and Capra worried about the Tarawa project becoming a dud.

The Sicilian-born director had been commissioned as a major in the U.S. Army Signal Corps in late 1941, five days after Pearl Harbor, leaving a lucrative film career and a salary of $250,000 per film, as well as hefty percentages of the gross. He joined other leading film-makers such as John Ford, William Wyler, and John Huston, who put country above commerce at the height of their careers. By then, Capra's film work already spanned more than twenty-five years, with scores of film credits that included light comedies such as *Our Gang* and more substantial pictures such as *It Happened One Night* starring Clark Gable and Claudette Colbert and his signature films *Mr. Smith Goes to Washington* starring Jimmy Stewart and *Meet John Doe* starring Gary Cooper.

Capra saw his Army service both as a way out of the Hollywood rat race and as a powerful statement of his patriotism. Yet as Capra biographer Joseph McBride notes, the Italian-American filmmaker may have had another motive in joining the Army: after the U.S. declared war on Italy, Capra's sister, Antoinette, was shocked to find she had never achieved American citizenship (Capra made the same discovery when he first enlisted in the Army during World War I). When his sister was labeled "an enemy alien," Maj. Frank Capra promptly wrote a letter to the government on her behalf, attesting to her loyalty and explaining the mix-up over her citizenship status. His sister was then granted citizenship.[14]

As he started the Tarawa film, Capra's early concerns over film quality soon dissipated when one of his lieutenants described a treasure trove of black-and-white newsreel clips. Once he saw the action-packed footage, Capra called Hatch to congratulate him and invite him to narrate a work on Tarawa for an autographical piece, *I Was There: Tarawa*. The brief documentary was part of the *Army-Navy Screen Magazine* distributed worldwide to American military forces.

Capra's work continued the long-running collaboration between Hollywood and Washington under the auspices of the War Activities Committee (WAC) of the motion-picture industry. Continuing the backing of the military that dated back to the 1920s, Hollywood was only too happy to lend its production services—and thousands of movie houses—to the war effort. In return for serving as an agent for the government's Office of War Information, WAC "made a deal with the Roosevelt Administration," writes film historian Peter Maslowski. "The government promised not to draft leading movie actors or compete with Hollywood in producing feature-length films." (Many actors of the day volunteered to serve anyway.)

WAC secured promises from the nation's 16,500 movie theaters to devote 10 percent of their screen time, free of charge, to government-sponsored films, including the first effort, director John Ford's *The Battle of Midway*, which was released in September 1942.[15]

The viewing public thrilled to see American fighter planes shooting down Japanese Zeros, but was it ready for closer images of war from Tarawa, including the heartbreaking images of dead Marines floating face down in the lagoon at Betio?

President Roosevelt already had opened the door a bit with his easing of print and photo restrictions. Now "the combat footage represented an order-of-magnitude change from the usual sugarcoated war news," Alexander writes. One day in early 1944, the president noticed Bob Sherrod in a crowd of White House reporters and "asked him privately for his advice about releasing the documentary. Sherrod believed the public knew little about the real nature of the war with

Japan and recommended the film be shown without restriction. FDR did so."[16]

Released on March 2, 1944, Hatch's twenty-third birthday, *With the Marines at Tarawa* was an immediate hit that boosted war bond sales. It was more of a mixed bag for the Marines, as recruiting dropped off as once-eager recruits could now see for themselves the real cost of combat. The film was praised by critics for its gritty realism and how it captured the often chimerical Japanese fighting force. The *New Republic* called the documentary "the most descriptive account of American men in combat" of the war.

Another distinction of *With the Marines at Tarawa* was that unlike some early documentaries produced by the armed services, this was obviously the real deal. It was known in documentary-making circles that some filmmakers weren't above staging combat scenes. In one of the best-known episodes of fakery, as the Army landed in North Africa in the summer of 1943, President Roosevelt was eager to see film of Operation Torch, the risky amphibious invasion of Morocco and Algeria. But the footage shot by one of Frank Capra's underlings had been lost when the ship carrying his footage was sunk. So along with directors John Huston and George Stevens, they staged what Huston would later call "a huge counterfeit operation simply to deceive the President." Working at an Army training camp in the Mojave Desert of California, they reenacted parts of the North African campaign, using officers involved in the original desert warfare to produce a film called *Tunisian Victory*.[17]

So it was not altogether surprising that Hatch would get a few inquiries even as plaudits kept coming in about his work. "How did you stage that combat sequence with the Japanese troops?" asked Richard de Rochemont, who had succeeded his brother, Louis, at *The March of Time.*

"Dick, those shots are real," Hatch flatly replied.

De Rochemont would then write in *Life* magazine that the photography from Tarawa was "one of the finest service-produced pictorial records of actual combat in this or any war."[18]

With the Marines at Tarawa starts with the strands of the "Marines' Hymn" and cuts to footage of troops exercising on the deck of a ship. "It won't be long now," the narrator says in a dramatic baritone. Pre-battle planning is shown, with officers gathered around a sand-table map of Betio. In short order, weapons are test-fired, then a church service is held on a ship's deck the evening before D-Day. An unidentified chaplain conducts a service, the pages of his prayer book flapping in the sea breeze.

The film quickly shifts to battle footage, first with the Navy's big guns firing offshore, seemingly pulverizing the island. Then the amtracs start crossing the reef—images captured by Hatch from his perch in Major Crowe's Higgins boat.

Navy dive-bombers sweep from above. Machine guns fire, bombs explode (unbeknownst to movie audiences, the sound effects were added back in Hollywood, since most of the cameras used at Tarawa had no sound equipment). Marines duck and weave their way across the smoke-filled beaches and seawalls. Before long, the dead and wounded begin to pile up; some Marines exhibit bloody wounds as they're carted off on stretchers.

Marines creep cautiously toward the enemy pillboxes and then let loose with torrents of flame and hand grenades. "We use all the fire-power we have," the narrator intones. Of the Japanese, he says, "They're savage fighters. Their lives mean nothing to them." (Watching the film later, Hatch commented, "That's a big lie.")

The *rikusentai* dash from a bunker to counter Major Chamberlin's charge. The Japanese are overmatched, though, and their dead soldiers are splayed across the sand. Mortars, tanks, more machine-gun fire—it all seems to merge into one big inferno as the Marines prevail in the fighting. Korean laborers emerge with hands held high in surrender.

As the fallen Americans are wrapped and gently laid in Navy transports, still more Marines float in the waters lapping the shore, their bodies pale in the tropical light. "These are Marine dead," the narrator says, stating the obvious. "This is the price we have to pay for a war we didn't want."

Amid the ruins of blown-up Japanese bunkers, the narrator proclaims, "Tokyo once boasted it would take 100,000 of our men to take Tarawa. We lost less than a thousand. The Japs 4,000." (The final death toll would count nearly all of the 3,000 members of the Imperial Landing Force defending Tarawa and Makin Islands, along with another 1,500 civilian employees of the Japanese Navy.)

The film ends with patriotic music and *Semper Fidelis*.

Though the Marines had developed a grudging respect for their tough nemesis, the film's promotional poster succumbed to comic-book racial stereotypes of a grimacing, evil foe stabbed with bayonets by superior Americans. "THRILL TO THE FIGHTING YANKS!" one poster declares (movie theaters could buy the largest 22-by-24-inch posters for 40 cents, with smaller ones selling for a dime). "ADS THAT SELL THE STORY OF HISTORY'S GREATEST BATTLE," a large poster declared. "Tarawa is ours! The Marines' own blood-and-guts story of the taking of the tiny strategic island. It will stand forever as one of the most thrilling pages in U.S. battle history. . . . The real thing at last . . . filmed under fire by the Marines' own fighting photographers!"

Back home, there were rations on everything from food to fuel to foil, but there appeared to be no limit on purple prose: "America's biggest moment since Pearl Harbor . . . the Marines' revenge for Wake Island . . . it hits the heart like a two-ton blockbuster!"

The government provided catchphrases for theaters to promote the film, including, "This is the picture that will wake up America."

Along with the posters, a promotional brochure designed like a newspaper bore such headlines as "Marines Marked Their 168th Birthday by Greatest Fight" and "Tarawa No South Sea Idyll for the Marines." The latter piece sounded a bit like a travelogue: "Ever since the voyage of Captain Cook, back in the 18th Century, the South Sea Islands have been the escapist's paradise . . . blessed with happy idleness, cloudless skies, calm waters and singing and dancing natives. . . . Today, the war in the Pacific has changed this island into an inferno."

In another promotional article, "Red Mike" Edson, by now a brigadier general, delivered a more sober and analytical view of Japan's "forty years of planning and preparation" to dominate the Far East: "We must realize that, at the moment, the Japanese have in their possession everything for which they started this war—domination of the coast of China; control of vast territories in China itself; the natural resources of the Phillipines [sic]; Malaya, and the Dutch East Indies; a far-flung outpost system to protect their homeland against attack and invasion—in other words, the sinews with which to wage a more successful war in the future. In spite of our successes since August 7, 1942, we have so far won only outpost engagements. We have not yet taken from the Japanese a single thing which they held before this war began. . . . As fighters they are cunning, strong and courageous. Their leaders have openly stated their determination to make this war so costly at every step of our advance that we will willingly accept a negotiated peace short of complete victory."

Noting the loss of American lives at Tarawa, Edson tried to put the battle in perspective, once again countering the criticism from Main Street to Capitol Hill: "No single battle or campaign should be assessed by casualties alone, but by the importance of the objective won in relation to the final outcome of the war. In that respect, Tarawa was not a costly victory. The losses there were not out of proportion of the advantages gained."

Edson also sounded the same warning that correspondent Bob Sherrod had made in the wake of the battle: "There will be other

Tarawas before we reach our final objective—Tokyo and a lasting peace. Unless we, as a nation, have the stamina to take such losses and to carry this war through to the complete defeat and unconditional surrender of the Japanese people, it is my opinion that we leave as a heritage to a succeeding generation the horrors of another war—and one that may be conceivably be fought upon our own soil."

The other lead article, "Marine Photographers Faced Death at Work," noted, "Staff Sergeant Norman Hatch, Washington, D.C., who took many of the newsreels later shown in American theaters throughout the country, spent all of his time with the most advanced elements of the Marine striking force. Hatch constantly exposed himself to danger, within a stone's throw of the big Japanese emplacements, to get action shots. That he escaped is considered something of a minor miracle by the men who saw him go forward with his camera."

Adm. Chester W. Nimitz wrote in a Navy Commendation Ribbon citation to Hatch, "For outstanding work as a motion picture photographer, cool-headedness under fire. . . . He landed with the assault waves the first day, coolly taking pictures on the beaches and throughout the action, always at great risk of life and limb. Not only did he exhibit great personal bravery, but his work was such that authorities say the best combat pictures yet filmed during this war were obtained."

CHAPTER NINE

"This Thing Doesn't Smell Right to Me"

In many ways, Norm Hatch's wartime experiences were a unique microcosm of what his fellow service members and civilians endured, whether they were on the battlefield or humbly working in support roles back home. As the war entered its third full year in 1944, the country experienced wide mood swings of public exuberance and expectation—the invasion of Normandy on June 6, 1944, for example—even while suffering in private when the dreaded telegram came bearing news of the loss of a loved one. Amid the drama, everyday people had to get up to do the necessary, if mundane, work of producing bombs and bullets and keeping up morale on the home front. And in both spheres—glorious battle and inglorious public relations—Hatch, still a young man in his early twenties, proved to be a natural.

After his debriefing in Washington and visits to Quantico, Hatch was assigned to temporary duty at Marine headquarters and at the Treasury Department, where for the next six months he was called upon to promote war bonds as part of the Fourth War Loan Drive. For someone who had never addressed more than ten people at one time, acting as a government spokesman seemed like quite a stretch. His first assignment took him to a Palmolive soap plant in New Jersey, where he calmly marched up to a platform to speak to a huge crowd milling about in the company parking lot.

Several thousand factory workers, men and women alike, peered up at the Marine in dress blues. No one in Washington had told him what to say, and so, working without a script, Hatch did all he really could do: he told his own story of what it was like to be a combat cameraman sent into battle. Mostly, he tried to convey the bravery of the Marines at Tarawa. The blue-collar audience listened raptly, and when he finished, the men and women of Palmolive burst into applause.

Once again, Hatch demonstrated his knack for seizing the moment. He became an effective spokesman for the war effort, and during this break from combat, he managed to spend some time at home with Lois. It was good having her husband back for a change, though she was none-too-happy to learn about his week-long run of appearances with Kathryn Grayson, a pretty singer and actress with Mickey Rooney in *Andy Hardy's Private Secretary*.

Grayson, an operatic soprano, was the headliner for nightclub events. Then Hatch was introduced, strode onstage, and talked about Tarawa. He brought along various Japanese souvenirs—flags, helmets, and bayonets—to auction off in exchange for war bonds.

He was told that his appearances helped generate more than $1 million in bond sales. Asked if he ever felt guilty about touring the country while his fellow Marines were fighting and dying, Hatch replied, "Christ no! It was my duty. I didn't have any particular feelings" about it.

Hatch became a regular on the Washington-area speakers' circuit, including an appearance at the Red Cross headquarters in suburban Alexandria, Virginia. There he learned the importance of being circumspect in his remarks to the volunteers, who were known as "grey ladies" for the aprons they wore over their dresses while entertaining or helping hospital patients. He spoke warmly about his old commanding general, Maj. Gen. Julian C. Smith, and his knack for showing compassion for his troops.

After his talk ended to polite applause, Hatch was approached by a local newspaper publisher and a city official. "We've got somebody we'd like you to meet."

"Who is that?"

"Just come on over here," they said. "There's a grey lady we'd like you to meet. This is Gen. Julian C. Smith's wife. This is Happy Smith."

He gulped and shook hands with the general's wife. Had he said the right things? It seemed so, because Mrs. Smith enthusiastically thanked him for his kind words. She subsequently wrote her husband about a "fine, upstanding young staff sergeant."

Around this time, on March 15, 1944, Happy Smith's husband traveled to Hollywood, where he accepted an Academy Award presented to the Marine Corps for *With the Marines at Tarawa*. It was named best short-subject documentary. Since there was no television coverage at the time, Hatch learned about the award some time later. Rather than handing out an actual statue, the Academy—constrained by the shortage of metal during the war—presented a wooden plaque to the genial general, who promptly took it to his home in Virginia. (Only after the war would the Oscar be given to the Corps. The statuette then seemed to take on a life of its own, starting out in the commandant's office, then getting shifted from place to place by different generals and their aides. "Nobody could find it for a while," Hatch recalled. It is now ensconced at the Marine Corps Museum in Quantico.)

By the summer of 1944, America was making major strides against the Axis powers, with the Marines applying the hard lessons of Tarawa against a much larger island target, Saipan, home of the Japanese Central Pacific Fleet. In Europe, the Allies were launching their invasion of France on the beaches of Normandy. And the Russians were crushing Hitler's forces on the Eastern Front.

No one knew how long the war would last, and combat cameramen and filmmakers kept distinguishing themselves in battle. On
Saipan, two Marines who had recently trained at Quantico, Bill
Genaust and Howard McClue, stormed ashore with the 4th Marine
Division. Unlike the small, flat terrain of Tarawa, Saipan was a mountainous atoll in the Marianas, fourteen miles long and six miles wide.
Nearly 30,000 soldiers from Japan's 31st Army were dug in and waiting for the American Marines and GIs. The Marines alone took 2,000
casualties on the first day of fighting. The bombs and bullets were bad
enough, but Saipan also offered a noxious mix of malaria-spreading
mosquitoes, bluebottle flies, and huge, stinking crabs.[1]

Early on, Genaust was injured by mortar fire. He could have
shipped out to Pearl Harbor for medical treatment, but chose to stay.
Hooking up with McClue, he set out for the front, and along with a
Marine scout, the trio was asked by a tank driver to help rid several
buildings of Japanese. They obliged, but when the tank was hit by a
land mine, the Marine cameramen were on their own.

After a firefight and a *banzai* charge by the Japanese, Genaust
wound up fighting by himself. McClue sought to bring back reinforcements. When he returned with help, Genaust stood up to direct
the Marines, taking a bullet in the thigh.

Eventually, Genaust was evacuated, but McClue did not know that;
thinking his buddy was was still in harm's way, he set out to find him.
"He never returned," writes film historian Peter Maslowski. "The next
day a search party found McCue's corpse, his heart pierced by a bullet."[2]

This time around, the wounded Genaust could not avoid getting
shipped back to Pearl Harbor and should have gone home to the mainland to rest. Instead, he requested to stay with the 5th Marine Division
in Hawaii as it prepared for the invasion of one of the final obstacles to
reaching the Japanese homeland, Iwo Jima.

By now, Norm Hatch was one of the Corps' most experienced motion-picture men, receiving a promotion to tech sergeant ("technical" ranks were given to skilled support positions, which photographic services were considered to be; a tech sergeant was roughly equivalent to gunnery sergeant). In August 1944, he was transferred to Camp Pendleton to join the photography unit of the 5th Marine Division as the senior NCO. The senior photo officer, Maj. Richard Day, was another Hollywood veteran who chose to join the Marine Corps.

While serving as senior art director at Twentieth Century Fox in the early days of the war, Day created a training area for the military to teach the fine art of camouflage. He was well suited to the task: Day began in 1919 as a set decorator for the legendary director Erich von Stroheim. Day went on to create a body of work over the next two decades that was known for its attention to detail. Indeed, his re-creation of a Welsh village in the 1941 John Ford film *How Green Was My Valley* was so admired that it was used for the next two decades in a variety of other pictures. Day would later serve as art director for *On the Waterfront*, the 1954 Elia Kazan drama that became the breakthrough picture for young Marlon Brando.

Though he was in his early fifties, Day applied his considerable aesthetic genius to the war effort, training Marines in the fine art of camouflage. Like the geckos, lizards, and brown tree snakes that the Marines found at Saipan, the Corps was becoming more adept at adapting to its natural setting.

"He knew how to fake colors of the areas the Army and Marines were operating, so they could camouflage their equipment, their guns, or whatever," Hatch said. Eventually, Day received orders to be photographic officer of the 5th Marine Division. His assistant was a second-unit director from Metro-Goldwyn-Mayer named DeHaven, who had traveled the world shooting film for background imagery, including the jungles of Laos, Cambodia, and Thailand, used in the Tarzan films of Hatch's old YMCA swimming instructor in Chicago, John Weissmuller.

Dick Day finally decided he was too old to go into combat and was allowed to return to his camouflage school in Hollywood. And DeHaven was seen as an intelligence asset and ordered back to Washington to be debriefed by Naval Intelligence about his knowledge of Southeast Asia.

That left Hatch, "by osmosis," he said, to serve as photo officer of the 5th Marine Division, yet another turn of events that gave him a front-row seat to history. He was glad to be reunited with Obie Newcomb, his buddy from Tarawa. Hatch was twenty-three years old, and Newcomb was about ten years his senior. Both men had recently been promoted to warrant officer.

Though the youngest man in the twenty-man unit, Hatch's reputation allowed him to train and lead cameramen and lab technicians twice his age. No one knew for sure where the next battle would be waged, but the Marines were preparing by adding forces at an astronomical rate, from the initial 18,000-man force when Hatch had enlisted in 1939 to nearly 600,000 men and women by late 1944. Naturally, this presented enormous problems with training and logistics.

Hatch used this time to help his men hone their camera skills as the Marines conducted amphibious landing exercises on the beach at San Onofre at Camp Pendleton, California. The camp was in the middle of the Pendleton Ranch, some four miles from the Pacific. The loud cracks of rifles, pistols, grenades, and Browning automatic rifles reverberated off the oceanside hills, along with explosions from mortars and artillery. Learning from the mistakes made at Guadalcanal and Tarawa, the division's commanders were practicing new tactics for their tankers, demolition teams, and infantrymen.

For the next major assault on Japanese forces, the division would employ combat teams comprised of three infantry battalions (about 950 officers and men), each with three infantry companies augmented by 60-millimeter mortar and light-machine-gun units. There were battalion landing teams (BLTs) with platoons or small units of specialists, such as engineers, for handling mines and demolitions. There were forward observers, who controlled artillery fire, and a joint assault signal company detachment to call in naval gunfire and air support. And, inevitably, there were casualty-handling sections.

Adding to the punch of the combat team was a weapons company of 175 men equipped with four 75-millimeter half-tracks, twelve 37-millimeter antitank guns, and heavy machine guns—all to support the three infantry battalions in the field.[3]

As the Corps regrouped for this next big push in the Pacific, Hatch faced his own domestic logistical problem: a telegram from Lois informed him she was taking the next train from Washington along with a girlfriend and wanted to stay with Norm until he shipped out for Hawaii. It was one thing to face Japanese machine-gun fire, but quite another to face an unhappy spouse after a cross-country train ride. Hatch knew that with the huge military buildup in southern California, he had about as much chance of renting a cottage as getting an invitation to stay at the White House. So he scrambled all weekend in Laguna Beach, knocking on doors to see if anything was available. Just as he suspected, the glut of Navy and Marine personnel had soaked up all available housing. On a whim, he hung around a real-estate office, where he overheard someone brag to an agent that he had just closed on a nice beachfront house. Sight unseen, Hatch asked if he could rent the property, and—*Voila!*—Hatch had just the place for Lois and her friend, a hillside bungalow overlooking the Pacific Coast Highway. The cottage was the perfect launching pad for the girls, who spent the week touring Hollywood and the area. And it gave Norm and Lois a place to return after dancing the night away to big band music, right before Norm had to ship out once again.

After arriving on the big island of Hawaii in August 1944, Hatch and Newcomb—by now experts in scrounging film and photo equipment by any means short of outright theft—began working their contacts. As warrant officers, they had more clout than they had as sergeants. Hatch contacted a fellow warrant officer with Hollywood ties, Howard Schwartz. "This is Norm Hatch," he said, "and I have next to nothing in supplies and I need a lot of things. I need, among other things, pistols." The lessons of Tarawa remained, and Hatch did not want to get caught unarmed in a pinch. Schwartz said he would see what he could do, which turned out to be a great deal. When Hatch walked through a big supply depot, he felt like a kid at Christmas, pointing and saying, "I'll take two of those, and three of that, and four of those."

The latest equipment was theirs for the asking. The preferred still camera had changed from the Speed Graphic used at Tarawa to the better-protected Combat Graphic, which could better withstand the heat, humidity, sand, and dirt of island combat. For motion pictures, the Marines had switched almost completely to the 16-millimeter Bell & Howell. Hatch's beloved 35-millimeter black-and-white Eyemo was in short supply, but he kept one anyway for old time's sake. The Marines also used Kodak cameras such as the Cine and the Cine Special—all handheld and spring wound, with no motors. They also tried to keep one large Wahl camera capable of sound recording, usually for special events such as awards ceremonies.

Late 1944 and early 1945 were spent training and planning for the coming invasion. The 5th Marine Division's officers drove their men hard to apply small-unit tactics and innovative assault techniques. No one knew for sure where they would tangle with the Japanese next, but after the hard-won victories at Guadalcanal, Bougainville, Tarawa, Saipan, Tinian, Guam, Peleliu, and other islands, no longer would the Marines underestimate the enemy's guile and fortitude.

Hatch thought they would probably hit Truk in the western Carolines, a deep-water harbor and home to Japan's Combined Fleet. Eventually, Lt. Col. George A. Roll, the division's intelligence officer, steered him straight. Not Truk, he said, but rather a godforsaken piece of volcanic rock called Iwo Jima.

Several weeks before the February 19, 1945, amphibious assault on Iwo Jima, a planning meeting for the military's photographic services was called in Honolulu. Besides Hatch and Newcomb, officers from the 3rd and 4th Marine Divisions showed up to coordinate coverage. All told, the three divisions had ninety photographers assigned to them for the massive operation. This would be the first attempt to coordinate such widespread coverage of a joint Navy-Marine assault, and the planners wanted to learn from earlier mishaps and miscues. The meeting was run by a Navy officer, Cmdr. John W. McLain. Though he wasn't a photographer, McLain was a respected columnist for the *New York Daily News* and was well connected to the motion-picture and theater industry. Second in command was Lt. Dave Hopkins, son of Harry Hopkins, FDR's top advisor and one of the architects of the New Deal.

The purpose of the meeting with Hatch and other photo officers from the 3rd and 4th Marine Divisions was to avoid the duplication of battle footage that had at times occurred at Tarawa and some other landings. They assigned each photographer or motion-picture man to follow a particular unit, whether it was infantry, aviation, medical, artillery, and up the line to division headquarters. They also created an expedited system to get the film and print dispatches off the island, with pickup stations on the beach. They created special signals from the ships at sea to let the photo stations know when a boat was coming for a pickup.

The plan was to fly all film and print dispatches from Iwo Jima to Guam on a Martin PBM Marine flying boat. After clearance by military censors, the material would be flown back to the States via Pearl Harbor.

As they steamed toward the volcanic island, Hatch ran into an old friend from Tarawa, Bob Sherrod, who was on board to cover the invasion. When they made a port call in Saipan, they went ashore and found what appeared to be the world's biggest bar, easily filling at least six Quonset huts. The cigarette and cigar smoke was thick as men stood six deep, downing cheap booze. After Sherrod struck up a conversation with an Air Force colonel, he heard a remarkable tale of some young pilots recently restricted to their quarters under house arrest.

Sherrod's ears perked up, and he asked why pilots would be arrested.

"They won't fly," the colonel explained. It seemed there had been a serious problem with Japan-bound B-29s using too much fuel while flying the nearly 3,000-mile round trip to Tokyo and back. Not everyone, it seemed, had the brave heart of Lt. Col. James Doolittle, the first man to fly across the United States in twelve hours, the first to land a plane blind-folded, and, in early 1942, the first American pilot to lead an air assault on Tokyo.

Doolittle had set a high bar for all American pilots in the war. He executed an audacious plan, one that came straight from the top. Shortly after Pearl Harbor, President Roosevelt remarked that he would like to bomb the enemy mainland at least to serve as symbolic punishment for December 7. This led to the retrofitting of the carrier *Hornet* to launch modified twin-engine B-25 bombers. Before they took off—some 700 miles from Tokyo—one of his pilots asked what to do in case of a crash-landing in Japan. That was up to each man, Doolittle said, but he did not intend to be taken prisoner. "I'm going to bail my crew out and then dive it, full throttle, into any target I can find where the crash will do the most good. I'm forty-six years old and have lived a full life."[4]

With planes strapped with ten extra five-gallon cans of gasoline, Doolittle's intrepid squadron made it to Japan, flying so low that Doolittle could see a group of officers, "their swords flashing in the sunlight."[5] They flew over the Imperial Palace, but dropped no bombs: Doolittle had issued clear orders to avoid the palace grounds as well as schools and hospitals.

The bombs dropped on Tokyo did no significant damage, and three men died in crash landings or bailouts, while eight were captured and brought to Tokyo for trial. Doolittle and most of the rest of the bombers made it to China and landed behind Chiang Kai-shek's lines.

But FDR's audacious plan had worked, lifting the national morale that had been so badly shaken early in the war by the fall of Bataan in the Philippines, along with Gen. Douglas MacArthur's exit and vow to return someday.

Now at Saipan, Hatch was disappointed to see some flyboys forgetting Doolittle's courageous example. It was all the more galling because the Marines were preparing to fight 625 miles to the north at Iwo Jima, all in an effort to save these airmen by cutting the air route to Tokyo by about half. It seemed outrageous that these guys were too scared to fly.

Sherrod interviewed the pilots and took notes about the episode, and as they left the colonel at the long bar, Hatch asked, "Are you going to write a story about this?"

"Nope," Sherrod replied, "I'm not going to send it in. It would be too discouraging to the public to think these guys were in this situation."

Iwo Jima (Sulphur Island) is part of the Nanpo Shoto island chain that dangles like a necklace from Tokyo Bay to within 300 miles of the Marianas: first the Izu Islands, then the Bonins, and last the Volcanoes, a trio of islands that run north to south, with Iwo in the center of the Volcanoes. From the sea, Iwo Jima was said to resemble a half-submerged whale, while from the air it looked like a generous porkchop. But its most distinctive feature was the extinct volcano at its narrow, southern end. The imposing volcano that rose up from the sea was Mount Suribachi, Japanese for "cone-shaped bowl."

In early October 1944, the Joint Chiefs of Staff issued a strategic mandate that made the volcanic island the likely choice for the next big push toward Tokyo. The chiefs were looking for an island big enough for an airfield to cover American bases in the Marianas and provide fighter cover for the ongoing bombing campaign of Japan.

Iwo Jima fit the bill perfectly. It had two operational airfields and was considered a "critical base in the inner ring of [Japan's] defenses, meant to serve as a sort of speed bump, slowing down the inexorable American drive toward Kyushu and Honshu," according to Maj. Gen. Fred Haynes and James A. Warren. "Tokyo wanted [Lieutenant General Todamichi] Kuribyashi to buy that most precious commodity in war—time."

Less than a century before, the United States had a chance to gain a foothold in the area when, in 1853, Commodore Matthew C. Perry landed with plans to make it a provisioning stop for American naval ships and mail steamers. But President Franklin Pierce refused to extend America's influence in the western Pacific, and in 1861, Japan annexed the Izus, Bonins, and Volcanoes. The islands were later placed under the rule of the Tokyo Prefectural Government, which made them, at least jurisdictionally, part of the homeland. Five miles long and half a mile wide—about a third the area of Manhattan—Iwo Jima was viewed by the Japanese as native soil.

Yet if the Sulphur Island was part of Japan's family, it remained something of a stepchild. Perhaps it was its boiling sulphur pits or the lingering fear that its dormant volcano might explode. Or it might have been a case of simply seeing the limitations of a Gibraltar-like rock where about 1,100 colonists were trying to eke out a living by subsistence farming of vegetables, bananas, papayas, sugar cane, and grain.

Iwo did have one major asset: its location as a gateway to Japan's home islands. In 1940, Mabuchi Construction built an airfield with two strips nearly a mile long near the foot of Mount Suribachi, along with gun positions. But it would be four more years before Imperial Headquarters sent in a garrison of more than 5,000 sailors and began clearing a second airfield in the central plateau. The Army sent in another garrison of 5,170, along with thirteen artillery pieces and more than 200 machine guns. The Navy brought in 14 coastal defense guns, 12 heavy pieces, and 150 25-millimeter machine guns for anti-aircraft defense.

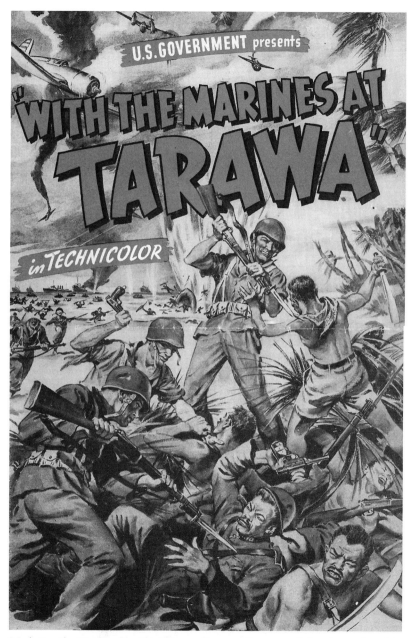

Marketing the Marines. President Roosevelt personally approved the release of graphic war footage, including With the Marines at Tarawa. *Distributed by the U.S. Office of War Information, this eight-page brochure promoted the film as though it were a commercial picture, a "two-ton block-buster."*

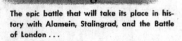

The real thing at last...

The epic battle that will take its place in history with Alamein, Stalingrad, and the Battle of London . . .

No punches pulled . . . no gory details omitted . . .

IT HITS THE HEART LIKE A TWO-TON BLOCK-BUSTER!

Play it
for THRILLS!
for ACTION!
for AMERICA!

Play it
right now while its story is hottest!

Mat 23

Anybody home? A patrol of men starts into a dug out to clean out the Japs who are trapped inside. One of the exciting scenes from "With the Marines at Tarawa" now at the .... Theatre.

Marines' Bloodiest Battle Shown in Tarawa Films

Fighting that cost the United States Marines a life for every square yard of ground gained, the bloodiest casualty list in American military history, is shown in "With The Marines At Tarawa," which comes to the .... Theatre on ......, in conjunction with ...... In storming the fortified island of Betio, 2½ miles long and 500 yards wide in the Tarawa formation, the Marines suffered fewer than 1,000 killed and 2,500 wounded, before achieving a brilliant and total victory by wiping out the 4000 Jap defenders of this Tarawa atoll strong point.

Marine Combat Photographers went ashore with the landing parties and filmed the action on the firing line, right up to the loopholes of the massive, concrete Japanese blockhouses. They made this cinema record of actual war, in technicolor. It cost two of them their lives to get these two reels of heroism and destruction. The photographers carried pistols and knives as well as their cameras and fought while filming.

Tarawa Destined To Rank Among Greatest U.S. Battles

The high point of American valor, up to November 20th, 1943, has usually been considered to be Pickett's charge at Gettysburg, when 3393 men of the 4500 in that general's division fell dead or wounded in advancing 1800 yards from the Confederate lines to the crest of Cemetery Hill on July 3rd, 1863. United States Marines eclipsed this mark last November when three battalions of them stormed the Jap Gibraltar of Betio on Tarawa atoll in the far Pacific at a cost of fewer than 1,000 Marines killed and 2,500 wounded.

This battle, the fiercest in American history was filmed in technicolor right on the firing line by Marine Combat Photographers. The result is the two reel picture, "With The Marines At Tarawa," being shown at the .... Theater on ....

Two Killed Making Films on Tarawa

(Opening Day)

A picture that cost a human life a reel, comes to the .... Theatre on ...., in conjunction with .... It is the two reel film, "With The Marines At Tarawa," photographed in technicolor under heavy gunfire during the bloodiest battle in 169 years of Marine Corps history, by Marine Combat Photographers who stormed in across the beaches of the fortified Jap atoll with the fighting troops. Two of the Combat Photographers, Lieut. Ernest A. Matthews Jr., of Dallas, Tex., and Staff Sgt. Wesley Lee Kroenung, Jr., were killed getting these two priceless reels.

Tarawa, a coral atoll in the Pacific Ocean, 31 miles long, was so heavily fortified, especially on its main island of Betio, that the Japs boasted its capture would cost 100,000 lives. After four days of bombardment by sea and air, during which 2400 tons of explosives struck Betio, three battalions of Marines landed on the islet, Nov. 20th, 1943, and in three days of desperate fighting took its massive concrete and log forts. Virtually all of the 4000 defending Japs were slain. Our casualties were fewer than 1,000 Marines killed and 2,500 wounded.

The action of "With The Marines At Tarawa," starts with seaborne expedition, then the troops going ashore in landing boats and proceeds to the completion of the airplane landing strip on the island. It shows the Marines holding a 20 foot deep stretch of exposed beach against the fire of massive Jap blockhouses. The men had no food but their K rations and no drinking water but what they carried in their canteens. Special detachments then landed, equipped to distill drinking water out of the salty Pacific surf.

Tarawa General Writes Own Story of Battle

By Brig. Gen. Merritt A. Edson

The war in the Pacific, to date, has not been an easy one, nor will it be in the future. There can be no doubt, however, but that the Japanese has met his master, for in every fight in which he has met the Americans since August 7, 1942, he has been soundly defeated.

Nevertheless, the American people should realize the task which confronts us before it can be said that the Japanese nation has been defeated. This war is not a mad, unplanned venture so far as the Japanese are concerned. It is the culmination of forty years of planning and preparation. Their ultimate objective is the domination of the Far East. The mastery of the entire Pacific area. The present conflict is only one step in the road to their final attainment of that objective.

Mat A
Brig. Gen. Edson

We must realize that, at the moment, the Japanese have in their possession everything for which they started this war—domination of the coast of China; control of vast territories in China itself; the natural resources of the Phillipines, Malaya, and the Dutch East Indies; a far-flung outpost system to protect their homeland against attack and invasion—in other words, the sinews with which to wage a more successful war in the future. In spite of our successes since August 7, 1942, we have so far won only outpost engagements. We have not yet taken from the Japanese a single thing which they held before this war began. Their casualties have been as nothing compared to their potential fighting strength. Their shipping losses, both naval and maritime, have been relatively heavy but they are not irreplaceable if they be left the wherewithal to replace them.

Japanese Cunning

The Japanese are a nation of 85,000,000 people, capable of sustaining an armed force of eight and a half million men. As fighters, they are cunning, strong, and courageous. Their leaders have openly stated their determination to continue the fight for a hundred years if that be necessary to gain their ends. It is their intention to make this war so costly at every step of our advance that we will willingly accept a negotiated peace short of complete victory. They are prepared to accept heavy casualties to achieve this end because they do not believe that we, as a nation, can or will take the losses involved. It is my opinion that any negotiated peace, regardless of the terms imposed, will be, in effect, a victory for them and will result only in another armistice of 20 to 30 years duration.

The American people must realize, too, that war is a two-sided business—that both sides get hurt. If the Japanese hold something which is necessary to us for the furtherance of the war, there are but two courses open to us. Either we can take it, with our attendant losses, and eventually win through to victory, or we can let the Japanese keep it and eventually lose the war.

Final Objective Tokyo

No single battle or campaign should be assessed by casualties alone, but by the importance of the objective won in relation to the final outcome of the war. In that respect, Tarawa was not a costly victory. The losses there were not out of proportion to the advantages gained; the grimness of the problem that beset us can be seen in the official film record of the battle, titled "WITH THE MARINES AT TARAWA." There will be other Tarawas before we reach our final objective—Tokyo and a lasting peace. Unless we, as a nation, have the stamina to take such losses and to carry this war through to the complete defeat and unconditional surrender of the Japanese people, it is my opinion that we will leave as a heritage to a succeeding generation the horrors of another war—and one that may conceivably be fought upon our own soil.

Tarawa Accented on First Syllable Say the Marines

Since Tarawa is a name which will be immortal in United States history, with Bunker Hill, Gettysburg, Belleau Wood and the rest, on the list of America's greatest battles, the correct pronunciation of the word is important. Most folks are inclined to call it "Tar-*aw*-a," with the accent on the "aw." According to the Marines who killed about 4000 Japs there and captured the island at a cost of fewer than 1,000 killed and 2,500 wounded, this is not correct. The word should be pronounced "*Tar*-aw-a," with the accent on the first syllable.

Tarawa, which provided the setting for "With The Marines At Tarawa," the two reel technicolor picture of the actual battle, which comes to the .... Theatre on ...... in conjunction with ...... , is a string of tiny coral islands in the Pacific, 31 miles long, 500 yards wide, and no more than 6 feet above the ocean at low tide. The Japs had fortified it with immense concrete and log blockhouses. They boasted it could never be captured and would exact a toll of 100,000 lives if attacked, but a U. S. amphibious task force with air support took it in 4 days of bombardment and 3 days of assault tactics by Marine shock troops. The picture shows every phase of the bitterly fought action.

Servicemen Only Stars Of Battle Of Tarawa Films

There is a picture without actors, now playing at the ...... Theatre, in conjunction with.... This picture is "With The Marines At Tarawa," a two reel record of the bitter battle on that Pacific island, which took place last November, when a U. S. amphibious task force of battleships, planes and infantry captured it in seven days of fierce fighting. The cast of this film is made up of the soldiers, sailors, Marines and airmen who engaged in this bloodiest conflict in American history, suffering many casualties out of the three Marine battalions that stormed the Japs' concrete forts.

Only one Hollywood actor had anything to do with the picture. He served as one of the daring Marine Combat Photographers who filmed the battle. Two of them were killed.

Horror of War Shown In Actual Tarawa Film

(Review)

Modern war in all its appalling horror and devastation stalks across the screen of the .... Theatre for two terrifying reels and leaves you shaken, but exalted. The picture is "With The Marines At Tarawa," that much heralded factual record of the capture of the string of coral islands in the Pacific which the Japs had built into a miniature Gibraltar, and which was taken by an American combined operations force late in November, 1943. Fictional war films seem pale beside the real thing in this picture.

Americans who are inclined to be complacent because of the success of the Allied cause during the past year, should be obliged to see "With The Marines at Tarawa." It shows what a gigantic task lies ahead of us to dig the Japs out of the empire they have established in the Pacific. Tarawa is nothing but an atoll 31 miles long and a half a mile wide, with one fairly lage island Betio. This islet was studded with concrete and log forts and machine gun emplacements.

Despite the small area of the Jap strong point, it took seven days; four of sea and air bombardment and three of infantry assault, to capture Tarawa. Some 2400 tons of explosives were hurled at the atoll. The film pictures this with terrifying vividness, technicolor adding to the horror of the sight as immense tongues of fire and huge pillars of smoke mount up into the calm Pacific sky. Yet, after this tornado of steel, the Japs were still there in their underground warrens. The Marines had to go in and blast them out with torpedoes and flame throwers. Practically all the 4000 Jap defenders were killed. Just under 3500 Marines were killed and wounded.

There are many Tarawas on the way to Tokyo and the road will be longer and harder if Americans take victory for granted. This priceless picture record of a brilliant American victory will do much to prevent any slackening of the all-out war effort.

Marine Photographers Faced Death at Work

By Master Technical Sergeant Jim G. Lucas
Marine Corps Combat Correspondent

Death stalked every Marine Corps Combat Photographer on Tarawa from dawn, November 20th, until the last shot was fired at 1.30 P. M. November 23rd, 1943.

The saga of the fighter-photographer who braved death to bring the American public one of the most complete picture records of any battle in which their men have participated is one of the most thrilling chapters of World War II. These actual under-fire scenes comprise the official film, "WITH THE MARINES AT TARAWA," coming soon to the .... theatre on ....

Combat photographers landed with the first wave and plunged immediately into the thick of the fight. Staff Sergeant Norman Hatch, Washington, D. C., who took many of the newsreels later shown in American theatres throughout the country, spent all of his time with the most advanced elements of the Marine striking force. Hatch constantly exposed himself to danger, within a stone's throw of the big Japanese emplacements, to get action shots. That he escaped at all is considered something of a minor miracle by the men who saw him go forward with his camera.

Photogs in Thick of Fight

No spot was too hot for these camera-sergeants. When the Japs finally were flushed out of their blockhouses, Marine Corps cameramen were there to record it. Perhaps the highest tribute came from a veteran photographer from one of the newspaper services, when asked if he intended to be present when the American flag was raised over Tarawa.

"No," he said, "I couldn't get it without two Marine photographers in the background."

Nor was it always possible to get action shots at the front without the crouching figure of a Marine picture man somewhere on the film.

Two Photographers Killed

Two Marine Corps photographers were killed at Tarawa, and a third was wounded. Valuable equipment was lost in the surf and on the beach. Staff Sergeant Roy E. Olund of Pasadena, California, lost all of his equipment when Japanese shells sank the assault boat in which he was headed for shore. Sergeant Olund attempted to swim in carrying his camera, but was forced to drop it in the sea when the swimmers were machine gunned.

Marine Corps photographers served under the direction of Captain Charles Louis Hayward, U.S.M.C., of Los Angeles, California, a former motion picture actor, and Warrant Officer John F. Leopold of Wooster, Ohio. The fifteen officers and men of the Leatherneck photographic crew fought for 76 hours, until Tarawa was secured.

Films Rushed to U.S.

Their work has been generally acclaimed as superlative and was considered so valuable that it came out of Tarawa and to the United States in the first plane to leave the Gilbert Islands after the fighting was secured.

In all, they took approximately 900 still photographs and 5,000 feet of color movie.

Warrant Officer Leopold said it was the first time combat photographers have gone in with the first wave in an amphibious landing. Like every man present, they were fighting Marines first and specialists - photographers - second.

"Before the landing," he explained, "we determined that we were going to get just as good pictures as the Russians, who have been taking them at the front."

And they did.

Mat 23

Landing craft with men aboard in the rendezvous area awaiting signals to go into the beach. One of the exciting scenes from "With the Marines at Tarawa" now showing at the .... Theatre.

No High Hat in Marines Brass Hats

There is nothing high hat about the brass hats of the U. S. Marines. Scenes of "With The Marines At Tarawa," the two reel technicolor film now playing at the .... Theatre in conjunction with .... show Major General Julian C. Smith, who was in charge of operations in the Tarawa battle, and his second in command, in the thick of the bloody action that caused under 3,500 casualties. They did not fight the battle from bombproof headquarters far to the rear of the firing line.

"With The Marines At Tarawa" is a factual picture of the fiercest action in U. S. military annals. It was filmed by Marine Combat Photographers who fought with troops through the fray. Two of them were killed.

History Wrote Script of Battle of Tarawa Films

History wrote the script of "With The Marines At Tarawa," the two reel, technicolor picture of the fiercest battle in American military history, which is being shown at the .... Theatre now, in conjunction with .... The natural sequence of events from the start of the expedition to take the Japs' miniature Gibraltar of the Pacific, to its final reduction in three days of ferocious fighting which cost Marines under 3500 dead and wounded, built up the drama of the battle to its mounting crescendo of action.

Hollywood's best script writers could not have packed into the brief space of this short film, the drama, adventure, tragedy, horror, beauty, and even grim humor, which modern war has piled into the two reels of "With The Marines At Tarawa." It was filmed by Marine Combat Photographers, two of whom were killed cinematizing there reels.

Tarawa No South Sea Idyll for the Marines

Ever since the voyage of Captain Cook, back in the 18th Century, the South Sea Islands have been the escapist's paradise. Pictured in numberless books, plays and films as a part of the world blessed with happy idleness, cloudless skies, calm waters and singing and dancing natives, they have always been the place people went to escape to when the battle for existence in the Western world gets too severe. Today, the war in the Pacific has changed this island paradise into an inferno.

What modern war has done to the South Sea dream world, is vividly shown in the two reel technicolor picture, "With The Marines At Tarawa," which is shown at the .... Theatre on .... in conjunction with .... Before Pearl Harbor, Tarawa was a string of palm tufted coral dots in the Pacific Ocean, 31 miles long and about half a mile wide, inhabited by a few peaceful natives. In their southern drive of 1941-1942, the Japanese took Tarawa and turned it into a vest-pocket Gibraltar which they boasted would cost 100,000 American lives to attack. On November 20th, 1943, U.S. Marines landed on the atoll and captured it in three days. Marine Combat Photographers, right on the firing line with the troops, filmed this whole fight, the bloodiest in Marine Corps history, to make "With The Marines At Tarawa."

Four days of American sea and air bombardment poured 2400 tons of explosives on the little atoll. Every tree on the islet was hit. Most were stripped of their foliage. The sandy beach and coral surface of the place were torn to pieces by shells and bombs. Thousands of gallons of gasoline, set afire, scorched the island to a cinder. The bright blue surf and white sand of Tarawa were reddened with the blood of almost 4000 Japanese casualties and fewer than 1000 Marines killed and 2500 wounded before a great Allied victory was won.

Marines Marked Their 168th Birthday By Greatest Fight

In 1943, the United States Marines as a military unit, were 168 years old. They celebrated this anniversary by fighting the most ferocious battle in their history, and in all American history. This battle, in which they captured the Japs' Pacific stronghold of Tarawa atoll, killing 4000 Nipponese and losing fewer than 1,000 Marines killed and 2,500 wounded, is now to be seen at the .... Theatre in the two reel technicolor picture, "With The Marines At Tarawa," which is playing in conjunction with ....

For four days, U. S. battleships shelled Tarawa with 16 inch shells. Then dive bombers attacked the island. Two thousand four hundred tons of explosives battered Tarawa, an average of a ton and a half to the square yard. Despite this storm of fire, the 4000 Jap defenders held out in their huge concrete and log forts. The Marines had to land and rout the Nipponese out of their defenses, inch by inch with bangalore torpedoes and flame throwers before victory was won.

SYNOPSIS

The men of the Second Marine Division are on their transports, sailing under sealed orders. They are escorted by ships of the Navy and Coast Guard. A few days before "D" Day, they are told their objective is Tarawa. They examine relief maps and soon know every inch of the terrain. They load ammunition, test-fire weapons and go over plans with Navy and Coast Guard coxswains. Religious services are held on the last evening before "D" day.

Before the dawn of "D" day, the naval vessels open fire, pounding Tarawa with high explosives for four hours. When the ships stop firing the Navy's planes take over. The planes then withdraw and the ships open up again.

"H" hour comes and the attack nears. The landing craft move in. From a Jap hulk, mounted machine guns constantly strafe the assault waves. A plane finally scores a direct hit on the hulk, knocking it out.

As the Marines approach there doesn't seem to be any organized resistance. They have the feeling the show is about over. However, they take no chances.

Suddenly, they're met by heavy machine gun and mortar fire. It takes a heavy toll of boats and men. But the Marines fight their way onto the beach. They get a good toe-hold but the Jap fire pins them down for hours. Casualties are tough.

Later, forces are reorganized and the Marines start moving up. They knock the Japs out of their pillboxes using hand grenades, rifle fire, mortars and flame throwers. It's tough blasting 'em out. . . .

At the end of the second day, they breathe a little easier. The Japs are licked and they know it. Snipers tie themselves in trees. At the beach there's constant activity. Fresh supplies are moved in. The chaplain's assistants tend the dead. The force's commanders confer.

The Marines dig the Japs out of their holes. A few prisoners are captured. Wounded Marines are carried to boats. The prisoners are lined up and their clothes cut away to make sure they're not concealing weapons. Not a Jap escaped. The Marines lost less than 1,000—the Japs 4,000. The holocaust was terrific. The island is a shambles. The Seabees land and clear the air strip and soon Navy pilots are taking off from it. Relief finally comes and the Marines sail away after four days of the toughest, hardest kind of fighting.

Mat 12

Belts of fresh ammunition are brought up by hand to established machine gun positions on the beach at Tarawa. One of the exciting scenes from "With the Marines at Tarawa," now at the .... Theatre.

Tarawa Film Reveals Terrible Cost of War

(Review)

War as it is, with the price of victory dramatically displayed, is revealed in the Technicolor picture, "With the Marines at Tarawa," filmed by their own combat photographers, which opened an engagement of .... days at the .... theatre yesterday, in conjunction with ....

Major General Julian C. Smith, Marine commander at Tarawa, was quoted as saying that this battle was the worst in the history of the Corps. The picture corroborates that opinion and at the same time it reveals in action the glorious fighting tradition of the Marines.

The combat photographers began shooting as the first wave of Marines came over the shallows of table reef toward the island of Betio. About 1000 feet off the beach, the amphibian boats were hit by heavy shell fire. Marines piled overside, carrying guns, radios, ammunition and equipment. Jap machine guns and mortar fire caught them mercilessly. Many of them died in the shallow water.

The film shows the survivors pushing forward and at last establishing a meager beachhead twenty feet in width. It follows them up across the sand to the barricades, through barbed wire and out to open flat territory where steel from the machine guns formed a sort of wall. It sweeps along with them when they get up to the palm-log forts and thrust bangalore torpedoes into the gun ports.

In about 76 hours the Marines killed 3000 Japs and lost fewer than 1000 killed and 2500 wounded. They took Betio — a stretch of barren coral two and a half miles long and 500 yards wide—wiping out what it took the enemy two years to build.

The picture shows the Japanese Imperial Special Navy Landing Force — or Marines — at its best. They were the picked fighting men of Japan. Few prisoners were taken. When it was certain that the Americans were coming through, the half-mad Japs thrust the muzzles of their guns against their heads and tripped the triggers with their wiggling toes.

This battle picture on the screen at the .... will stir American pride beyond the power of any fictional drama. This is the real thing. This is it. That's what the Marines said to one another when they went into Tarawa. The film is distributed and exhibited under the auspices of the War Activities Committee—Motion Picture Industry.

EYEWITNESS STORY

CALL OUT THE MARINES!

Marine Corps recruiting centers and stations throughout the country have received a directive from Washington headquarters, to cooperate whenever possible with theatres on the showing of this picture. The men in these centers will help you put over this picture. Call on them for assistance. They'll prove invaluable in promotion.

It's the Real Thing

The authenticity of the picture is the keynote of any campaign on it. The fact that it is the real thing, photographed on the spot by Marine photographers is the best selling angle you have. There's not a single foot of fake or studio stuff in it. Every frame was taken right there on Tarawa under battle conditions with Japanese snipers taking pot shots at the cameramen as they maneuvred for better photographic angles. For the first two days of the battle, the Marines held a 20 foot strip of beach AND NO MORE. On this narrow and precarious foothold, the photographers stayed with the troops, risking death at every moment. It's of such stuff that the picture is made. This is the idea you have to sell to your audience. Get this point over in all your selling—in talking with newspapers—in tieups—in every means at your disposal.

Local Heroes

Get any local boys who have returned from the Tarawa campaign, or any other Pacific Island battle to appear on the stage in connection with your showing of this picture. They should be interviewed on their opinion of the picture, perhaps writing reviews of it for the local papers. Perhaps they can be induced to appear on the stage in connection with it and a War Bond Drive.

One-Sheet On A-Board

The Marine Corps Recruiting Stations generally have A-Boards which they use outside and in various strategic locations. Right now they are being used to a large extent in recruiting women for the Marine Corps. Because of the authenticity of the picture, the one-sheet shown on the back page of this press book may be posted on this A-Board and even in Post Offices, which are ordinarily banned for the commercial picture but which are available for this picture because it is official.

Tack Cards

Print a quantity of 8 by 10 cards with headline reading. "MARINES TAKE TARAWA." Additional copy about the picture can be featured underneath. These cards can be spotted on poles, fences, billboards and trucks.

Impressive Throw-away

Because of the paper shortage no herald was made for this picture. Exhibitors, however, can make their own herald by selecting ad mat No. 2X and having a solid slug cast, using this as the art display for the throwaway as illustrated.

Window Display

Department stores throughout the country will feature a Marine Corps window in connection with a Marine Corps picture, especially if it is an official picture like this one. Obtain Marine equipment and accoutrements either through the recruiting center or the nearest Marine Corps League. Be sure a placard accompanies the display indicating that these are the items carried and used by the Marines in the capture of Tarawa.

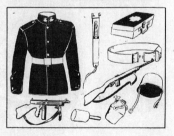

Draft Board Tie-Up

Local Selective Service Boards should be contacted to arrange a tieup whereby boys who are soon to be inducted can see the picture. The Boards may also assist your showing by putting some posters or advertising material around their offices.

ADS THAT SELL THE STORY OF

TARAWA IS OURS!

The Marines' own blood-and-guts story of the taking of the tiny strategic island. It will stand forever as one of the most thrilling pages in U. S. battle history!

U. S. GOVERNMENT presents

WITH THE MARINES AT TARAWA in *Technicolor*

PHOTOGRAPHED BY COMBAT PHOTOGRAPHERS OF THE SECOND MARINE DIVISION

THE REAL THING AT LAST ... filmed under fire by the Marines' own fighting photographers!

2 Reels

Distributed by Universal for War Activities Committee!

Ad Mat 2A—230 lines—30c

TARAWA IS TAKEN!

The actual, living story of the Marines' greatest victory... in all its terrible fury!

America's biggest moment since Pearl Harbor! ...the Marines' revenge for Wake Island!

U. S. GOVERNMENT presents

WITH THE MARINES AT TARAWA in *Technicolor*

PHOTOGRAPHED BY COMBAT PHOTOGRAPHERS OF THE SECOND MARINE DIVISION

They did it ... you'll see them do it! Filmed under fire by the fighting Marines photographers!

2 Reels

Distributed by Universal for War Activities Committee!

Ad Mat 1A—112 lines—15c

THE REAL THING AT LAST!

You've heard about it!
You've read about it!
NOW you'll see it in all its terrible fury!

U. S. GOVERNMENT presents

WITH THE MARINES AT TARAWA in *Technicolor*

PHOTOGRAPHED BY COMBAT PHOTOGRAPHERS OF THE SECOND MARINE DIVISION

The battle that starts the Japs on the road to Hell...

2 Reels

Distributed by Universal for War Activities Committee!

Ad Mat 2B—140 lines—30c

THE REAL THING AT LAST!

U. S. GOVERNMENT presents

WITH THE MARINES AT TARAWA in *Technicolor*

2 Reels

Filmed under fire by the Marines' own photographers!

Distributed by Universal for War Activities Committee!

PHOTOGRAPHED BY COMBAT PHOTOGRAPHERS OF THE SECOND MARINE DIVISION

Ad Mat 2C—56 lines—30c

U. S. GOVERNMENT presents

Extra Attraction **WITH THE MARINES AT TARAWA**

Distributed by Universal for War Activities Committee!

Ad Mat 1B—25 lines—15c

EXTRA ATTRACTION U. S. GOVERNMENT presents **WITH THE MARINES AT TARAWA**

Distributed by Universal for War Activities Committee!

Ad Mat 1C—18 lines—15c

Page Six

HISTORY'S GREATEST BATTLE

U. S. GOVERNMENT presents

Extra Attraction

WITH THE MARINES AT TARAWA

Distributed by Universal for War Activities Committee!

Ad Mat 2D—100 lines—30c

Extra Attraction U. S. GOVERNMENT presents **WITH THE MARINES AT TARAWA**

Distributed by Universal for War Activities Committee!

Ad Mat 2E—42

IT HITS THE HEART LIKE A TWO-TON BLOCK-BUSTER!

The actual, living story of how it was done...in official pictures filmed under fire by the Marines' own fighting photographers!

U. S. GOVERNMENT presents

WITH THE MARINES AT TARAWA in TECHNICOLOR

Furious, thrilling...wonderful!

2 Reels

PHOTOGRAPHED BY COMBAT PHOTOGRAPHERS OF THE SECOND MARINE DIVISION

Distributed by Universal for War Activities Committee!

Ad Mat 1D—70 lines—15c

MONTAGE OF HEADLINES

↓

Since headlines told the story of the capture of Tarawa by the Marines, a montage of them would make an excellent and appropriate lobby display. It might be difficult to get some of these headlines so we have made a montage which can be reproduced directly from this press book. Simply give this to your local photo service to enlarge to any size you like. Put any other copy on it that suits local conditions; set it in lobby for smash display.

Fierce Battling on Tarawa

Tarawa Dearest Marine Victory

Fighting ty Armada

On Tarawa Invaders Still

A BITTER PILL for the Japs

the loss of Tarawa

U.S. CO. TARAWA LOSSES THEIR HEAVIEST

MARINES

GILBERTS Of Raid on Tarawa

Bombardier's View

AMERICANS LAND ON THIRD GILBERT ATOLL;
GAIN IN BATTLES ON TARAWA AND MAKIN

...es Land On 3d Atoll in Gilberts Fight

Pacific Fleet Supports Marine-Army Landing on Makin and Tarawa

MEN
Marines Won-- at Highest Cost

Abemama Is Invaded as Fighting Continues on Tarawa and Makin

Posters

THRILL TO THE FIGHTING YANKS!

WITH THE MARINES AT TARAWA
in TECHNICOLOR

ONE SHEET

THRILL TO THE FIGHTING YANKS!

WITH THE MARINES AT TARAWA
in TECHNICOLOR

U.S.M.C.

THREE SHEET

14 X 36

22 X 28

4—11 X 14's

The rifts between the Japanese Army and Navy that had plagued the country's military throughout the war continued. A cloud of doubt and doom enveloped the island's command under Lieutenant General Kuribayashi. "The entire Army and the nation will depend on you for the defense of that key island," Prime Minister Tojo had told the fifty-three-year-old general. Two weeks after his arrival in June, fifty-one American carrier planes knocked down sixty-six Japanese interceptors and pummeled Iwo.

Over whiskey with a key aide, Maj. Yoshitaka Horie, the general was horrified to learn that the once-vaunted Combined Fleet had been decimated off the coast of the Marianas. Any thoughts of holding off the Americans until the fleet came to the rescue were foolish.

Kuribayashi accused his aide of drunkenness, declaring, "This island is under the jurisdiction of the city of Tokyo!"

Major Horie refused to back down. "When I saw this island from the air today, I thought the best thing to do would be to sink it to the bottom of the sea." He declared his readiness to die and pulled out a packet of potassium cyanide to show he was serious.[6]

Kuribayashi evacuated all civilians and made the fateful decision to ignore military doctrine to defeat the enemy on the beach. Instead, he ordered construction of a complex of some eleven miles of reinforced tunnels and caves. It was a controversial decision that later drew protests from other naval officers on the island. What they did not know, however, was that their fleet had been scattered after the "turkey shoot" by the Americans in the Marianas. Nonetheless, Japan's Army General Staff continued to send communiqués reflecting the outmoded doctrine of fighting the enemy at the shoreline. They urged construction of pillboxes to counter the coming American juggernaut.

Now Major Horie took Kuribayashi's side. "How long did our guns last along the beaches at Saipan and Guam? Will you please show me how effective the beach pillboxes at Tarawa were?" Frontal defenses against the Americans' naval guns and aircraft would be futile, he said. "The lessons we learned at Saipan, Guam, and Tinian have taught us beyond any doubt that the best defense is to snipe at the enemy from caves. We must realize we can't defend a beach."

Instead, Kuribayashi ordered the garrison of 14,000 Army and 7,000 Navy troops to fight a delaying action against an invasion force that would prove to be more than five times as large—110,000 men in all, with three reinforced Marine divisions and supporting forces. "Once the enemy invades the island, every man will resist until the end, making his position his tomb. Every man will do his best to kill ten enemy soldiers." The island was divided into five sectors, including 1,860 men assigned to Mount Suribachi. Caves were dug into the slopes facing the beaches, with entrances built at angles to resist blasts and flamethrowers. "Inside the mountain," historian John Toland wrote, "work was almost completed on a vast storied gallery—complete with steam, water, electricity and plastered walls."[7]

The grimly determined Japanese were waiting at the gates of what the Marines came to call "Hell's Volcano."

In the weeks before the massive amphibious assault, U.S. Navy and Army pilots bombed Iwo Jima through the summer and fall of 1944, culminating in a seventy-four-day-long round of steady strikes by bombers based in Saipan. Yet intelligence reports clearly showed that by the end of January, the number of fortifications on the island actually *increased*—an estimated 900 primary and secondary heavy weapons installations. Most of them were camouflaged and would have to be "uncovered the hard way—by Marines fighting on the ground, drawing their fire."[8]

Then, under the command of Tarawa veteran Lt. Gen. Holland M. "Howlin' Mad" Smith came D-Day at Iwo Jima, February 19, 1945. Before the landing, Smith, a devout Methodist, was reading his Bible in the command ship, the *Eldorado*. Several weeks before, he had expressed grave doubts to Lt. Gen. Alexander Vandegrift, the new commandant: "On two separate occasions I protested that naval gunfire is insufficient, with the result that it has been increased to some extent, but not enough, in my opinion, to suffice. I can only go so far." He predicted some 15,000 casualties among his landing force. "We have done all we could to get ready . . . and I believe it will be successful, but the thought of the probable casualties causes me extreme unhappiness . . . would to God that something might happen to cancel the operation altogether."[9]

Three days before D-Day, Adm. Richmond Kelly Turner, commander of what was then the largest Navy-Marine operation, held an emotional press conference on board the *Eldorado*. "Iwo Jima is as well defended as any fixed position that exists in the world today," he told the tense gathering of combat correspondents. The plan of attack had already been given to all of the officers in the amphibious force. Capt. Williams Sanders Clark of Cleveland, a veteran of Saipan, wrote in his war diary: "The 5th [Marine] Division was to land near the base of Mount Suribachi. Its mission was to secure the volcano, thus denying the Japs perfect positions from which to subject our landing beaches to severe enfilade fire. When this was accomplished it was to turn north and drive up the west side of the island." The 4th Marine Division, where Clark was attached as a radio operator, was to land near the center of the island. Its "mission was to cut directly across the island, capturing Motoyama Airfield No. 1. This was the primary enemy airstrip. This accomplished, the division was to make a right pivot and drive up the east side of the island. The 3rd Marine Division was to be a floating reserve to be used only in case of emergency."[10]

The reporters in Turner's boardroom were told the "frontal assault" would be a slow slugfest, yard by volcanic yard. There was no room for maneuver or strategy. At least one of the generals was "misty eyed," according to the ubiquitous Bob Sherrod; the meeting generated "the sort of the pit-of-the-stomach emotion one feels when he knows that many men who love life are about to die."[11]

Before the invasion, the Navy conducted what another correspondent, author John P. Marquand, called "a slow, careful probing for
almost invisible targets." It reminded him of "the weaving and feinting
of a fighter watching for an opening early in the first round. To put it
another way, our task force was like a group of big-game hunters surrounding a slightly wounded but dangerous animal."[12]

As hundreds of amtracs raced toward the blackened shoreline, the
island was eerily quiet, almost like a practice landing. The surf was
light, so that unlike the long, bloody slog at Tarawa, the landing at Iwo
Jima seemed ideal at first. Within twenty minutes, the first five assault
waves had been ferried ashore, and the amtracs were returning to the
ships for cargo. The Marines had made a "dry" landing, with a few
shells crashing among them and some bullets whizzing by, but the initial resistance was light and not particularly well-organized.

"There's something screwy," muttered Cpl. Leonce "Frenchy"
Olivier, a short, black-haired Louisianan, one of the first Marines to
land. A smoky mist floated over the black sand, and the air was perme-
ated by the acrid smell of cordite from the naval barrage.[13]

Hatch knew that Japanese battle doctrine would allow attacking
forces to reach the beach before launching a major counterattack on the
volcanic ash beaches. "That's why I also endeavored to get in on the first
wave." As he lumbered ashore from a wooden Higgins boat, Hatch felt
himself sinking in the black sand. He clung to his 35-millimeter
Eyemo—still his camera of choice—and walked alongside Obie
Newcomb, who was shooting stills. They hoped to reach the area designated as division headquarters near the foot of the airfield on the
mountain plateau, Motoyama No. 1.

As they crossed the bomb craters left by the Navy battleships and
destroyers, Hatch remarked on the lack of enemy resistance, "Obie, this
thing doesn't smell right to me. What we're going to do now, I'm
going to keep a lookout forward, and Obie, you keep an eye out to the
rear because I'm afraid some Japs are down here in the hole someplace
and they're going to come up behind us and bushwhack us."

Newcomb grimly nodded and watched his back. Division intelligence estimated it might take them a day or more of fighting to reach the airfield. They were surprised to reach it within half an hour of landing as only sporadic small-arms fire was coming from the Japanese. Hatch shot some film, capturing images of Marines strolling ashore with their rifles shouldered.

Then he found the perfect spot for the 5th Marine Division's photographic office: an abandoned machine-gun position off one corner of the airstrip. It was well protected, surrounded by fifty-gallon drums filled with sand. Its doorway was cleverly constructed at an angle to protect against explosions, and there were gun mounts for what probably was a .50-caliber machine gun. "Obie, that's just like a tent pole. See if you can find a tarp someplace."

As Hatch unloaded his gear, his resourceful colleague returned with a huge tarp. They found a tent pole, stuck it in the mount, and, before long, had erected an effective command post with a panoramic view of Mount Suribachi and the rest of the island's southern tip.

Soon Lieutenant Colonel Roll stopped by, and the intelligence officer informed them that their fine command post might be taken from them as the division command exercised a form of battlefield eminent domain. The 5th Marine Division's commander, Maj. Gen. Keller B. Rockey, was not too pleased to be hunkered down in a nearby shell hole filled with rain water—hardly a fitting division headquarters. Yet Hatch persuaded the lieutenant colonel to let him stay put to protect the photo section from the rain and to supervise the filming and shooting ahead. It would turn out to be yet another example of Hatch being in the right place at the right time.

Roll shrugged and let the bull-headed photo chief stay put.

Hatch was well prepared for the battle ahead—or at least as organized as one can be facing the same enemy that had nearly killed him at Tarawa. After the planning conference in Hawaii, he and Newcomb had teamed up to get men into place so that each one was embedded with a designated unit assigned two weeks before the landing. Beyond that, he kept his orders simple but firm: "You have to come back in every day to turn in the film you've shot and get your camera inspected." He had a camera repairman to ensure they were not getting their cameras clogged with the fine, volcanic ash. Once men came in, they could load up on film or equipment and get back to the fighting.

Once the naval gunfire stopped, the Marines who landed "were seared by machine gun and rifle fire from skillfully concealed emplacements. At the same time, mortar and artillery shells began exploding all along the beaches. The lull had ended."[14]

The big guns hidden at the foot of Suribachi erupted, along with guns on the island's northern end. Columns of water shot up around the waves of amtracs, which only minutes before seemed to be booking it to shore. Now Kuribayashi's gunners were training their mortar and artillery on the invaders. Seven battalions of Marines were landing abreast on a two-mile swatch of volcanic beach. Each battalion had a 500-yard stretch.

The 28th Marine Regiment was to swing around the base of Mount Suribachi and seal it from the rest of the island, while the 27th Marines were to move straight across Iwo's beaches, then swing north up the island. The 23rd Marines would seize the airfield and head north, while the 25th Marines would pivot as the right flank.

Only now, as one young captain pinned down on the beach put it, "The honeymoon is over." Not far from Hatch, 20-millimeter dual-purpose guns dug into the side of Suribachi fired down on the Marines even as beach-level pillboxes caught them in their crossfire. The enemy gunners had taken refuge in thick-roofed blockhouses and ridden out the naval bombardment. The "mysteriously silent beach" had exploded, taking a ghastly toll on the Marines. Their advances

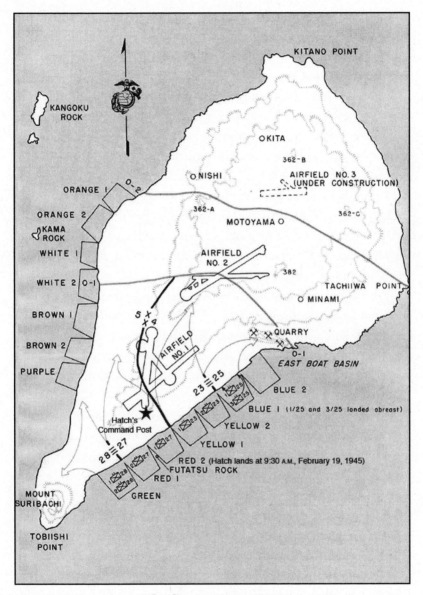

Iwo Jima. U.S. MARINE CORPS

slowed, and the number of dead and wounded climbed. In response, Navy gunboats maneuvered offshore near the base of Suribachi's cone and began to blast away at the enemy observation posts that were calling down fire from above.

The beach itself presented the "one enemy they had underestimated—the soft, loose volcanic sand in which they sank to their ankles with every step," according to accounts by Marine combat correspondents. Trucks, jeeps, and antitank guns also became mired in "the seemingly bottomless sand." Even if they made it across the beach, tanks and half-tracks faced a rocky terrace they could not surmount and "began to wallow as they struggled to get off the beach—like giant beetles stuck on a strip of fly paper." As the LVTs started exploding offshore, the Marines faced the same carnage as they had experienced at Tarawa: piles of wreckage and bodies floating in the water.

"I was beginning to know what it must feel like to be crucified," said 2nd Lt. Benjamin F. Roselle of Chicago, part of a six-man naval gunfire liaison team. After getting 200 yards onto shore, they were hit by mortars that tore into his left leg. He was wounded three more times, but despite the intense pain, he said, "I was so mad I think it kept me alive."[15]

Corpsmen crawled from casualty to casualty to apply bandages and administer morphine and plasma. A supply of litters had been lost on a sunken boat, so corpsmen had to improvise, turning ponchos into stretchers. Rescue boats sank, leaving little chance for the corpsmen to get the wounded off the island. Eventually, the landing ships were transformed into huge operating rooms, with the wardroom tables used as operating tables.[16]

If General Kuribayashi was resigned to waging a futile battle, he did not show it in the deadly defense he mounted against the bleeding, battered Marines. And it would only get worse as Iwo Jima quickly turned into a "troglodyte war on a primitive level with modern refinements that burned men to ashes, blasted through concrete masses, split the earth with seismic effect . . . entomb[ing] thousands alive."[17]

Despite the carnage, by the morning of the second day, Hatch's command post at the captured airfield was surrounded by a veil of relative quiet. So when Roll called for a meeting of the D-2 intelligence personnel, Hatch walked over to the division headquarters without wearing a helmet. After the meeting in the shell hole began, the Japanese opened up with antiaircraft guns firing shells that exploded in midair and sent flak flying. Hatch hit the deck and wound up on top of the public-affairs officer, Capt. Bob Jones, who started yelling, "I'm hit! I'm hit!"

Hatch was skeptical. "How the Christ are you hit?" he roared back. "I'm covering you with my body!"

Once again, his uncanny luck had held; a piece of shrapnel pierced the public-affairs officer's hand, barely missing Hatch's posterior. An intelligence officer bound up Jones's hand and offered him a shot of whiskey. Jones gratefully accepted and downed the whole thing. "That's my only bottle!" the officer protested with a grudging laugh. Any humor, however painful, was a welcome respite from the grim reality of the pitched battle with 22,000 Japanese defenders. Entire companies were getting wiped out as they tried to penetrate the enemy's subterranean base.

Hatch kept his combat photo shop going—checking on the locations of the photographers, setting up channels to retrieve film, and taking care of his men.

If someone did not check in with him, Hatch would try to find him. That happened one day when he had not heard from photographer PFC Donald Fox, assigned to the 3rd Battalion, 8th Marines. The lines were always changing, so when he came across a tank, he grabbed a phone on the back of the vehicle.

"Do you know where the 3/8 is?" Hatch asked.

"You're in advance of their lines," the tank commander said, "and you better get the hell out of there because we're about to engage a hidden gun position up on that hill."

As if on cue, a door slid open on the hillside about 1,000 feet away. The door was painted black to blend in with the volcanic rock. The tank fired and scored a direct hit. Hatch ducked out in the other direction, just before enemy machine-gunners opened up on the tank. He did not hang around to see the tank demolish the Japanese position. (He eventually found cameraman Fox, who was later killed in action.)

As the battle raged, Hatch was proud of his unit's performance. The planning with Newcomb was paying dividends as photographers had gotten to know their assigned units, winning the trust of officers and NCOs alike. As a result, the camera and film men got the kind of behind-the-scenes access that leads to great coverage. For instance, photographer Frank Cockrell shot the medical battalion caring for wounded Marines in the harsh and treacherous field conditions. "He was in the operating room," Hatch recalled, "and how he did it, I'll never know, but he photographed with a light in one hand and a camera in the other hand." Cockrell was a former script writer in Hollywood. "He was excellent behind a camera because he could tell a story."

The Navy medics later said they were happy with the pictures because it showed what they could do and what battlefield operating conditions were really like. It was combat reporting at its best, telling the best story of all: how the Marines and Navy corpsmen and doctors were doing their jobs.

Similarly, on the fifth day of battle, a patrol of Combat Team 28 was just doing its job atop Mount Suribachi when it raised a flag so Marines and sailors below could see America's colors raised in victory over the Japanese island. By itself, the flag raising was a routine field ceremony, but it would set off an extraordinary controversy that would shake the American public's confidence in news coverage as well as raise other questions that may never be completely resolved about the events of February 23, 1945.

CHAPTER TEN

Raising Doubts

Early on February 23, the commander of the 2nd Battalion, Combat Team 28, Lt. Col. Chandler W. Johnson, sent a small reconnaissance patrol to the crest of "Hell's Volcano." The patrol leader, Sgt. Sherman Watson, led the perilous trek and met little resistance as the Japanese stayed holed up and held their fire. But Watson observed a number of weapons emplacements at the crest of Suribachi; his reconnaissance mission complete, he scrambled with his men back down the rocky hill to report their findings.

This intelligence gave Johnson the impetus to order Capt. Dave Severance of Company E to bring a platoon over to battalion headquarters for further orders. Severance picked 1st Lt. Harold G. Schrier's platoon to seize and occupy the strategic mountaintop that had given the Japanese a bird's-eye view of the island, allowing them to dial in artillery fire on the advancing Marines. Before dismissing the platoon, Johnson asked for an American flag he kept in a map case. "If you're able to get up the mountain," he said, handing it to Schrier, "I want you to take this flag. . . . If you can't make it all the way up, turn around and come back down. Don't try to go overboard."[1]

The forty-man patrol carefully zigzagged up the steep, rocky incline, alert for mines and booby traps. Two teams of stretcher bearers brought up the rear, along with a Navy corpsman named John H. Bradley from Appleton, Wisconsin. Years later, Severance would tell Bradley's son, James Bradley, author of *Flags of Our Fathers*: "I thought I was sending them to their deaths. I thought the Japanese were simply waiting for a larger force [than the initial patrol]."[2]

It took the platoon about thirty minutes to reach the volcano's rim at 1015 hours. They met a small enemy force and had a brief skirmish that drove off some Japanese defenders. During the action, other Marines found a piece of Japanese iron pipe, part of a broken water cistern. Following Johnson's order, they tied the stars and stripes to the end of the pipe, and at about 1020, they raised the flag over Mount Suribachi. S/Sgt. Lou Lowery, a combat photographer for *Leatherneck*, took a series of photos of the ad hoc ritual.

The flag wasn't the only thing that was raised: the morale of Marines and sailors who glimpsed the waving flag also soared. "All hell broke loose below," recalled Cpl. Charles W. Lindberg, one of the members of the flag-raising team. "Troops cheered, ships blew horns and whistles, and some men openly wept. It was a sight to behold."

Hatch was busy working in his command post and did not see the first flag go up. But when he heard the cheers and whistles across the beachhead, he peered out from the tent and felt immense relief "because it signified that Mount Suribachi was in our hands and would no longer be an observation post for Japanese artillerymen in the north who were continually and accurately firing on our positions."

The flag, though inspiring, was hard to see, measuring only fifty-four by twenty-eight inches—four and a half feet wide by two and a half feet tall. Hatch wasn't the only Marine who felt the flag was too tiny to properly send such a big message not only to the Marines, but to the Japanese, into whose native land the Americans were driving a stake. So Johnson told a subordinate, 2nd Lt. Albert T. Tuttle, to go down to one of the ships on the beach to fetch a more formidable flag, "large enough that the men at the other end of the island will see it. It will lift their spirits also."

The question of who actually requested the second flag remains in dispute today among Marines as well as historians. In *The Lions of Iwo Jima*, Maj. Gen. Fred Haynes, USMC (Ret.), and James Warren contend that Johnson gave his order after hearing that the newly arrived secretary of the navy, James Forrestal, "had expressed a desire to have the small flag." In this version of events, Johnson wanted to find a replacement flag in order to save the original colors as a battalion memento. (Johnson was later killed in action, so his version was never told.)

Hatch has his own take on the flag flap, one that led to a long-running editorial dispute with then-Col. Dave Severance over the battle-flag narrative, a story that seemed to strike a deep chord not only within the Marine Corps, but with the country at large.

"Dave and I have disagreed on the why's and the wherefore's of the flag story for a number of years," Hatch wrote in 2004 to Col. John W. Ripley, the Vietnam War hero who headed the Marine Corps' History and Museums Division. "He has relied heavily on an unsupported rumor that Secretary Forrestal asked for the flag to take back to Washington with him."

However, Hatch notes, "Forrestal was a meticulous diary keeper even to the minute he first set foot on Iwo. There is no mention of his asking for the flag. Furthermore, he was with 'Howlin' Mad' Smith so undoubtedly his request would have been to him, and then to [General] Rockey." Any such request would have then gone down the chain of command, but there's no record of this among the many commanders on the island. "As far as I can discern, none of the journals report such a request," Hatch wrote. Adding to the mystery is this: because it was only a replacement flag, there's no official record of the second flag ever being raised—and thus no record of the motives or thoughts of the officers in the field. (Years later, Hatch would impress the point on senior commanders: make sure you have photographers on hand to chronicle key battles and events in order to create a photographic record. For without the visual record provided by two quick-thinking combat cameramen at Iwo Jima, PFC Bob Campbell and Sgt. Bill Genaust, the Marine Corps leadership would have lacked an essential tool when the flag-raising itself raised a red flag of controversy.)

For his part, Forrestal reportedly told Smith as they set foot on the shore of Iwo Jima that morning and witnessed the first flag flapping in the breeze: "Holland, the raising of that flag on Suribachi means a Marine Corps for the next 500 years." Little did either know that even this heartfelt prediction, which seemed so true at the time, would be severely tested when the war drew to a close.

According to Hatch's eyewitness account, he first got wind of plans for a second flag when Roll came by his photo shop around 1100 hours. "Norm," he said, "the general [Rockey] wants a second flag put up there—a larger one so that everyone can see it."

"Where the hell are they going to get a big holiday flag with everyone fighting on the beach?" Hatch skeptically asked.

"I don't know," Roll replied, "but just send your guys up there in case it happens."

"But I don't have anybody here," he protested. "I can't get a-hold of anybody."

"Well," Roll said on his way out, "do what you can because the general would like to have a still and motion-picture camera man up there." General Rockey, it appeared, knew the importance of recording the fast-moving events atop Mount Suribachi.

Hatch was left to sweat out the general's order when Sergeant Genaust, one of his best motion-picture men and winner of a Bronze Star Medal for gallantry at Saipan, and Private First Class Campbell, a promising young still photographer, walked in. They were stopping by to replenish supplies.

"Guys," Hatch said urgently, "you've got to give me your film, get your new film, and have a quick look at your cameras." He explained the mission, and within a couple of minutes, he sent them out with fresh film. "Hurry!"

On the way up Suribachi, the cameramen encountered an old friend of Campbell's from the *San Francisco Chronicle*, Associated Press photographer Joe Rosenthal. At just under five feet, five inches, and 140 pounds, Rosenthal, thirty-three, looked more like a frumpy art professor than a battle-hardened photographer. Indeed, his poor vision required thick glasses and caused his rejection from the Army, Navy, and Marines when he volunteered to serve after Pearl Harbor.

After a stint as a photographer in the Maritime Service, Rosenthal joined the AP in 1944 in hopes of photographing the Pacific War. Now he was lugging his bulky press camera, the 4x5 Speed Graphic, and bantering with the Marines. "I understand that there's a flag up there and I want to go up. You guys have rifles," he said jokingly. "You could protect me."[3]

About a third of the way up the mountain, the trio encountered S/Sgt. Lou Lowery, limping and bruised after taking a fifty-foot tumble down a steep slope to avoid a Japanese grenade. Rosenthal asked the *Leatherneck* photographer if it was worth his time to trek to the summit of more than 500 feet. No, Lowery replied, the ceremony's over. But there is a great view of the beach.

When they reached Suribachi's summit, Lieutenant Schrier already was positioning his men for a makeshift ceremony: lowering the first flag and then raising the second one at the end of another pipe. The second, larger set of colors had been found on a landing ship on the beach below; it had originated in a ship's stores in Pearl Harbor.

Four men—Sgt. Michael Strank, Cpl. Harlon H. Block, PFC Franklin R. Sousley, and PFC Ira I. Hayes—furiously worked to tie a rope on to the makeshift flagstaff, a heavy pipe about twenty feet long. Once the flag seemed secure, the foursome worked to get it firmly planted in the rocky, debris-strewn ground. Noticing their difficult task, two onlookers, Pharmacist's Mate Second Class Bradley and PFC Rene A. Gagnon, hustled over to lend a hand.

Initially, Rosenthal hoped to capture the lowering of the first flag and the raising of the second. But as he backed up about thirty-five feet, he discovered that because of the steep slope, he could not see what was happening. The diminutive photographer pushed some old Japanese sandbags and rocks together to gain a higher perch.

Meanwhile, Campbell and Genaust also prepared to shoot the simultaneous lowering and raising of the colors. The moment had arrived, but Schrier walked into Rosenthal's viewfinder, followed by Genaust.

"I'm not in your way, am I, Joe?" Genaust asked.

"Oh, no," Rosenthal said politely, adding, "Hey, Bill, there it goes!"

He swung his Speed Graphic camera around and waited as the six Marines, whose names weren't known to him at the time, leaned into their work. The wind blew, and the stars and stripes unfurled against a partly cloudy midday sky. Like a lepidopterist capturing a rare butterfly, Rosenthal caught the moment in a single frame of film.

A few days later, Hatch heard radio reports about a fantastic picture taken by Joe Rosenthal at Iwo Jima. When he saw the AP photographer, who was still covering the battle, he asked, "What was it, Joe? What did you take?"

"I'll be damned if I know," Rosenthal replied. "The only thing I can think of it must have been the picture when I got all the guys at the base of the flagpole and they're all raising their rifles and yelling, 'Banzai!'"

All told, Rosenthal had taken eighteen pictures on Iwo Jima the day of the flag raising. But since his packet of film was sent by a mail plane to Guam for processing and security review, he was in the dark about the fate of his picture and the stir it created back home. He didn't know that an AP photo editor took one look at the glossy print of the flag raising and declared, "Here's one for all time!" And he was unaware that the expertly cropped photo was transmitted to AP headquarters in New York and subsequently ran on nearly every front page in America.

Indeed, when he was asked later on Guam whether "the flag raising picture" had been posed, Rosenthal innocently replied, "Sure." He thought the reporter was referring to the "banzai" picture where more than a dozen Marines—the men who raised both flags—held up their helmets and rifles and mugged victoriously for Rosenthal as the second flag flew in a straight line above them.[4]

But before this misunderstanding came to light—followed by years of controversy and even an official investigation by the Marine Corps—the single frame of the second flag raising had a monumental impact on the folks back home. Within two days, Rosenthal's picture ran on front pages across the country, from the *New York Times* to the *Los Angeles Times*. It ran on the cover of *Life* and was praised on all of the radio networks. It was the rarest of photojournalistic feats, the perfect picture for the moment. It came at a time when national morale was wearing thin; even as Hitler's Third Reich appeared ready to fall, many Americans were starting to wonder if they would force the implacable Japanese to surrender.

Like a glimpse of a glorious sunrise, Americans' spirits were lifted en masse by the stirring sight of the Marines atop Mount Suribachi. Readers marveled at this tableau of teamwork in the thick of combat. And now, because Colonel Johnson or General Rockey had the foresight to take time out to recognize this moment in the war—acknowledging, long before the battle was won, the sacrifices of his fellow Marines—the stars and stripes were flying majestically over the Japanese homeland. The message was as powerful as it was simple: America had turned a corner in this long, brutal journey to win the war. Uncle Sam was now approaching the stretch run toward Tokyo. Adding to the picture's subliminal power, its "dramatic composition was unforgettable, symbolizing simultaneously heroism, suffering and accomplishment."[5] It served as a reminder for weary Americans that an end to the war—and the dreaded deliveries of telegrams of death—was in sight.

It's worth noting that Rosenthal shot what he considered a horizontal picture, but the print was cropped by an enterprising AP photo editor in Guam to create a powerful vertical thrust. Instead of showing piles of dirt, rock, and wood in the foreground, the picture that captured America's imagination focuses on the raw power and grit of the Marines, starting with Corporal Block at the base of the pole, his back and thighs rippling with exertion, followed by the other men grasping the pipe—except for Hayes, who let go of it before the camera clicked, but his hands, reaching upward, have their own transcendent quality.

Rosenthal was always humble about what has been called the most famous single photograph of all time. A decade later, he wrote that "of all the elements that went into the making of this picture, the part I played was the least important. To get that flag up there, America's fighting men had to die on that island and on other islands and off the shores and in the air. What difference does it make who took the picture? I took it, but the Marines took Iwo Jima."[6]

Back in Washington at the Marine Corp's public-information division, Brig. Gen. Robert L. Denig was furiously trying to determine the identity of the six flag raisers. Private First Class Gagnon, the first to be sent home, was given an enlargement of the Rosenthal photo, and while getting most of the identities correct, he initially named one as Sgt. Henry O. Hansen, who helped raise the first flag but was soon killed in action. Ironically, the fatally wounded Hansen would be treated by Corpsman Bradley, who raised the second flag.[7] Hansen's place on the flagpole was actually taken by Cpl. Harlon Block, a Texas farm and oilfield worker who also died on the island. Two other members of the second flag-raising team never made it home: PFC Franklin Sousley, a former factory worker from Flemingsburg, Kentucky, and

Sgt. Michael Strank of Conemaugh, Pennsylvania, who served in the Civilian Conservation Corps before enlisting in the Marines in 1939.

President Roosevelt ordered that any survivors be located and returned to the United States as a boost to national morale—and to the Seventh War Loan Drive. But it didn't take long before questions started cropping up about the authenticity of Rosenthal's work. *Time-Life's* Sherrod had talked with Lou Lowery of *Leatherneck*, who was bitterly complaining about the amount of attention the second flag raising was getting. "Lou was very upset over this because, after all, he had risked his life to climb that mountain and he had gotten pictures of the first flag raising," Hatch said.

Lowery's feelings are still more understandable since the military cameramen, whether in the Army, Navy, or Marines, typically received little or no credit for their work (except in the case of Hatch at Tarawa). "Lou was convinced that his stuff had been held up and Joe's had been sent through" because Rosenthal worked for the Associated Press, Hatch recalled, "and that's why he was getting all this acclaim."

Sherrod, a consummate professional, had told his editors to check with the AP about the allegations of posing the picture. But before anyone checked with Rosenthal for his side of the story, a New York radio station, WJZ, picked it up, feeding the rumors questioning the picture's veracity.

Rosenthal later observed, "Had I posed that shot, I would of course have ruined it. I'd have picked fewer men. . . . I would have made them turn their heads so they could be identified for AP members throughout the country, and nothing like the existing picture would have resulted."[8]

As the flag-raising flap continued, Hatch received orders on March 8, 1945, D-Day plus 18, to detach from the division and return to

Marine headquarters near Washington. It was part of the plan developed with other photographic officers to bring film from the Iwo Jima battle back to the United States and ultimately to Hollywood so that movie audiences would get the latest newsreel accounts of the fighting.

So just over two weeks after the invasion, Hatch boarded a DC-4 airplane bound for Guam and home. He was told to bring all of the motion-picture footage of Marine and Navy combat taken in recent days for viewing by the Joint Staff. Then he would go on to Warner Brothers in Hollywood to help with film editing.

After nearly a week of travel, Hatch landed at National Airport ready to go home to Lois—and shave, shower, and sleep. He would deliver his film to headquarters the next day. His plans were short-lived, however. Hatch was met at the bottom of the plane's stair ramp by Lt. Col. Ed Hagenah, deputy director of public affairs of the Marine Corps. *How nice*, thought Hatch, *he's come over to greet me.*

Hatch saluted him, smiled, and said, "Well, colonel, it's awfully nice of you to meet a warrant officer and take me home."

Carrying Hatch's gear to a waiting staff car, the senior officer shook his head. "I'm not taking you home, Norm. I'm taking you to headquarters."

Touching his beat-up battle fatigues and field jacket and his two-day growth of beard, Hatch said, "You're not taking me to headquarters looking like this! I'm not walking in there and everybody's dressed to the nines and me looking like a wreck. I only live five minutes away. Why not drive me there?"

"Get into the car," Hagenah insisted, "and I'll tell you."

After the door slammed, the lieutenant colonel explained, "You've got to go inside the commandant's office. He wants to see you."

"Well, what's happened?" Hatch said. He thought of Tarawa and his fear of failure then. Had his luck finally ran out and had he screwed up somehow? Was he being called on the carpet? Were some photos or film out of whack?

His mind raced. But if they were messed up, how would anyone know yet? Most of the film was in his possession, with the rest sent to Hollywood.

"No," Hagenah reassured him, "it's a very simple thing. We've got a problem concerning the Iwo flag-raising pictures."

He briefed Hatch on the controversy generated by Sherrod's reporting from Iwo, based on the interview with Lowery. Hatch was friends with Lowery and knew that if he had been able to see Rosenthal's picture—with the Marines' backs to the camera in a way no professional would have posed—he probably would not have spouted off to Sherrod and raised suspicions about the iconic photograph. But the damage was done, and now the Marine Corps' leadership was in full damage-control mode. Hatch was the first Marine from the island to arrive in Washington (aside from battle casualties), and the leadership wanted to pick his brain.

The staff car raced along the George Washington Parkway, where the dogwoods and cherry trees had yet to bloom. The Washington Monument and Jefferson Memorial shone brightly across the river, which rippled dark green in the sunlight. They whisked past the 14th Street Bridge, then the Memorial Bridge. On the hillside above, Arlington Cemetery stood in silent testimony to past and present sacrifices. It was almost too much to take in after all the dirt and heat and losses of Iwo Jima, where the battle still raged.

Hagenah continued to brief him about why he had been summoned to headquarters. Commandant Vandegrift was meeting with two executives from Time-Life and the Associated Press to discuss the allegations about Rosenthal's photo and related matters. What had started as such a public-relations boon for the Corps had quickly devolved into a controversy. Someone from the front needed to answer his questions, and Hatch happened to be that someone, or as he later put it, "the interlocutor of the news industry." He didn't relish this role.[9]

The car swung southwest to the Navy Annex on Columbia Pike, on a hillside overlooking the sprawling new Pentagon complex. Before he could protest any more about his grubby appearance, Hatch was ushered into General Vandegrift's office. He recalled the words of the commandant's predecessor, General Holcomb, when they had stood side by side in the head: "Be good to the Corps, and it will be good to you."

Would the general's advice still hold true?

Vandegrift had gone through his own share of personal and public grief over Iwo Jima, including frantic phone calls from worried parents. In his memoirs, he related a frantic phone call from a woman in Chicago who thought her son was wounded. She wanted to know whether this was true and where her son had been taken.

"I just don't know," Vandegrift responded. "I don't even know your name."

The woman gave her name, adding, "You must know how my son is, where he is."

Vandegrift responded, "I want to tell you something. My own son was badly wounded on Iwo Jima. I don't know how badly, and I don't know where he is. I know he has been evacuated and is receiving excellent care, and I know the same is true of your son."[10]

When Vandegrift rose to shake Hatch's hand, the commandant acted cordial enough. He introduced the rugged-looking Marine to his visitors—Allen Dibble, Washington bureau chief for Time-Life, and Alan J. Gould, senior vice president of the Associated Press. "How are you?" Vandegrift asked.

"Fine, sir, just a little tired."

"So gunner," he said, settling back behind his desk, "what's the story on the two flags?"

Hatch was glad he had brought along a copy of the division intelligence journal and could cite the time of the first flag raising at 1020, though no time was given for the second event.

After Hatch reviewed the log, Vandegrift asked what was on everyone's mind: was the second photo a phony staged by Rosenthal?

"No, sir," he replied, "There wasn't anything phony about that picture."

He told him what he knew about the reason for the two flags and recalled Roll's order at about 1100 to get some men up on the mountain. It was his understanding that General Rockey had ordered the second flag raising. His own photographers, Genaust and Campbell, had taken motion-picture and still footage that showed one flag coming down and the next one going up. No fakery at all, just two different flags and two different sets of pictures.

Vandegrift nodded and seemed pleased to have the confusion cleared up by someone who clearly had no axe to grind and had just returned from the fighting. But another ticklish issue remained. Rosenthal's photo was a great public-relations boon and could help the Marine Corps for recruiting purposes, so Vandegrift asked the AP executive if he would allow the Corps to copy it.

Gould replied that the AP would provide duplicate negatives and the Corps would have to pay $1 for each eight-by-ten print made by the wire service. Vandegrift grimaced, and a chill seemed to fill the room. Hatch, keeping his own counsel, reflected that the AP never would have had its stunning photo if the Marines hadn't beaten back the Japanese at such an enormous cost. Now the Corps had to *pay* for a picture representing its own sacrifice?

Vandegrift turned to him. "Gunner, what do you think about that?"

Hatch's thoughts raced like the runaway mustang that almost hit Mrs. Roosevelt. The wrong answer might doom his career. He understood where the AP executive was coming from: Gould's request for reimbursement was standard operating procedure. But the flag-raising photo had acquired an instant status—the word "iconic" had not yet been turned into a cliché—and had become a national treasure that required special handling.

So Hatch took the biggest gamble of his young life. "Well, sir," he said, "we have 16-millimeter color film taken by Sgt. Bill Genaust, and even now it's at Warner Brothers being processed. We could make color and black and white blow-ups from that and have the exact same picture of the flag raising. Genaust's an excellent photographer."

As professionals, Hatch and Gould both knew that the quality of any prints made from a 16-millimeter film negative would never equal the sharpness and clarity of Rosenthal's four-by-five photo.[11] But Hatch felt the bluff was worth taking. A hush fell over the room as the wire service executive thought it over: there might be two similar, if not identical, images out on the market. One would be good, the other not so good, and perhaps the public would be confused about which one the AP produced. Still, the AP had the upper hand: it owned the rights to Rosenthal's photo. Would he call Hatch's bluff?

Gould finally spoke up. "On second thought," he said, "I'll give the Marine Corps the rights to use the image in perpetuity at no cost, as long as the AP receives photo credit."

General Vandegrift smiled and his aides heaved sighs of relief. He thanked Gould for his offer and dismissed Hatch. Soon after Hatch got home, after hugging and kissing Lois, he ran to the phone and called Hollywood.

"Have you seen Genaust's film of the flag raising?" he asked Lt. Herb Schlosberg, photo officer of the 4th Marine Division. "Yes," Schlosberg said. "It's beautiful."

"Thank God," Hatch replied, "because if it had gone the other way, I'd be sent to Iceland."

The battle of Iwo Jima lasted for thirty-six days, from February 19 to March 26, 1945, exacting a horrific toll on the Marines as they fought cave by cave, ridge by ridge, and gorge by gorge: 5,931 killed in action and 17,372 wounded. The death toll meant that of the 19,000 Marines killed in World War II, about one third died at Iwo Jima. It was the only campaign in the Pacific in which the total number of American casualties was higher than Japan's.

Among the dead was the cameraman who had helped Hatch get off the hot seat in Washington, Genaust. On March 4, the intrepid Marine traded his camera for a rifle because of poor lighting conditions. He was with an infantry team clearing caves and tunnels, joining in the fighting as he had at Saipan. At one cave, the Marines discovered a Japanese soldier sitting at a table, apparently doing routine paperwork. The Americans tried to get his attention, but he wouldn't look at them. So they got an interpreter, a lieutenant who called into the cave in Japanese. Still, the soldier remained silent. The patrol leader prepared to go underground to investigate, but he needed a flashlight. He asked Genaust for his, but the cameraman told him he'd go down and talk to the paper-shuffling soldier. Two thirds of the way into the cave, machine-gun fire opened up from a hidden entrance on the other side, killing Genaust in the darkness.

"Close the cave up!" the interpreter ordered, and the Marines complied, setting TNT charges to blow up the cave. Genaust's body was buried in the blast. "Genaust has been lost to time," Hatch said. "There have been a number of attempts to find him, but none have been successful."

Besides Genaust and Donald Fox (both with the 5th Marine Division), two other cameramen with the 4th Division, Leo Harry McGrath and Donovan R. Raddatz, died at Iwo Jima.

Hatch was spared a return trip to Iwo. Instead, he spent some time at the Naval Photo Center in Washington, processing film with former employees of Eastman Kodak. Then he was ordered out to the Warner Brothers lot in Hollywood to work on a documentary, *To the Shores of Iwo Jima*. He worked with a familiar group of Navy and Marine photo officers, including Cmdr. John McClain, who was in charge of the Iwo Jima photo coverage; his assistant, Lt. David Hopkins; and Capt. Milton Sperling, a Marine and former producer and writer at Twentieth Century Fox.

They spent more than a month poring over 300,000 feet of Technicolor film taken by 106 combat cameramen. The Office of War Information, in typical Hollywood fashion, boasted that the film "marked the first time a picture was filmed according to a carefully worked out battle-plan 'script.'"

Hollywood "was sort of a fantasyland in those days," Hatch recalled. "It was still in the heyday of the . . . major studios and the star system." It wasn't unusual to go into a snack bar and wind up sitting next to the likes of Errol Flynn, the swashbuckling star of *The Adventures of Robin Hood* and other action movies. When Hatch went out at night, he had a standing invitation to dine and drink at a classy restaurant, Romanoff's, where he met other actors and writers of the day. In the America of late World War II, he recalled, "You just could not do anything for yourself if you wore a uniform. You couldn't walk down the streets. Somebody would stop and say, 'Do you want a ride?'"

If he stuck out his thumb, someone would inevitably stop and say, "Where are you going, Marine?" He received free rides daily through the Hollywood hills over to the Warner Brothers studio.

On June 7, 1945, *To the Shores of Iwo Jima*, a nineteen-minute documentary, was released for nationwide distribution by United Artists. It starts with a globe and a narrator saying, "This is the Pacific as you know it," with wide stretches of water. "But this is the Pacific as the Joint Chiefs of Staff views it." A well-drawn color map of key Japanese strongholds appears, including one tan island in the blue-green water—Iwo Jima, "the most heavily fortified island in the world," with "20,000 of [Japan's] toughest fighting men [who] waited for us to make the first move."

Navy battleships fire salvo after salvo; planes launched from aircraft carriers strafe and bomb enemy positions; at night, the naval gunfire creates a strobe-like effect as the national anthem plays in the background. Then the narrator announces, "D-Day—beginning of the toughest thirty-six-day period in Marine Corps history."

A line of 500 landing craft races like an armada of sea turtles, leaving a white wake behind them. The problems of D-Day are shown as Marines are pinned down on the beach. "We want to pull the beach over our heads like a blanket," says the narrator.

The film doesn't flinch in showing dead Marines, such as one with a helmet strapped on, his head turn to the right, and his chin resting on the ashen sand as though he was sleeping. It describes the taking of Mount Suribachi, with supporting ships offshore "delivering point-blank fire."

Then comes Genaust's footage of the second flag raising: the group of five Marines and one Navy corpsman planting the flag on the rocky mountaintop with a cloudy sky in the distance. They gaze as one at the red, white, and blue, and the announcer intones, "Suribachi is ours." There's no mention of Joe Rosenthal or the ensuing controversy.

More pictures follow of wounded and bandaged Marines, some being helped along by buddies, pain etched in their faces. "The show was just beginning. We never saw a Jap, but fire was coming out of every hole and every rock. . . . We have to go in and dig them out one by one. When we can't dig them out, we burn them out."

Here the soundtrack sounds more like an Errol Flynn sea-faring adventure as the Marines unleash swirling streams of flame. Burning corpses of the enemy are shown twisted in agony on the ashen earth.

The film ends with funerals, white crosses, and pictures of "helmets of 4,000 men who died to take a tiny island somewhere in the Pacific." And there's a voice-over by FDR, who declares, "We will gain the inevitable triumph, so help us God."

General Rockey awarded Hatch a Bronze Star "for meritorious achievement in connection with operations against the enemy" during his time as 5th Marine Division photographic officer from October 15, 1944, to June 22, 1945. He was cited for "expert professional and administrative ability," in particular "a photographic plan, whereby all agencies in the division were fully covered." The resulting pictorial record "was the finest both in quantity and quality to have emerged from the Pacific war up to that time." By spreading his men out among the field hospitals, tanks, artillery, communications, and infantry, he created films "of inestimable value in training the units of his division."

Noting the high praise for *To the Shores of Iwo Jima*, Rockey concluded that "the unparalleled success of his photographers and the high praise of the American Press and Public are in direct proportion to Warrant Officer Hatch's professional skill and untiring devotion to duty. His conduct throughout was in keeping with the highest traditions of the United States Naval Service."

Hatch, while thankful for the award, said the order of his medals was somewhat reversed. "What I did for the Corps and what I did for photography was more important at Tarawa because we had never done anything like that before."

CHAPTER ELEVEN

The Nagasaki Customs House

O n August 6, 1945, Norm Hatch returned to Pearl Harbor for
another planning conference, this time to discuss invasion of the
Japanese homeland. Code-named Downfall, the plan called for two
landings. The first assault, dubbed Olympic, would have 760,000 Army
and Marine troops land on the shores of Japan's southernmost island,
Kyushu, on November 1, 1945. The Americans would seize the island
and its seaport of Nagasaki, where they would build air and naval facilities to prepare to execute the second part of the plan, the invasion of
the main island and the Tokyo Plain, in early 1946.

Gen. Douglas MacArthur would direct the ground troops of the
first landing, with Adm. Chester Nimitz leading the naval armada and
attached forces, including six Marine divisions numbering more than
120,000 men. Hatch had transferred back to the 2nd Marine Division,
his home base for Tarawa. Now, less than two years later, he was prepared to lead the division's photographic services unit into this climax
of the war, an epic event that was sure to be filled with carnage,
courage, and unprecedented challenges. The invasion of the Japanese
mainland would dwarf even the Normandy invasion with 1.7 million
troops, the entire Pacific fleet, and 5,000 assault aircraft.

After President Harry Truman came to power after Roosevelt's death that April, he was told by Army Chief of Staff George Marshall to expect the Japanese to mount a formidable defense, with 900,000 defenders on Kyushu alone. American casualties in the first month would top 25,000, and estimates of total casualties after the second assault ran as high as 1.6 million, with 370,000 American dead. One measure of the coming carnage: 500,000 Purple Hearts had been stockpiled to cover the American wounded. Millions of Japanese civilian and military casualties also were anticipated.

Even as this planning took place in Hawaii, the United States continued to pay a steep price for the advance on the empire. After eighty-two days of fighting, the victory at Okinawa marked "the bloodiest campaign of the Pacific war" with 12,510 American dead and missing in action and 36,613 wounded. On the Japanese side, more than 107,000 died, but thousands more fighters were believed to be sealed in caves and never entered the death count.[1] Additionally, at least a third of the island's population perished—about 160,000 civilians—as Japan's declaration of "total war" came back to haunt its own people.

Yet the Battle of Okinawa paled in comparison to the combined death and suffering that had been exacted that spring on the people of Tokyo. Gen. Curtis E. LeMay, who at age thirty-eight was the youngest two-star general in the Army Air Forces, was looking for a way to bring the Japanese to their knees while providing better odds for the return of his B-29 crews.

Flying from Saipan, LeMay's fleet of 100 B-29s faced a perilous 1,300-mile trek to the Japanese mainland—an eighteen-hour, 2,600-mile round trip. Simply getting off the ground with so much fuel and bombs on board was extremely hazardous. And Japan's air defenses remained strong, especially with more than two hours' warning by the country's radar and air defense system, including those operating on Iwo Jima before it fell to the Americans.

Inspired by the *kamikaze* pilots who had sunk so many American naval vessels, Japanese fighter pilots charged into American bombers at closing speeds of 600 miles per hour, clipping the wings and engines of the B-29s and shattering their noses. "The Japanese lined up across the sky and came in to ram. They would swarm on the B-29 and finish it off," wrote John Ciardi, a B-29 gunner who would later become a leading poet and literary critic.[2] Faced with such peril, he wrote, "I had to condition myself to be a killer. This was remote control. All we did was push buttons. I didn't see anybody we killed."

Though the aerial combat was far from the close fighting and immolations Hatch witnessed on Iwo Jima, it remained a dangerous business. The pipe-smoking, scowling LeMay finally came up with a new approach that he thought would save his crews while raining ruin on Japan: use small, six-pound cylinders filled with napalm. A new weapon developed by Standard Oil and DuPont, the gelatinized gasoline produced "rivers of fire" that were too hot to put out by conventional means, according to historian Donald L. Miller. "Napalm would be shatteringly effective in Tokyo, LeMay reasoned, where 90 percent of the structures were built of wood or heavy paper." He ordered the planes stripped of guns and gunners and packed the B-29s with bundles of the napalm "fire sticks."[3]

LeMay's prediction proved tragically prescient on the first night of the Tokyo fire bombings: 300 B-29s dropped napalm bombs that leveled nearly sixteen square miles of the densely-packed capital, an area roughly equivalent to two-thirds of Manhattan, creating a conflagration that left an estimated 100,000 dead and more than 1 million homeless. "It was probably the worst fire in history," Miller wrote.

Several months later, after Hatch rejoined the 2nd Marine Division in Saipan, he divided his day between daily briefings by D-2 intelligence and D-3 operations officers and building a photo lab inside two twenty-by-forty-foot tents. In an effort to improve his lab and reproduction facilities, he sent men on foraging missions, always with their cameras handy. Led by a resourceful tech sergeant, Al Rohde, when they met anyone with access to building materials such as plywood and paint, they promised to shoot pictures of the supply bearer. Long before quick-stop photo finishing, Rohde promised quick processing and home deliveries—a promise that led to boat-loads of building materiel. It was classic scrounging and stealing within the military brotherhood. But Rohde's resourcefulness almost backfired when some senior officers saw Hatch's elaborate wood-and-linoleum darkroom.

"I want to take this over," a Navy chief surgeon said of the room, painted light green. "It's better than my hospital."

Later, a general on inspection railed about other signs of pilfering on the base, including an elaborate NCO club. "Why can't I get my materials?" the general shouted at his chagrined staff.

Pictures were Hatch's secret weapons, possessing their own talis-manic power. Since the troops were forbidden from having their own cameras—any pictures were considered security breaches—the divi-sion's photo unit provided a valuable service for anyone who wanted to let his wife or parents know he was still alive or just impress the folks back home.

While some jealous officers didn't like him, Hatch managed to make another kind of friend in Saipan, a tailless monkey named Eight Ball. Johnny Ercole had captured the creature in a bamboo grove and turned it into the photo unit's mascot. Eight Ball was tethered by a belt around her waist and was an impish monkey who enjoyed stealing the caps off anyone passing beneath her tree. She slept at the foot of Hatch's bed. •

After this monkey business on Saipan, Hatch returned to Hon-olulu in early August for the serious work of the Japan invasion plan-ning. Documenting Operation Olympic involved massive logistical challenges with hundreds of cameramen, filmmakers, editors, and sup-port personnel to chronicle the expected bloodbath.

A few weeks before they met, President Harry Truman listened to arguments, pro and con, from his top military and civilian advisors for a ground invasion. The pragmatic politician knew that it would lead to unspeakable losses. He knew from the experiences of Tarawa, Saipan, Iwo Jima, and Okinawa that air power alone would not win the war, at least not conventional air power.

Even as he prepared to meet with his Allied counterparts, Stalin and Churchill, at Potsdam, Truman was well aware that a new kind of bomb that unleashed the power of the atom had been successfully exploded in Alamagordo, New Mexico. Watching the explosion from about five miles away, an assistant to Gen. Leslie Groves, overseer of the secret Manhattan Project, exclaimed, "The war is over!"

"Yes, it is over," said Groves, "as soon as we drop one or two on Japan!"[4]

Even as the first atomic bomb was being assembled on the Mariana island of Tinian, the United States sent a message to Japan threatening "the utter destruction of the Japanese homeland" unless they surrendered unconditionally. The ultimatum made no mention of the atomic bomb, nor, after much internal debate, did it suggest that Emperor Hirohito could remain in place. It limited Japanese sovereignty to the four main islands, but promised that the Japanese would not be "enslaved as a race or a nation" and would be allowed "to maintain such industries as will sustain her economy," providing access to raw materials. The occupying forces would withdraw as soon as order was established and there was adequate proof that Japan's war-making capabilities were destroyed.

The Japanese government, deep in internal wrangling and denial, quickly ridiculed the peace overture—one newspaper called it a "LAUGHABLE MATTER"—while it also used diplomatic back channels to try to negotiate the terms of an honorable surrender.

It was too late, though. The first atomic bomb—ten feet long and twenty-eight inches in diameter—was assembled in an air-conditioned bomb hut on Tinian. Three days before, the commander of the 509th

Group, Col. Paul W. Tibbetts, had been told his mission: to drop a bomb on a city that thus far had been mostly spared war's destruction: Hiroshima, on the southeast coast of Honshu, Japan's largest island.

The B-29, named for Tibbetts's mother, *Enola Gay*, would drop a bomb containing the equivalent force of 20,000 tons of TNT.[5]

On the night of August 6, 1945, Hatch was at an open-air theater in Pearl Harbor watching a movie. Such films were prone to run off their sprockets or get jammed, often at the critical juncture of a movie. So when the projector spluttered to a stop that night, it wasn't particularly surprising.

"Turn the goddamn thing back on!" the men started yelling.

But someone came over the public-address system and, amid the booing, announced, "I've been informed to tell you that an atomic bomb has been dropped on Hiroshima today."

There was a pause, and Hatch joined the other men, yelling, "So what?!" No one knew what in the world an "atomic bomb" was. "Turn the goddamn projector back on." The movie started up, and the men enjoyed a distraction from their worries of invading Japan.

But by the next morning, everyone knew that the invasion could be called off. The streets of Honolulu resembled New Orleans at Mardi Gras. The main street of Waikiki was jammed with vehicles and soldiers, sailors, and Marines wildly celebrating this news—which remained somewhat incomprehensible—of a bomb that could end the war. The revelers could not have known the awful destruction that fell from the *Enola Gay* and the effects of what Colonel Tibbetts initially reported to General Groves: "First there was a ball of fire changing in a few seconds to purple clouds and flames boiling and swirling upward. . . . Entire city except outermost of dock areas was covered with a dark gray dust layer which joined the cloud column. . . . Estimated diameter of this dust layer is at least three miles. One observer stated it looked as though whole town was being torn apart with columns of dust rising out of valley approaching the town. . . . Its effects may be attributed by the Japanese to a huge meteor."

Later, Tibbetts added to his official account: "The giant purple mushroom . . . had already risen to a height of 45,000 feet, three miles above our altitude, and was still boiling upward like something terribly alive. It was a frightening sight, and even though we were several miles away, it gave the appearance of something that was about to engulf us. Even more fearsome was the sight on the ground below. . . . The city we had seen so clearly in the sunlight a few minutes before was now an ugly smudge. It had completely disappeared under this awful blanket of smoke and fire. A feeling of shock and horror swept over of us."[6]

Hiroshima lay in ruins, with more than 100,000 people perishing in the blast and at least that many dying later from burns, injuries, and a new disease, radiation poisoning—what the Japanese came to call "the atomic plague." Also perishing in the blast were twenty-two American prisoners of war held in Hiroshima.

Tragically, the razing of one of its major cities was not enough to persuade Japan's militarist government to surrender. U.S. planes dropped thousands of pamphlets across the country warning that "a single one of our newly developed atomic bombs is actually the equivalent in explosive power to what 2,000 of our giant B-29s can carry on a single mission." The pamphlets asked the Japanese to "petition the Emperor to end the war" and accept Truman's plan for "an honorable surrender." Even as the warnings from the American Office of War Information rained down on the increasingly jittery Japanese, Maj. Charles "Chuck" Sweeney, who had piloted one of the supporting aircraft over Hiroshima, was told he would drop a different kind of bomb over one of two possible targets, both on the southern island of Kyushu—either Kokura, home to an arsenal, or the seaport city of Nagasaki. This second bomb would be a spherical plutonium missile

measuring eight feet long and five feet in diameter. It was called "Fat
Man" in honor of Winston Churchill, who recently had lost his reelection bid as British prime minister.

As it happened, the city of Kokura, on Kyushu's northeastern coast,
was shrouded in smoke and haze. Sweeney banked his B-29 southward
to the alternate target, Nagasaki.

About six weeks later, on September 23, 1945, Norm Hatch was
standing at the rail of a troop transport entering the long approach to
Nagasaki harbor, trying to make sense of what was before him. But
there was simply no way to process the devastation: mountainous piles
of rubble, steel girders sticking out like broken matchsticks, the sides of
buildings peeled away like plastic strips. It was as if the city had been
blow-torched and then shaken to death. Hatch later wrote: "To think
that single explosive device had done all of this in a fraction of a second
was incomprehensible. Most of us had been exposed to bombs, artillery
and naval gunfire and knew the results of their explosive power. But
this knowledge provided no reference point to what we were seeing."[7]

To an animal lover, the strangest and most disturbing sights were
images left behind by horses and humans that been seared into the
sides of concrete as though the bomb's rays left negatives on Nagasaki's
buildings.

Hatch stood with the other Marines, elbow to elbow on the deck,
speechlessly surveying the ruins. They could see the remnants of the
Mitsubishi Steel and Arms Works and the Mitsubishi torpedo factory;
both facilities had been flattened like plastic toys under the boot of a
giant. The mid-air blast crushed everything in its path up the Urakami
River Valley.

Once a city of 200,000, Nagasaki invited favorable comparisons to
San Francisco. With a bay facing the East China Sea, the city had many

western touches, such as its Victorian homes, picturesque schools, and classic churches. One of the most popular tourist attractions was Glover's Mansion, the legendary home of Puccini's Madame Butterfly, overlooking the harbor. Nagasaki was known for its "harmonious blend of the cultures of East and West" and was considered the most Europeanized and Christianized city in Japan.[8]

"Fat Man" erased much of that cherished history in a flash the Japanese called *pika*. Some 40,000 people died instantly, while 30,000 more men and women and children later died of wounds and illnesses. Among the first to die were Roman Catholics who worshiped at the city's Urakami Cathedral, about 500 feet from the epicenter. The shrine traced its roots back to the missionary work of St. Francis Xavier in the sixteenth century. One of the cathedral's parishioners, Dr. Takashi Nagai, a professor of radiology at the University of Nagasaki's medical school, had been tossed like a puppet and lost his wife in the blast. After setting up a relief center, he went on to live a monk's life, dying in 1951 with these parting words: "Grant that Nagasaki may be the last atomic wilderness in the history of the world."[9]

As Hatch entered this wilderness, he set out walking with some of his photographers, searching for a suitable place to set up shop. Their mission was to chronicle all aspects of the division's work—intelligence, operations, training, and any human-interest stories. The Marines' immediate task was to locate all fortifications and weaponry and render them useless. Hatch's unit was to record their images for intelligence purposes. In addition, they were asked to cover the restoration of civil law and order by American occupation troops, as well as the rebuilding of infrastructure like public utilities.

Aware of the radiation risk, they wore dosimeters—small buttonlike instruments—pinned to their jackets. Yet no one was too concerned about the ill effects of the A-bomb, and the Marines were as clueless as their vanquished foe about the poisoned water and soil under their feet.

Hatch had more immediate concerns, such as angering the Japanese soldiers returning from Manchuria and other parts of the empire where they were still in control. General MacArthur had issued an edict about this, warning his troops not to antagonize the returning Japanese soldiers, especially considering the shock and anger at seeing entire cities and populations wiped from the face of the earth. Against such feelings of loss and shame, it wouldn't take much to enflame their patriotic fervor.

Searching for a suitable command post, Hatch could see that most of the buildings that survived the blast were made of steel-reinforced concrete. Their roofs and windows may have been destroyed, but the structures remained intact. Near the waterfront, he found one imposing building not far from the mid-air blast over the harbor, which appeared to have suffered remarkably little damage. It was the former customs house for the port of Nagasaki.

The former clearinghouse for goods entering the port had hot and cold running water as well as a laboratory, just the thing for a darkroom. (Asked if he worried about drinking water in the atomic blast zone, Hatch replied, "I don't think we really understood the full import of it. We didn't know enough about it." He never suffered any ill effects.)

The pentagon-shaped structure was ideal for shooting and developing photos and, with multiple offices, for managing the 2nd Marine Division's photo section. Its central location was the perfect jumping-off point for Hatch's photographers to come and go around the city whose streets were clogged with refugees and troops. The next logistical problem to solve was housing. For the first few days, Hatch camped out, but he grew tired of this, especially with the cold nights. So as he sped around the city in a jeep, he noticed another facility that had somehow escaped the carnage: the Kawasi School, atop a hill with a grand view of Nagasaki harbor. As a warrant officer, he drew a private room with a bath—a luxury after so many nights in the field or barracks.

The school was the perfect habitat for Eight Ball, the monkey mascot who arrived in a custom-made box built with wire and air holes. Hatch had stowed her aboard ship and continued his tradition of mooching goods and services from the Navy. To feed the mascot, he asked the ship's senior chief master-at-arms for a favor: did he have any bananas and oranges?

"Whatever for?" the old salt replied.

"We have a monkey on board," Hatch replied honestly.

Then Eight Ball found a home at the Customs House courtyard, where she was tied to a tree. This arrangement worked until some of the Japanese day laborers were surprised by the dive-bombing primate stealing their rice balls from lunch buckets. The monkey, who was accustomed to tropical climes, developed a sniffle, and a doctor told Hatch that she wouldn't survive the cool autumn. With the pet's health in mind, he sold Eight Ball to the crew of a Philippines-bound ship for $100—money that purchased booze for a party in her honor.

Such high jinks provided a welcome diversion from the grim scenes of the ruined city. Hatch marveled at the resilience of the survivors, especially those who were badly burned or blinded and helplessly wandered the streets seeking relief.

George Weller, a Pulitzer Prize–winning reporter, preceded Hatch into the city by several weeks, entering Nagasaki in early September despite a media blackout ordered by General MacArthur. "The atomic bomb's peculiar 'disease,' uncured because it is untreated and untreated because it is undiagnosed, is still snatching away lives here," he wrote on September 9. "Men, women and children with no outward marks of injury are dying daily in hospitals, some after having walked around for three or four weeks thinking they have escaped."[10] The people of Nagasaki were awaiting help from the Americans that was a long time coming. (Weller's dispatches were censored by the occupation forces, including eyewitness accounts of the Nagasaki bombing by American prisoners of war held outside the city. "We discussed the smoke rising over Nagasaki and wondered whether it was bombing or a cloud," said one, "and could not make up our minds."[11])

Hatch's first photo opportunity came shortly after the transport ship tied up at the dock. The Japanese military commander in the area and the mayor marched aboard a gangplank and were greeted by Maj. Gen. Leroy P. Hunt, commanding general of the 2nd Marine Division. It was a short, solemn meeting to sign the formal terms of the American occupation.

The Japanese may have expected the worst, since their propaganda portrayed the 20,000 U.S. Marines as marauding killers and rapists. MacArthur gave orders to change that perception, and efforts to rule with a soft hand appear to have succeeded, since no widespread unrest or organized opposition developed.

For Hatch, Nagasaki still held vestiges of old-world charm, including farmers entering the city with horse and buggies. Of course, the city was firmly planted in the twentieth century, and like any big city, it offered a variety of services to servicemen. One of the more unusual assignments for Hatch's crew was photographing ladies of the evening as they were being examined by military doctors for venereal disease. The examinations were part of a larger plan to meet the pressing needs of the occupying forces.

"The Army was in command of the whole operation," Hatch recalled, "through General MacArthur's headquarters in Tokyo, and the Army had a different outlook on life than most everybody else did regarding prostitution. . . . So it was finally decided that we would take this whole Joro area and turn it into a big R&R center for the Marines."

The working girls agreed that in preparation for fraternizing with the Americans, they would take a two-week hiatus until they could all be examined by the doctors to make sure they were "clean and healthy," Hatch said. There were two "entertainment houses" in the compound, along with restaurants, "so essentially a Marine could go in at the gate . . . surrender his ID card or his dog tags, and get a shot of penicillin [to protect against venereal disease] and stay all night."

The plan was to control prostitution and venereal disease, which explains why Hatch and his men took pictures of the medical area (Asked about his own participation in the nocturnal services, he replied, "No, I didn't go in. I was a very straightforward guy with my wife, and I just didn't fool around. In Hawaii, it was very easy to do.")

He was surprised to learn that the Joro area ladies had once been under the protection of Western church workers, who had helped them set up a union with a pension fund. The union also provided care for any children born out of wedlock.

Everything appeared ready to go for the eager Marines and their hostesses, until two chaplains from the division got wind of the affair. The chaplains complained that the sanctioned sex would corrupt the morals of the young Marines, a point Hatch recalled arguing with a red-haired Jewish chaplain. "How can you do this?" Hatch protested. "You know these guys are going to go out anyway and mix with the women, and they're going to come down with all kinds of diseases. This way we can control it."

But the rabbi was adamantly opposed to the sanctioned prostitution and, along with another chaplain, relayed his grievance to General MacArthur's headquarters in Tokyo. If the gates of Joro opened to the Marines, he warned, they would resign from the division, return to the States, and broadcast the affair to Congress.

The clerics won the day. By now, the Americans were several weeks past the end of the hiatus for the Joro women. They were growing impatient and poorer by the day. "Finally," Hatch remembered, "guys were slipping over the walls and going into a house here and winding up in a bed there, and the gonorrhea and syphilis rate went up in the division."

The chaplains may have blocked the military's Joro area plan, but they hadn't stopped the Marines' hormones. "I still think it was a mistake not to do it," Hatch would say years later, "because men being what they are and women being what they are and sex being what it

is, there's no way they were going to keep 20,000 guys from that particular area."

For Hatch, the occupation of Japan allowed him to peek behind
the curtain of the nation's fascinating culture. After MacArthur issued
an edict for the citizens of Japan to surrender all weapons to their local
police stations, Hatch photographed a treasure trove of goods that
seemed to come from the proud *samurai* past: sabers, swords, long pikes,
and halberds, the combination spear and battle-ax that dates back to
the fifteenth century. He also took pictures of farm implements such as
axes and scythes that could double as weapons.

Before long, the Marines realized that the region's homes had
been turned into micro-industrial sites. The discovery reflected the
severe damage caused by General LeMay's bombers on the empire's
manufacturing capability. In response, the Japanese government had
farmed out weapons-making and created a kind of cottage industry.
Marine patrols that ventured out into the hilly countryside discovered
the homespun weapons-making: lathes and drill presses and saws in
living rooms, running off electricity from overhead light sockets. The
equipment produced vital parts for airplanes and weapons, one part at
a time.

The 2nd Marine Division remained busy destroying larger threats,
such as antiaircraft and shore batteries—"spiking" the big guns with
explosives. One photograph of this work shows a huge pile of dozens
of Japanese planes taken from airfields across Kyushu and tossed like so
many model airplanes into a giant bonfire. The planes were "stripped
of useful parts before burning" and consisted of a variety of Japanese
aviation, from the early Zeros to late-model carrier-borne dive-
bombers and other improved models.[12]

Hatch sensed there was more to be seen of Japan's hidden defense industry, so he set out with a jeep and a photographer to the west coast of Kyushu. Once they got out of the city, he was amazed to see the beautiful mountainous countryside, not unlike the Poconos or Adirondacks back home.

Riding along with S/Sgt. Marty Cohen, a diminutive Jewish lad from New Jersey, he could see flickers of fear on the faces of the men, women, and children in small villages they passed along the way. After a day's drive, they rolled into a fishing village, Shimabara, and found the chief of police. He was amicable enough, but spoke no English. Eventually, the chief found his mistress, a young lady who looked to be in her late teens, named Sadie. She was the child of a Japanese mother and a British soldier who had married in Burma. When the war broke out, Sadie's father was killed in fighting with the Japanese who overran Burma. The grieving mother and her child were sent back to Kyushu. Sadie eventually was sent to work in a coal mine as punishment for her British ties. But she was rescued from the mine when the Shimabara police chief noticed her and she became his mistress.

The next morning, Sadie acted as interpreter for the Marines as they toured the area and documented the cottage munitions industry. The lack of ill feeling toward the Marines—at least on the part of the police chief and his girl—was evident that evening when Sadie issued an invitation: "We're going to see a movie for the first time in years that's not a propaganda film. It's a Japanese love story." The theater would be packed, but the chief rated his own box. "Would you like to come?"

Hatch accepted the intriguing invitation and drove everyone in the jeep to the theater. But as they rumbled down a narrow dirt road into town, they came upon a figure looming in the middle. A tall young man in a soldier's uniform was blocking the road.

When Hatch honked the horn, the soldier looked back defiantly and uttered what sounded like an epithet. What was he doing out in the middle of nowhere? The chief yelled at him, and he finally stepped aside. But as they passed him, the soldier was still agitated and threw a rock that barely missed the jeep.

They went on to the theater, which true to the chief's prediction, was packed with about 150 people. As they took their box seats, all eyes turned to watch the lone Americans in the house—and perhaps the first natives of the enemy nation they had ever seen. A low murmur of dissatisfaction filled the place, especially among men who appeared to be of military age. Cohen shifted nervously in his seat.

"Just stay loose, Marty," Hatch whispered, "and keep your hand on your pistol in case we need it."

It didn't help matters when the chief leaned over to speak to Sadie, then walked off. "He said he has to leave for a while," she said, without further explanation.

Five minutes later, Sadie followed suit, saying, "I've to go out for a minute."

So far the chief and his lady had been completely trustworthy and hospitable. Yet Hatch could not shake the suspicion that this might be some kind of set-up. So he also got up to leave. "You stay here, Marty, and I'll find out what the hell happened to the other two."

Cohen was not happy to be left behind. "You're going to leave me here?"

"Yes," Hatch said. "We can't show any kind of fear. Just stay here and I'll be right back."

Hatch marched up the steps, through the lobby, and went outside. He arrived in time to see the police chief using some kind of jujitsu move on the young soldier who had blocked their way. He threw him over his shoulder as Sadie looked on.

Hatch asked what happened.

"Well," Sadie explained, "when we passed him he'd yelled that he was going to get us, the American bastards." So the chief decided to keep an eye out for him, and sure enough, he found the man with a knife, ready to slash the jeep's tires. He apprehended him and took him to the lock-up.

Sadie and the Americans returned to watch the Japanese romance. Though Hatch couldn't understand a word, he could see from the acting that a love story was unfolding onscreen. The earlier paranoia was left behind.

The next morning, when Hatch and Cohen returned to the jail-house, they found a distraught old lady in the reception area, crying her eyes out.

"Sadie, what gives?" Hatch asked.

She was the mother of the arrested soldier. He had been drunk and did not know what he was doing, and now great shame would be brought on their family.

"What would the chief normally do on something like this?" Hatch asked, trying to understand Japan's justice system.

"Well, probably give him sixty days at hard labor," Sadie said.

Hatch thought it over. The drunk, angry soldier hadn't done any harm to their jeep or to them. "Let's just show him that we can be for-giving and just tell him to stay out of sight whenever we're around."

Sadie translated the proposal, and the police chief agreed, bring-ing the young man out of his cell to apologize. His mother came to retrieve her son, but before she left, she grabbed Hatch's hands, dropped to her knees, and thanked the American profusely. It needed no translation.

It was time to get back to Nagasaki, but on the way back, they stopped at a mountain resort, Unzen. The Victorian wooden frame hotel had hundreds of rooms, but no guests except these passing Amer-icans. The staff rolled out the red carpet for the visitors, starting with a thermal bath and followed by a traditional massage with women walk-ing on their backs. The food was great, too.

The same couldn't be said back in Nagasaki, where feeding the troops was an ongoing problem. The Marines had been cautioned not to eat Japanese food because it was grown with fertilizers that would make the Americans sick (apparently radiation was not factored into the warning). But after several weeks, the Marines were living on C-rations and getting sick of the canned food. Every time a refrigerator ship came into the harbor, they expected fresh food. But instead, the cold lockers were filled with random items such as barbed wire and ping pong balls. Hatch could guess what was happening: down in the Philippines, the supply officers were keeping the fresh stores of food, but shedding items they didn't want, sending them up to the troops in Japan.

Faced with such supply shenanigans, the mess officers in Nagasaki finally broke down and started buying vegetables on the open market. The Marines ate better, and no one seemed any worse for the wear.

Of everything he witnessed in the moonscape of Nagasaki, Hatch was most fascinated by the juxtaposition of two surviving religious symbols: a round Shinto shrine, a symbol of the worship of nature and ancestors and ancient heroes and, until war's end, Japan's state religion; and a Christian church with a steeple. Both religious edifices remained standing when everything else had fallen.

He reasoned that there may have been aerodynamic reasons for this: for example, the roundness of the Shinto shrine might have provided the least resistance to wind, and the conical shape of the Christian church whose denomination he didn't know might have had a similar effect. "But at the time," he would later write, "it almost seemed like the Supreme Being was protecting His own from mankind."[13]

It was one of Hatch's more revealing statements and one of the few times he opened the lens a bit on his inner life.

Asked if he had ever had nightmares about the horrors of Nagasaki or anything at all from combat, he answered with his Yankee candor: "I never did. Well, I apparently am not an emotional person to a great extent that others are." He continued, "It may be because I have been a reporter all of my life, being a cameraman, and one of the things you try not to do is to get involved with the subject you're documenting. If you do, you lose perspective altogether."

It was a point he would argue in years to come with more narcissistic journalists—first in print and later on television—who increasingly interjected themselves into the story. Hatch's core principle—remaining detached to achieve as much objectivity as possible—had worked for him from *The March of Time* through Tarawa and Iwo Jima. And his center still held: "Don't get emotionally involved in the story, or you won't be able to tell the best story you can."

CHAPTER TWELVE

Bombs over Tokyo

The 2nd Marine Division would occupy Nagasaki and the surrounding island of Kyushu for nine months, until it sailed for the United States on June 15, 1946. By then, the Marines had successfully helped demilitarize the region as well as supervise the repatriation of thousands of Korean and Chinese prisoners and workers.

But Norm Hatch wasn't on board the troop carriers that transported the division across the Pacific, through the Panama Canal, and through the Caribbean and up the Atlantic seaboard to its new home in North Carolina at Camp Lejeune. Once again, in the midst of a field assignment, Hatch had been ordered back to Headquarters, Marine Corps, for reasons unknown. Before leaving Japan, he heard the question that became a kind of mantra of his service: "Norm," asked a bewildered division adjutant, "what the hell have you been doing?"

He shrugged and said, "Nothing that I know of."

Unlike other points in his career—such as going back to boot camp when he applied to work as an English instructor in Washington—this time around he had not been hatching any kind of plot to increase his skills or professional standing. Yet for some reason he had been given a "highest priority" transfer to Washington, a designation that under normal circumstances would have rated a seat on the next flight home.

However, at this stage of the occupation of Japan, there was a lack of air service back to the States. So he was told to board a transport ship traversing a northern route across the Pacific to Seattle. The ship was filled with Army soldiers heading home as part of the military's massive postwar demobilization.

And so, once again, Hatch talked with the ship's executive officer and wheedled his way on to his favored spot on the ship's flying deck, thus avoiding the cramped quarters down below. The week-long voyage was uneventful except at the end, when the ship was buffeted by a mighty storm off the coast of Seattle.

"She was rolling so badly that I could almost touch the water from the flying bridge. I thought, 'This sonofabitch is going over!'" The ship pitched and rolled like a rubber duck in a bathtub. After surviving Tarawa and Iwo Jima unscathed, Hatch was having some serious doubts about his future, wondering whether this would be how his Marine Corps career ended, silently sinking to the bottom of the sea.

But the ship stayed afloat and sliced through the big waves. It finally arrived in Seattle and got in line with several dozen other troop ships and freighters. Before long, they were tying up at the pier. It was four days before Christmas.

Everyone was expecting a long disembarkation filled with paperwork and red tape when a Marine officer hollered up at Hatch from the dock below, "How many Marines have you aboard?"

"About twenty."

"Well, get them off!" the officer ordered. The Marines took care of their own, and several NCOs arrived to help the woozy men with their gear, process their orders, and drive them to downtown Seattle. A train was leaving that very night for Chicago, and before he knew it, Hatch was riding through the river valleys of the Pacific Northwest, headed for home. Like many of his fellow vets, he carried a couple of souvenirs, including a *samurai* sword and an Arisaka rifle found on a dead Japanese soldier at Iwo Jima.

He made it home to Lois by Christmas, and the next week, he reported to Headquarters, Marine Corps, still wondering why he had been brought back from Japan. The mystery was solved when he was greeted by Lt. Carlos P. Steele, an old friend from the 2nd Marine Division. Steele had been a staff sergeant in charge of the film training office in New Zealand and had wanted to leave with the division to go to Tarawa, so Hatch made him his administrative NCO. Now Steele headed the photographic services office at headquarters and, he quickly explained, requested Hatch's transfer to help fill the brain and talent drain after the war.

For after building up so much film expertise, now there was a mass exodus out of the Marine Corps and its sister services back into the civilian world as directors, cameramen, and key grips at Warner Brothers, Twentieth Century Fox, Paramount, and other studios. These film professionals feared that if they didn't get back to work soon, their jobs might be taken forever. Though they had some reinstatement rights as military veterans, they also knew the nature of the business: time waited for no one in Hollywood, New York, and Chicago.

The Marine Corps' film talent "bailed out like mad," recalled Hatch, "and that left nobody at the top level at the Navy Annex [site of the Marine headquarters in Arlington] to run the photographic setup." The photographic section, which had seventy officers at the peak of the war, was now down to five.

This reduction in force reflected a broader problem not only with the size, but with the very identity of the Marines. After the surrender of Japan, Congress drastically reduced the Corps' peacetime strength to 107,000, a force level that was about a quarter of its peak strength of more than 485,000 at the height of the war. Discharges were made by a point system based on length of service, time overseas, wounds, and medals.

While the postwar Corps would remain six times larger than the police department–size service Hatch joined in 1939, Congress's action represented a blow to a proud fighting force that had grown into six divisions and four aircraft wings in the Pacific, providing a superior level of manpower, equipment, and support personnel to win the battles of Iwo Jima and Okinawa. Those hard-won victories, the Corps' leadership argued, had paved the way for the airfields and logistics that allowed the Army Air Corps to launch the air strikes that finally brought Japan to its knees. In other words, the Marine Corps had played a vital role—equal to the Army and the Navy—in winning the war in the Pacific.

But even as Hatch took his new job as photographic operations officer, the peacetime Corps was becoming a shadow of its former swaggering self. It had shrunk into two branches based on either coast, Fleet Marine Force Pacific (with main bases in southern California at Camp Pendleton, San Diego, and the air wing at El Toro near Los Angeles) and Fleet Marine Force Atlantic (with main bases at Camp Lejeune, the air wing at nearby Cherry Point, North Carolina, and boot camp at Parris Island, South Carolina).

The seeds to shrink the Corps actually had been sewn several years earlier, in what Lt. Gen. Victor H. Krulak called "a carefully designed plan which, if implemented, would destroy the Marine Corps as a fighting force."[1] There had long been interservice rivalries between the Army and the Navy and, in turn, between the Army and the Marines. Part of this stemmed from the Army brass's belief that they could handle their own amphibious landings, as proven at Normandy and Sicily, even with the many mistakes and loss of lives that marked those battles. The other factor fueling this rivalry was the nature of power and politics in Washington, as each branch of the military lobbied for as big a piece of the defense pie as possible without giving Congress indigestion.

So as early as December 1943—even as the nation was watching Hatch's Tarawa footage and marveling at the toughness and courage of the Leathernecks—Army Chief of Staff George C. Marshall presented to the Joint Chiefs of Staff a plan for a "unified" Defense Department, one that included a separate Air Force. In his detailed account of the controversy, *First to Fight: An Inside View of the U.S. Marine Corps*, Krulak ruefully noted that as early as 1932, a similar proposal was made in Congress, prompting General MacArthur, then the Army's chief of staff, to voice his opposition to creating a separate Air Force. "Pass this bill and every potential enemy of the United States will rejoice." Those words would come back to haunt the Army in the hearing rooms of Congress.

It's easy to forget that during World War II, there was no separate Defense Department and no secretary of defense exercising civilian control of the military. Rather, the War Department, which dated back to the country's founding in 1789, consisted of the Army and Navy departments. It wasn't until 1947, following passage of the National Security Act, that President Truman named James V. Forrestal the first secretary of defense; in 1949, the War Department became the Department of Defense.

Before these changes, the armed services reported directly to the president through the Joint Chiefs of Staff, a leadership group that did not include the Marine Corps' commandant and was seen by the Marines as yet another reminder of their stepchild status. And things looked to get worse for the Leathernecks. Marshall's 1943 plan would have carved up the military's responsibilities into three elements: land, sea, and air. The Army would handle land combat, the Navy the sea, and the newly constituted Air Force would patrol the skies. The role of the Marine Corps was conspicuously left out of this new organizational chart.

In 1944, the House of Representatives appointed a study committee to prepare for a postwar military, with emphasis on streamlining operations. This committee agreed with Marshall that limits should be put on civilian control of the military by creating "a commander of the armed forces" with direct access to the president. The proposed appointment of a civilian secretary of defense, with other civilians heading each branch of the armed services, was put on the back burner.

As word of Marshall's plan spread, one advisor to Commandant Vandegrift described it as "pure militarism in the German image and a direct threat to the Corps."[2] It didn't help matters that President Truman, proud of his own Army service in World War I, sided with his Army's chief of staff. Worse yet for the Corps, Truman privately dismissed the Marines as a duplication, part of the Navy's "own little Army that talks Navy and is known as the Marine Corps."[3]

Meanwhile, Hatch waged his own battle for professional survival. After four months at headquarters, the Corps began an extensive review of its officers. During the war, as so many junior officers were killed leading companies and platoons in combat, their ranks had been filled by the "temporary commissioning" of enlisted men such as Hatch who were promoted to officer. Now all of those field promotions, including his own, were under scrutiny. Hatch was called before a Marine Corps review board, with officers asking what seemed like a lot of inane questions. Shortly afterward, he was informed he was being reduced in rank from warrant officer to master sergeant, a reduction in both pay and status. Hatch's mood further soured when he learned that his former assistant at Tarawa, Obie Newcomb, was granted permanent warrant officer status. It all depended on who was on your review board and what their mood was that day. For once, Hatch's luck hadn't held, and the Corps, though it had been good to him for more than seven years, had left him feeling disrespected.

Now he was at a fork in his professional road. As the Corps' ranks kept diminishing, Hatch knew that as a master sergeant, he could expect to move every three years or so between the West Coast (Camp Pendleton) and the East (Quantico), home of the Corps' downsized motion-picture units. By then, he had a one-year-old son, Norman T. Hatch Jr., who had been born while he was out in Hollywood working on *To the Shores of Iwo Jima.* With his young family, Hatch couldn't see much sense in moving Lois and Norm Jr. back and forth across the country.

So he told Lieutenant Steele that he was going to try to get out. But his old friend presented another option: stay, and Steele would get the job converted into a civilian billet. Working as a federal civil service worker, he said, "you'll do the same thing you did as an officer."

It took a bit of high-level string-pulling, but that's what happened. The commandant, General Vandegrift, had to ask Congress to authorize a special exemption to a law that prohibited servicemen from jumping from the military into federal civil service jobs. So after more than seven years of active-duty service, on September 14, 1946, Hatch was formally discharged from Headquarters Battalion of the Marine Corps.

He departed as a warrant officer, but on the following Monday, Hatch returned as a GS-9 in the Department of Defense, at $4,142 per year—not a bad salary in those days. He supervised a photo lab with about thirty employees working on the first floor of the Navy Annex. Hatch's discharge form notes his previous employment as an "able seaman" who steered a "three masted sailing vessel . . . knows navigation."

Hatch's navigational skills would be tested once again as the Marine Corps spent much of 1946 and 1947 fighting for its collective life in Congress and in the White House. What had started as a relatively quiet, behind-the-scenes spat among the military chiefs now bordered on open warfare. In response, a group of forward-thinking officers in Quantico and Washington faced the cold, hard political reality that their beloved Corps was facing, if not extinction, then at least an extreme shrinkage bordering on castration. And for a group of tough-minded men who prided themselves on training and planning, the military unification plan made it obvious they "had no plan or system for mustering congressional help or for generating favorable press support."[4]

These Marine activists were known at first as "The Little Men's Chowder and Marching Society," a self-deprecating term from a popular comic strip, *Barnaby*. They were some of the best and brightest and most highly decorated veterans of World War II, including Brig. Gen. Merritt "Red Mike" Edson, who had helped engineer the victory at Tarawa and won the Medal of Honor for his leadership at Bloody Ridge on Guadalcanal. "Fearless and truly patriotic," Krulak wrote of Edson, "he ultimately sacrificed his career to see the truth made public."

General Vandegrift had to tread softly in his congressional testimony, since he reported to Truman, whose animus toward the Corps dated back several decades to World War I. Truman, who as a captain had shaped up an unruly battery in the 129th Field Artillery, was justifiably proud of his Army service. He had provided support for George S. Patton's tank brigade during the Meuse-Argonne offensive, and on November 11, 1918, his battery had fired some of the last shots of the war into German positions. So he took it personally when so many of the press reports centered on the exploits of the Marine "devil dogs" helping turn the tide of the war against the Germans and committing countless acts of courage and bravado, including Col. Wendell Neville's response to a French colonel who ordered him to retreat at Chateau-Thierry: "Retreat, hell," Neville reportedly said. "We just got here."

Now it was another generation of Marines refusing to retreat, but this time, the battle lines were drawn in the halls of the Senate and House of Representatives. And instead of bullets and bombs, the right words and rhetoric were required, along with some state-of-the-art image making that would draw Norm Hatch into the fray. Even when he was out of the Marine Corps, he was destined to stay.

General Vandegrift relied on the cool, calculating mind of Col. Merrill B. Twining, a lawyer by training who spearheaded the Corps' political counterattack in Congress. This existential struggle was made even more formidable by the role of Gen. Dwight D. Eisenhower, then the Army's chief of staff, who adopted the line of his predecessor,

Marshall, that the Marines merely duplicated the Army's role in the last war and could easily be scaled down in form and function. Ike proposed a limited role for the Marine Corps, "initially bridging the gap between the sailor on the ship and the soldier on the land." The Marines—instead of continuing to grow as experts in amphibious warfare—would be relegated to second-class status, essentially operating landing craft and providing security for U.S. embassies and other interests abroad.

General Vandegrift, as a Medal of Honor winner and war hero, could see the historical irony of the Corps' sudden fall from official grace and was determined to do everything in his power to stop it. He recalled Navy Secretary's Forrestal's oft-quoted declaration that the raising of the flag on Mt. Suribachi "means a Marine Corps for the next five hundred years." Unfortunately, Vandegrift said, "events soon placed his prediction of the Corps' longevity in jeopardy."[5]

Even the Navy was getting drawn into the internecine struggle, Vandegrift learned. He was given a memo from the secretary of the navy that included remarks by an Army Air Corps general laced with "a bitter tirade against the Navy." After questioning the Navy's separate aviation assets, Army Air Corps Gen. Carl Spaatz went further, asking a group of aviation writers, "Why should we have a navy at all? The Russians have little or no navy; the Japanese Navy has been sunk; the navies of this world are negligible; the Germans never did have much of a navy."

He asserted "there are no enemies for [the U.S. Navy] to fight, except apparently the Army Air Force." Spaatz said the next war would be decided by atomic weaponry, especially the B-29 long-range bomber. "There is only one airplane that can carry the atomic bomb and that is the B-29. If they insist on a carrier, the only carrier that could do the job would be of a size so great that it would have a flight deck of 6,000 feet long."[6]

While dismissing this as "patent nonsense," Vandegrift and his top advisors were upset that such sentiments were finding a sympathetic audience in Congress. The Marines knew they had to take off the gloves in the ring of political and public opinion. With help from his bright aides, on May 6, 1946, Vandegrift soon delivered a riveting address before the Senate Naval Affairs Committee. In what became known as the "bended knee speech," Vandegrift began by warning members of Congress that the Army-backed plan would preempt their role—through approval of executive-branch appointments and in the budgeting process—in the civilian control of the military.

Then he attacked the most toxic part of the plan for the Corps: a current bill before the Senate that would "reduce the Marine Corps to a position of military insignificance" and might even abolish the service altogether. He explained how the bill to merge the services "would undoubtedly sterilize the Marine Corps" and stressed the importance of the service's ability to quickly mobilize as a "force in readiness" for the United States. Even before World War II, he noted, the Marines participated in fifty of the sixty-one landings conducted to protect American lives and property abroad. Acting cooperatively, he said, the Marines and the Navy developed the doctrine, techniques and equipment "which became the standard pattern of amphibious warfare adopted not only by our own Army but by the armies and navies of eight United Nations. In grim contrast, the Army failed miserably to develop two specialties that sprang up between the wars: airborne operations and armored warfare. How, then," Vandegrift asked, "could they reasonably claim to usurp our unquestioned pre-eminence in still another specialty?"

Vandegrift reminded Congress of its own long role in this debate over the shape and role of the armed forces. "In its capacity as a balance wheel, the Congress has on five occasions since 1828 reflected the voice of the people in casting aside a motion which would damage or destroy the Marine Corps. Now I believe the cycle has repeated itself and that the fate of the Marine Corps lies solely with the Congress."

Driving home his point, Vandegrift concluded, "The Marine Corps thus believes it has earned this right—to have its future decided by the legislative body which created it—nothing more. . . . The bended knee is not a tradition of our Corps. If the Marine as a fighting man has not made a case for himself after 170 years, he must go. But I think you will agree with me that he has earned the right to depart with dignity and honor, not by the subjugation to the status of useless-ness and servility planned for him by the War Department."

After this eloquent defense of the Marines' core mission, Vandegrift received a sympathetic hearing from some sympathetic senators who had been carefully briefed by the Corps' brain trust about the Joint Chiefs' secret plan to shrink the Corps into a shell of its formerly proud self. "Are there documents or papers drawn up by the Joint Chiefs of Staff which confirm your fears about the Marine Corps being rendered ineffective?" asked the committee chairman, Sen. David I. Walsh, a for-mer isolationist Democrat from Massachusetts. This question opened the door for Vandegrift to discuss what had been the top-secret plan of the Joint Chiefs that denigrated the Marines' amphibious warfare devel-opment, challenged the importance of close air support, and dismissed the Corps' claims to unique victories in the Pacific. Under this plan, the size of the Marine Corps would be "limited to small, readily available and lightly armed units no larger than a regiment."[7]

Vandegrift's dramatic speech and testimony had the desired effect, sparking a wave of protest about the chiefs' plotting and galvanizing supporters of the Marines in the public, press, and Congress. President Truman, Krulak wrote, was "stunned by the vigor of adverse public and congressional reaction to the measure" and was forced to abandon "the idea of a single chief of staff of the armed forces."[8] But the Corps' leadership knew that the unification genie was out of the bot-tle, and they needed to do something to stuff it back in forever. A new kind of magic was needed, and soon Hatch was asked to use film as part of the alchemy.

One day, Lt. Col. Victor Krulak, who had been helping to steer the lobbying effort on Capitol Hill, dropped by Hatch's office in the Navy Annex near the Pentagon. He told Hatch that General Vandegrift was gravely concerned that the congressional committee was not fully grasping the threat to the Corps' existence and had said, "I'm afraid I'm going to lose the Corps."

The issue remained very much in doubt, according to Krulak, known as "The Brute," a nickname he picked up as a midshipman at Annapolis for his diminutive stature and iron will. With his piercing gaze and no-nonsense bearing, Krulak—like his beloved Corps—may have been small, but he should never have been underestimated. In the days before Tarawa, he had earned a Navy Cross and Purple Heart for boldly leading a battalion of paratroopers on a diversionary raid in the battle of Bougainville. (Krulak's force had been evacuated by a young PT boat captain, John F. Kennedy; at the time, he promised to repay Kennedy with a bottle of whiskey, a pledge he fulfilled many years later when JFK was in the White House.)

Krulak briskly delivered the assignment: make a film—quickly—that will illustrate what the Corps accomplished in World War II to prove the point that the Marines' amphibious warfare techniques played a critical role in vanquishing the Japanese and building vital runways at Tarawa, Saipan, and Tinian, among others. The goal was to show that without the Marines, the high-flying Army Air Corps could never have bombed Tokyo—and the war would have been prolonged.

"Yes, sir," Hatch said. "We have plenty of war footage." All he and Lieutenant Steele needed was a script and some money, and they could stitch something together. The outline of a script was delivered, along with a budget. So for nearly a month, Steele and Hatch ventured across the 14th Street Bridge into Washington and over to the nearby Naval Air Station in Anacostia, Maryland. They pored over hundreds of reels of film at the Naval Photo Center. They were especially interested in grabbing as many images of the B-29s and General LeMay's air forces delivering the incendiary bombs that torched Japan.

The result was a piece of pure Marine Corps propaganda which appeared to pay homage to the Air Corps. The twenty-minute film, *Bombs over Tokyo*, starts with a panoramic sweep of Marine Corps history: landings on the Bahamas, the Indian Wars, the Civil War, World War I, and the Banana Wars of Central America. Then it leaps ahead to the close of World War II, with shots of Marines scurrying up sand dunes as they enter Tokyo as part of the American occupation. "This was their last amphibious operation of World War II," the narrator intones. "Now they stepped out of their landing craft onto the prostrate form of the enemy himself." With his experience making *To the Shores of Iwo Jima*, Hatch played a key role in finding the right mix of dramatic footage and over-the-top narration. The Marines, the narrator said, "found a desert of stone" in Tokyo, a result of the "awe inspiring" results of the fire-bombing.

Against images of factories reduced to rubble, the narrator declares, "Civilization itself had been erased in the Japanese home islands, reducing the people to a broken and dazed condition." Women trudge by with scarf-covered heads, as broken-looking men push carts—some of the same images Hatch captured on the busy streets of Nagasaki. "No Japanese could believe now in the invincibility of his race," the narrator continues, "nor could any Japanese hear the sound of airplane engines without knowing abject fear. . . . To the enemy homeland, the airplanes spelled doom."

Musical strands of "Off We Go into the Wild Blue Yonder" provide more martial background as bombs drift through the clouds. The movie's score segues into "America the Beautiful" as factory workers are shown building the B-29, "a tribute to the American man and woman."

Once the Air Corps and civilian factory workers were given their due, Hatch and Steele pivoted to make their central point to Congress: "But even more important to the success of the B-29 were the bases from which they operate effectively against Japan." Shots of amphibious landings follow, "the most difficult, the most complex, the most specialized operation in the military repertoire."

A map of the Pacific appears, showing the 1,500-mile flying radius of the B-29s and noting, "Thus were the wings of this giant bird clipped by space." As the "Marines' Hymn" starts to swell in the background, we learn that "the B-29 effort waited for the United States Marines, whose task it was to storm the beaches of the broad Pacific." The Tarawa footage follows, then more geography lessons about the Marines' island hopping from Saipan to Tinian and Guam, from Iwo Jima to Okinawa, "the key to the success of the B-29" as "again the Marines landed."

The film is all Marine, all the time. "Marines have been our amphibious expert since the birth of the nation, since Capt. Samuel Nicholas took his 270 Leathernecks ashore in 1776." More snippets of history follow, including the creation of the Higgins boats and LVTs as "the U.S. Marine Corps [developed] the reputation as the finest assault landing force in the history of warfare." More graphic combat footage is shown of the Marines firing away at Saipan, Tinian, and Guam. Thus, Hatch and Steele accomplished what no testimony, speech, article, or book could ever do: create that special pride and lump-in-the-throat feeling for anyone who pulled for the success of Marines.

The filmmakers' ace-in-the-hole, of course, was Iwo Jima, "a mission meant for specialists" and by then a mission tightly woven into the fabric of the nation's postwar psyche. Just in case anyone in Congress failed to get the point, the film hammers it home one last time: "The knockout blow" to Japan was a joint effort of the Army, Navy, and Marine Corps. "It was not machines alone that defeated the enemy, it was men"—close up here on the faces of battle-hardened Marines—"brave men with even more heart than heavy equipment. Brave men coupled with an amphibious idea born many years ago . . . by the United States Marine Corps."

As "My Country 'Tis of Thee" begins—first barely audible, then swelling at the end—the narrator concludes, "These Marines, with their incomparable know-how, are indeed unsung heroes of the bombing of Tokyo and the setting of the Imperial Sun."

The film had a quick and unique release, shown by appointment only in the offices of Washington's power brokers. "With film in hand," Hatch later wrote, "Krulak also carried, with the help of an assistant, a 16-millimeter projector and screen all over Washington to the power center he knew well, from the White House to Capitol Hill and the powerful civilian advisers," such as Clark Clifford. "After two months went by, [Krulak] came to my office and asked that 1st Lieutenant Steele also be present."

Unlike *With the Marines at Tarawa*, this film wouldn't win an Academy Award. It would, however, win something even more important for the Marine Corps: congressional support. Krulak "told us that the heads of the various committees said that the film was instrumental in the decision to keep the Corps as a separate military."

According to Hatch, "for a couple of young Marine Corps officers to know that by utilizing the film of our combat cameramen of World War II we had essentially helped save the Corps from extinction was heady stuff!"[9]

The passage of the National Security Act of 1947 would protect the Corps' core assets: three divisions and three aircraft wings. In the early 1950s, this would be turned into law, but only after Truman made the political blunder of writing a heated letter to a congressman who wanted to upgrade the Marine commandant's status as a permanent member of the Joint Chiefs of Staff. "For your information," Truman wrote, "the Marine Corps is the Navy's police force and as long as I am president, that is what it will remain. They have a propaganda machine that is almost equal to Stalin's."[10] (After yet another public outcry on the Corps' behalf, Truman was forced to write a letter of apology stating, "I am certain that the Marine Corps itself does not indulge in such propaganda.")

If *Bombs over Tokyo* was propaganda—as Truman clearly felt— Hatch was certain it was for a good cause, the same cause he had enlisted in as an unemployed eighteen-year-old and the same cause he would gladly serve as a reserve officer through the 1950s and 1960s and later as a defense official in the 1970s. It was the same cause that led Gen. Wallace M. Greene, then commandant of the Marine Corps, to write Hatch a personal letter when he retired in 1967 as a major in the reserves: "Your many-faceted assignments throughout the years have been marked with continuing accomplishments which have served to increase public awareness and support of the Marine Corps."

In war and peace, Hatch always trusted his own instincts, just as he trusted the thousands of men (and later women) he came to know and love in all of the armed services. He had mastered a new form of global communications—motion pictures—which in its day was every bit as revolutionary as the technology of the internet that he embraced in the twenty-first century. Long after he retired, Norm Hatch was always ready for a new adventure.

"I haven't been a John Kennedy or a big shot," he said, looking back on his life, "but for the average person, the average citizen, I've done very well."

NOTES

CHAPTER 1

1. Col. Joseph H. Alexander, *Across the Reef: The Marine Assault of Tarawa* (Washington, D.C.: Marine Corps Historical Center, 1993), 4.
2. Col. Joseph H. Alexander, *Utmost Savagery: The Three Days of Tarawa* (Annapolis, MD: Naval Institute Press, 1995), 33.
3. Ibid., 35.
4. Alexander, *Across the Reef*, 14.
5. Martin Russ, *Line of Departure: Tarawa* (Garden City, NY: Doubleday & Co., Inc., 1975), 7.
6. Richard W. Johnston, *Follow Me! The Story of the Second Marine Division in World War II* (New York: Random House, 1948), 75.
7. Benis M. Frank, *Denig's Demons and How They Grew . . . The Story of Marine Corps Combat Correspondents, Photographers, and Artists* (Washington, D.C.: Moore & Moore Inc., 1967).
8. Ibid.
9. Alexander, *Across the Reef*, 4–5.

CHAPTER 2

1. Victor H. Krulak, *First to Fight: An Inside View of the U.S. Marine Corps* (Annapolis, MD: Bluejacket Books, 1984), 76.

CHAPTER 3

1. Edwin H. Simmons, *The United States Marines: The First One Hundred Years* (New York: The Viking Press, 1976), 126.
2. Krulak, *First to Fight*, 1.
3. Simmons, *United States Marines*, 138.
4. Norman T. Hatch, "How I Almost Killed the President's Wife," *Leatherneck* (November 1997): 37.
5. Ibid., 37.
6. Ibid., 39.
7. John Toland, *The Rising Sun: The Decline and Fall of the Japanese Empire* (New York: Random House, 1970), 237.

CHAPTER 4

1. Frank, *Denig's Demons*.
2. Toland, *Rising Sun*, 247.
3. Ibid.
4. Wallace M. Nelson, letter, June 2, 1996.
5. Lawrence Suid, *Sailing on the Silver Screen: Hollywood and the U.S. Navy* (Annapolis: Naval Institute Press, 1996), ix.
6. Ibid., x.
7. Ibid., xi.
8. Ibid., 39.
9. Ibid., 39.
10. Nelson's account is based on a 1996 letter and family history from Nelson given to the author from Norman Hatch.
11. Rafael Steinberg, *Island Fighting* (New York: Time-Life Books Inc., 1978), 22.
12. Peter and James D. Neushel, "With the Marines at Tarawa," *Proceedings* (April 1999): 75.

CHAPTER 5

1. Norman T. Hatch, "All's Well That Ends Well," *Leatherneck* (December 2003): 42.
2. Ibid., 43.
3. Krulak, *First to Fight*, 73.
4. Ibid., 74.
5. Ibid., 92.
6. Ibid.
7. Ibid., 98.
8. Alexander, *Across the Reef*, 5.
9. Alexander, *Utmost Savagery*, 47.
10. Ibid., 87.
11. Russ, *Line of Departure*, 23.
12. Norman T. Hatch, "How I Almost Killed the President's Wife," 39.
13. Russ, *Line of Departure*, 31.
14. Alexander, *Across the Reef*, 6.

CHAPTER 6

1. Alexander, *Utmost Savagery*, 76.
2. Ibid., 77.
3. Neushel, "With the Marines at Tarawa," 75.
4. Alexander, *Across the Reef*, 13.
5. Alexander, *Utmost Savagery*, 136.
6. Ibid.
7. Alexander, *Across the Reef*, 18–19.
8. Ibid.
9. Robert Sherrod, *Tarawa: The Story of a Battle* (Fredericksburg, TX: The Admiral Nimitz Foundation, 1973), 68.
10. Ibid., 74–75.
11. Alexander, *Across the Reef*, 21.

12. Earl J. Wilson, et al., *Betio Beachhead* (New York: G.P. Putnam's Sons, 1945), 53.
13. Ibid., 56.
14. Ibid., 58.
15. Alexander, *Across the Reef*, 26.
16. Wilson, et al., *Betio Beachhead*, 150.

CHAPTER 7
1. Alexander, *Utmost Savagery*, 161–62.
2. Alexander, *Across the Reef*, 29.
3. Sherrod, *Tarawa*, 88–89.
4. Alexander, *Utmost Savagery*, 117.
5. Simmons, *United States Marines*, 137–38.
6. Alexander, *Utmost Savagery*, 187.
7. Ibid., 188.
8. Ibid., 188.
9. Alexander, *Utmost Savagery*, 188.
10. Norman T. Hatch, "Marine Combat Photographer," *Leatherneck* (November 1993): 48,
11. Oral history, Lt. Gen. William K. Jones, U.S. Marine Corps Command and Staff College, 24.
12. Alexander, *Across the Reef*, 27.
13. Sherrod, *Tarawa*, 88.
14. Alexander, *Utmost Savagery*, 34.

CHAPTER 8
1. Sherrod, *Tarawa*, 194.
2. Alexander, *Utmost Savagery*, 198.
3. Ibid., 199.
4. Ibid., 200.
5. Ibid., 201.
6. Ibid.
7. Wilson, et al., *Betio Beachhead*, 134.
8. Ibid.
9. Alexander, *Across the Reef*, 50.
10. Sherrod, *Tarawa*, 149.
11. "The Fight For Tarawa," *Life* 15, no. 24 (December 13, 1943): 27.
12. Alexander, *Utmost Savagery*, 206.
13. Ibid., 228.
14. Joseph McBride, *Frank Capra: The Catastrophe of Success* (New York: Simon & Schuster, 1992), 450.
15. Peter Maslowski, *Armed with Cameras: The American Military Photographers of World War II* (New York: The Free Press/Macmillan Inc., 1993), 259.
16. Alexander, *Utmost Savagery*, 229.
17. McBride, *Frank Capra*, 484.
18. Neushal, "With the Marines at Tarawa," 78.

CHAPTER 9

1. Maslowski, *Armed with Cameras*, 226–28.
2. Ibid.
3. Maj. Gen. Fred Haynes, USMC (Ret.), and James Warren, *The Lions of Iwo Jima* (New York: Henry Holt and Co., 2008), 25.
4. Toland, *Rising Sun*, 306.
5. Ibid., 308.
6. Toland, *Rising Sun*, 642.
7. Ibid., 644.
8. Haynes and Warren, *Lions of Iwo Jima*, 52.
9. Ibid., 650.
10. Donald L. Miller, *The Story of World War II: Revised, Expanded, and Updated from the Original Text by Henry Steele Commager* (New York: Simon & Schuster, 2001), 532–33.
11. Ibid., 533.
12. Toland, *Rising Sun*, 648.
13. *The U.S. Marines on Iwo Jima* (Washington, DC: Infantry Journal, 1945), 42.
14. Bernard C. Nalty and Danny J. Crawford, *The United States Marines on Iwo Jima: The Battle and the Flag Raisings* (Washington, D.C.: History and Museums Division, Headquarters, U.S. Marine Corps, 1995), 3.
15. *The U.S. Marines on Iwo Jima*, 49–50.
16. Ibid., 55.
17. Holland M. Smith and Percy Finch, *Coral and Brass* (New York: Scribner's, 1949), 238.

CHAPTER 10

1. Haynes and Warren, *Lions of Iwo Jima*, 126. For the basic narrative of what led to the flag raisings, I also draw from the Marine Corps' definitive account: Nalty and Crawford, *United States Marines on Iwo Jima*, as well as interviews from Norman Hatch, his oral history with the Marine Corps, and his writings.
2. James Bradley with Ron Powers, *Flags of Our Fathers* (New York: Bantam Books, 2000), 202.
3. Parker Bishop Albee Jr. and Keller Cushing Freeman, *Shadow of Suribachi: Raising the Flags on Iwo Jima* (Westport, CT.: Praeger Publishers, 1995), 58.
4. Joe Rosenthal and W. C. Heinz, "The Picture That Will Live Forever," *Collier's* (February 18, 1955): 62.
5. Toland, *Rising Sun*, 658.
6. Rosenthal and Heinz, "The Picture That Will Live Forever," 62.
7. Nalty and Crawford, *United States Marines on Iwo Jima*, 11.
8. Ibid.
9. Maj. Norman T. Hatch, "Flags over Mount Suribachi," *Marine Corps Gazette* (February 2004): 63.
10. Gen. A. A. Vandegrift, *Once a Marine: The Memoirs of General A. A. Vandegrift, Commandant of the U.S. Marines in WWII* (New York: Ballantine Books Inc., 1964), 284.
11. Ibid., 64.

CHAPTER 11

1. Miller, *Story of World War II*, 590.
2. Ibid., 446.
3. Ibid., 448.
4. Toland, *Rising Sun*, 767.
5. Ibid., 777.
6. Miller, *Story of World War II*, 618–19
7. Norman T. Hatch, "Nagasaki: Vision of Death," *Leatherneck* (September 1995): 40.
8. Toland, *Rising Sun*, 802.
9. Miller, *Story of World War II*, 648.
10. George Weller, *First into Nagasaki* (New York: Crown Publishing Group, 2006), 43
11. Ibid., 52.
12. Johnston, *Follow Me!*, 280–81.
13. Hatch, "Nagasaki," 42.

CHAPTER 12

1. Krulak, *First to Fight*, 17.
2. Ibid., 27.
3. Ibid., 31.
4. Ibid., 28-29.
5. Vandegrift, *Once a Marine*, 283.
6. Ibid., 315.
7. Krulak, *First to Fight*, 34.
8. Ibid., 38.
9. Norman Hatch, "Bombs over Tokyo," *Marine Corps Gazette* 93, issue 8 (August 2009): 52.
10. Ibid., 56.

SELECTED BIBLIOGRAPHY

Albee, Parker Bishop, and Keller Cushing Freeman. *Shadow of Suribachi: Raising the Flags on Iwo Jima.* Westport, CT: Praeger Publishers, 1995.

Alexander, Joseph H. *Across the Reef: The Marine Assault of Tarawa.* Washington, D.C.: Marine Corps Historical Center, 1993.

Alexander, Joseph H. *Utmost Savagery: The Three Days of Tarawa.* Annapolis, MD: Naval Institute Press, 1995.

Bradley, James, with Ron Powers. *Flags of Our Fathers.* New York: Bantam Books, 2000.

Frank, Benis M. *Denig's Demons and How They Grew . . . The Story of Marine Corps Combat Correspondents, Photographers and Artists.* Washington, D.C.: Moore & Moore Inc., 1967.

Haynes, Fred, and James Warren. *The Lions of Iwo Jima.* New York: Henry Holt and Co., 2008.

Johnston, Richard W. *Follow Me! The Story of the Second Marine Division in World War II.* New York: Random House, 1948.

Krulak, Victor H. *First to Fight: An Inside View of the U.S. Marine Corps.* Annapolis, MD: Bluejacket Books, 1984.

Maslowski, Peter. *Armed with Cameras: The American Military Photographers of World War II.* New York: The Free Press/Macmillan Inc., 1993.

McBride, Joseph. *Frank Capra: The Catastrophe of Success.* New York: Simon & Schuster, 1992.

Miller, Donald L. *The Story of World War II: Revised, Expanded, and Updated from the Original Text by Henry Steele Commager.* New York: Simon & Schuster, 2001.

Nalty, Bernard C., and Danny J. Crawford. *The United States Marines on Iwo Jima: The Battle and the Flag Raisings.* Washington, D.C.: History and Museums Division, Headquarters, U.S. Marine Corps, 1995.

Russ, Martin. *Line of Departure: Tarawa*. Garden City, NY: Doubleday & Co., 1975.

Sherrod, Robert. *Tarawa: The Story of a Battle*. Fredericksburg, TX: The Admiral Nimitz Foundation, 1973.

Simmons, Edwin H. *The United States Marines: The First One Hundred Years*. New York: The Viking Press, 1976.

Smith, Holland M., and Percy Finch. *Coral and Brass*. New York: Scribner's, 1949.

Steinberg, Rafael. *Island Fighting*. New York: Time-Life Books Inc., 1978.

Suid, Lawrence. *Sailing on the Silver Screen: Hollywood and the U.S. Navy*. Annapolis: Naval Institute Press, 1996.

Toland, John. *The Rising Sun: The Decline and Fall of the Japanese Empire*. New York: Random House, 1970.

Vandegrift, A. A. *Once a Marine: The Memoirs of General A. A. Vandegrift, Commandant of the U.S. Marines in WWII*. New York: Ballantine Books Inc., 1964.

Weller, George. *First into Nagasaki*. New York: Crown Publishing Group, 2006.

Wilson, Earl J., et al. *Betio Beachhead*. New York: G. P. Putnam's Sons, 1945.

ACKNOWLEDGMENTS

The seeds of this book were sewn by Col. Walt Ford, USMC (Ret.), who introduced me to Norm Hatch and encouraged my research into his life and times. Ford, publisher and editor of the *Marine Corps Gazette* and *Leatherneck*, also provided invaluable editorial comment after reviewing the book's first draft.

My longtime editor at Stackpole Books, Christopher Evans, helped shape this book, along with his able and thorough assistant, David Reisch.

I am grateful to the Marine Corps University Foundation for providing a research grant to continue my work, along with a grant from the Marine Corps Heritage Foundation. Thanks to Brig. Gen. Thomas V. Draude, USMC (Ret.), president and CEO of the Marine Corps University Foundation, and Lt. Col. John R. Hales, USMC (Ret.), its secretary and chief operating officer.

Col. Joseph H. Alexander, USMC (Ret.), was kind enough to review an early draft of the book and provide invaluable editorial suggestions and historical perspective. His seminal work on the battle of Tarawa—*Utmost Savagery: The Three Days of Tarawa*—was my chief historical resource in reconstructing the dramatic events Hatch described.

Colonel Alexander's earlier work, *Across the Reef: The Marine Assault of Tarawa*, also shed light on the battle. Thanks to the U.S. Naval Institute Press for permission to quote from Colonel Alexander's *Utmost Savagery* and from Lt. Gen. Victor H. Krulak's *First to Fight: An Inside View of the U.S. Marine Corps*.

The Admiral Nimitz Foundation generously granted permission to quote from Robert Sherrod's classic work, *Tarawa: The Story of a Battle*.

Thanks to Mike Miller, head of Archives and Special Collections at the Library of the Marine Corps, and library archivist Greg Cina. Benjamin Kristy, aviator curator at the National Museum of the Marine Corps, showed me some of the camera equipment used by Hatch and other World War II–era cameramen and was kind enough to share his photographs of those cameras.

Carol E. Ramkey, director of the Library of the Marine Corps, helped me navigate the research library in Quantico, Virginia. Dr. Charles P. Neimeyer, director of the Marine Corps History Division, also provided timely assistance.

As I tried to preserve more of Norm Hatch's story for posterity, I am grateful to Richmond-based documentary producer Lindsay Stone for filming him and editing the interview for this book's website.

Gen. James L. Jones Jr., USMC (Ret.), took time out from his busy life as national security advisor to write the book's foreword.

I am grateful to Norm Hatch for opening up his home, his personal archives, and his memories.

Finally, my deepest thanks go to my wife, friend, and professional collaborator, Deborah White Jones.

INDEX